CRACKING THE COMMON CORE

Also from the Authors

Differentiated Reading Instruction in Grades 4 and 5:
Strategies and Resources
Sharon Walpole, Michael C. McKenna,
and Zoi A. Philippakos

How to Plan Differentiated Reading Instruction:
Resources for Grades K–3
Sharon Walpole and Michael C. McKenna

The Literacy Coach's Handbook, Second Edition:
A Guide to Research-Based Practice
Sharon Walpole and Michael C. McKenna

Reading Assessment in an RTI Framework
Katherine A. Dougherty Stahl
and Michael C. McKenna

CRACKING THE COMMON CORE
Choosing and Using Texts in Grades 6–12

William E. Lewis
Sharon Walpole
Michael C. McKenna

Foreword by Jeffrey Menzer and Jacob Nagy

THE GUILFORD PRESS
New York   London

© 2014 The Guilford Press
A Division of Guilford Publications, Inc.
72 Spring Street, New York, NY 10012
www.guilford.com

Printed in the United States of America

This book is printed on acid-free paper.

Last digit is print number: 9   8   7   6   5   4   3   2   1

Library of Congress Cataloging-in-Publication Data

Cracking the common core : choosing and using texts in grades 6–12 / by
William E. Lewis, Sharon Walpole, and Michael C. McKenna
      pages cm
   Includes bibliographical references and index.
   ISBN 978-1-4625-1318-5 (hardback) — ISBN 978-1-4625-1313-0 (paper)
   1. English language—Composition and exercises—Study and teaching
(Secondary)   2. Language arts (Secondary)—Curricula—United States.
3. Language arts (Secondary)—Standards—United States.   I. Lewis,
William E.
   LB1631.C69 2014
   808′.0420712—dc23

                                                                    2013032244

*We have been blessed to work with talented teachers
and administrators, all willing to take chances with us.*

We are grateful for our partnerships with

Capital School District (Dover, Delaware)
Caesar Rodney School District (Dover, Delaware)
Harrisonburg City School District (Harrisonburg, Virginia)
New Castle County Vocational Technical Schools (Wilmington, Virginia)
Shue–Medill Middle School (Newark, Delaware)
Staunton City School District (Staunton, Virginia)
William Penn High School (New Castle, Delaware)

This book is for them.

About the Authors

William E. Lewis, PhD, is Assistant Professor in the School of Education at the University of Delaware, where he teaches undergraduate and graduate courses in content-area literacy, English language arts methods, writing, and young adult literature. Before going to the University of Delaware, he taught secondary English language arts for 20 years in the Pennsylvania public schools. Dr. Lewis has served as a consultant to both the Delaware and Georgia education departments and presents a range of professional development seminars on content-area literacy at the local and state levels. His research interests focus on persuasive writing and argumentation and secondary content-area reading and writing.

Sharon Walpole, PhD, is Professor in the School of Education at the University of Delaware. She has extensive school-based experience, including work as a high school history teacher. Dr. Walpole has also been involved in federally funded and other schoolwide reform projects. Her current work focuses on the design and effects of schoolwide reforms, particularly those involving literacy coaches. She has coauthored or coedited several other books with Michael C. McKenna, and her articles have appeared in numerous journals. Dr. Walpole is a recipient of the Early Career Award for Significant Contributions to Literacy Research and Education from the National Reading Conference.

Michael C. McKenna, PhD, is Thomas G. Jewell Professor of Reading at the University of Virginia. Before becoming a professor, he taught middle school math and English. Dr. McKenna has authored, coauthored, or edited more than 20 books and over 100 articles, chapters, and technical reports on a range of literacy topics. His research has been sponsored by the National Reading Research Center and the Center for the Improvement of Early Reading Achievement. Dr. McKenna is a corecipient of the Edward B. Fry Book Award from the Literacy Research Association and the Award for Outstanding Academic Books from the American Library Association.

Foreword

According to a Russian yarn, an excited peasant ran into the constable's office one morning, crying out for help. It seems his friend, Ivan, had fallen into a bog and was already up to his ankles in mud.

"Up to his ankles?" said the constable. "That doesn't sound very alarming."

"But you don't understand," cried the peasant. "He fell in head first."

At William Penn High School, we're definitely up to our ankles in the Common Core State Standards (CCSS), and we have turned many a time-honored notion on its head as well. The transition has been both challenging and unifying. It has broadened us as leaders and helped our faculty develop as educators. Although *Cracking the Common Core* would have been an ideal guide as we got started, we had the advantage of working with its authors. As they make clear, the importance of leadership cannot be overstated in addressing the new standards and the special challenges they pose for secondary schools.

Before you begin, we offer a few insights from two different leadership perspectives: that of the principal and that of the literacy coach. Our own experiences as school leaders may help you see how the contents of the book can be applied in a particular school context.

The Principal

Politics aside, secondary teachers tend to be among the most conservative people on the planet. *Change* is the most feared word in their vocabulary. Many work in schools that function almost identically to the way they did decades ago. When a principal announces a change, whether it involves grade levels or content areas—or even classroom assignments—a wave of angst sweeps through the school. Imagine, then, the level of consternation brought about by the need for real change, change of the kind mandated by the CCSS, the corresponding Next Generation Assessments, and Race to the Top. These initiatives compel teachers to change the very foundation of their instructional practices at the secondary level, especially in high school. No more business as usual, no more comfort zone, and no more self-fulfilling prophecies about struggling students. And although the mandate for implementing the CCSS can be traced up the line to the district and the state, the ultimate responsibility for implementation lies with the school principal.

This book offers principals a refreshing perspective on how to strategically and thoughtfully impact the most valuable resource a school possesses: the instructional core. The interaction among teacher, student, and content through research-based strategies is at the heart of a school, and it is the principal's job to nurture, protect, and support it. This goal seems easy enough to accomplish in the abstract. But as every principal knows, the reality is very different. Schools are complex systems in which change efforts are affected by many factors that compete for a principal's attention. Many of these, such as discipline, have no direct link to instruction and yet demand immediate attention. In the past, it was easy to become immersed in these day-to-day problems and to lose sight of the important task of instructional improvement. A principal might rationalize inaction by assuming that efforts to alter instructional practice would fail in any case because of the virtually immutable system in place in American high schools. No longer is this possible. The CCSS demand that serious change must happen and happen now.

In order to achieve change on this scale, principals must first acknowledge that they cannot achieve it alone. They must work with others to bring about change by guiding without controlling and by sharing leadership. Toward this end, principals must carefully identify and select teachers who demonstrate the willingness to change their practices, share student achievement data, and openly reflect on their ability to deliver high-quality instruction. These teachers need to be the quiet leaders who begin the grassroots movement to improve instruction. While I was able to find a team of courageous teachers who were willing to become change agents at William Penn, I still needed one more person to lead the charge: a literacy coach. The literacy coach must be an expert in the foundations of literacy strategies, understand student achievement data, be a master practitioner in the classroom, and possess the leadership skills to provide professional development to all stakeholders, including the principal. Luckily, I found just such a person.

The Literacy Coach

The school's tech guy told me he could not find my account because I was not listed under the "admin logins" with the elevated privileges. Neither was I under the teacher directory. My folder was alone and sandwiched between everyone else's folders. I laughed because it seemed oddly fitting. Being a coach is like existing between two worlds. I was no longer a teacher, but I lacked the authority (and the paycheck) of an administrator. It was a jarring transition, one that seemed to leave me on the outside at first. As odd as it felt, it was necessary and actually carried important advantages.

My position represented a change to our rather typical high school system, one that frequently involved the standard us-versus-them divisions. The teachers, tired of a battery of new initiatives, felt that the administration didn't understand their efforts. The administration, in turn, believed that the teachers weren't really giving any of the new initiatives a fair evaluation. It is in these divisions that I believe most school initiatives fail. Luckily, I had a principal who was committed to making instruction the focus. The principal had already given a handful of teachers the opportunity to pilot these initiatives in a safe haven. He ensured that the scheduling, time, and resources were protected in order to truly evaluate these literacy practices. Once we saw a change in achievement, which validated the new approaches in our school context, he recommitted to creating a coaching position for me to facilitate the buildingwide implementation of these strategies. Since I was now freed from these entrenched sides, my goal was to seize the high ground and attempt to make everyone see how together we were going to improve instruction.

Using the work of the authors of this book, I navigated between these worlds as fluidly as I could. It wasn't always easy, but they provided a clear map to reach the goal of buildingwide instruction that would actually allow our challenging student population to meet the lofty standards of the CCSS. Finally, as a unified team, we have a singular focus: showing students how to learn anything though the use of texts. We can work on teaching them content, while improving the literacy skills that had been so frequently neglected in a No Child Left Behind world.

Moving Forward Together

Working with these authors, we were able to refocus the efforts of our school to make the instructional core better than it had been in years. We had been adrift in a sea of initiatives, buzzwords, and acronyms, but we found a unifying lifeline in the advice contained within this book. We moved forward only because we made the constant effort to base all decisions on cultivating and protecting solid, literacy-based instruction throughout the school. It has not been quick or easy. It has been a monumental task for our staff from top to bottom, and we are still not finished. However, for the first time in a very long while, we are starting to see our population of students complete work that they themselves did not think was possible. For our teachers, witnessing that realization has become a powerful justification for continuing the struggle.

If your own school is contemplating how best to meet the mandate of the new standards, *Cracking the Common Core* can be indispensable. But you must do more than read it like one more abstract text. You must allow it to guide the steps you take. And, like Ivan, you must simply jump in head first.

JEFFREY MENZER, Principal
JACOB NAGY, Language Arts Coach
William Penn High School
New Castle, Delaware

Preface

The Common Core State Standards (CCSS) are changing the state of play in American secondary schools. Their mandate for the use of more challenging texts is not limited to English classrooms but extends to other content subjects as well. Moreover, the influence of the Standards is felt even in the few states that have yet to adopt them or that adopt the new tests being developed by the two assessment consortia, the Partnership for Assessment of Readiness for College and Careers (PARCC) and the Smarter Balanced Assessment Corsortium. This is because the standards in these states are being revised upward, as are the tests that measure their attainment.

Wherever you teach and however your students are assessed, there can be no doubt that a new era has dawned. It is characterized by an aggressive new set of expectations, and their implications affect middle and high school teachers on a comprehensive scale. Successful implementation will not occur if it is left to the efforts of individual teachers working alone. It will require a schoolwide initiative that begins with professional learning and ends with ongoing collaboration. Our hope in writing this book is that it might serve as the cornerstone of that learning and as a guide to teachers working collaboratively to take the measure of their practice against new approaches.

We begin with a brief overview of the CCSS, including their history and the give-and-take they have occasioned within the educational community. It is important that educators understand the structure of the Standards, how to interpret them, and how they are complemented by the essential, but easily overlooked, appendices. Accordingly, the opening chapter contrasts the instruction embraced by the Standards with the status quo in many secondary schools. The differences can be jarring, but they can also serve as a wake-up call to create a new mindset from the beginning.

The second and third chapters provide some background for effectively translating the CCSS into instruction. Chapter 2 describes the unique qualities of adolescent readers and offers suggestions for taking advantage of these qualities to motivate them to read, not only in English classrooms but also in content subjects. Chapter 3 addresses the nature of text complexity and the challenges of helping students traverse the more demanding textual terrain required by the

CCSS. We provide a list of key exemplars and a clear description of how text difficulty is gauged. The chapter concludes with specific suggestions for choosing texts that are appropriate for meeting the demands of the Standards.

Chapter 4 is a natural follow-up. In it, we explore how several texts can be taught together as a set ranging in content, format, and difficulty. We introduce our idea of a quad text set, which is thoroughly grounded in comprehension research. The idea is that most students can successfully read a challenging target text as long as they are supported in advance with easier related texts. These include a video component, an information text, and an engaging young adult selection. Complete examples from literature, history, and science are provided in the appendices.

Chapters 5–7 address the before, during, and after components of any lesson that includes reading a challenging text. Chapter 5 suggests ways in which teachers can introduce vocabulary and supply relevant knowledge required for comprehension. Chapter 6 explores effective and viable approaches to ensuring that students are engaged and supported while they read. We have included well-established strategies such as reading guides and Reciprocal Teaching together with techniques of more recent vintage, such as Peer-Assisted Learning Strategies. We stress the need for collaboration and accommodation, and we explain how these approaches are within the reach of any classroom teacher. In Chapter 7 we offer suggestions for conducting relevant and engaging discussions. We begin by describing the nature of classroom dynamics and then present specific approaches, such as Reciprocal Questioning, Collaborative Reasoning, and Questioning the Author.

Chapters 8 and 9 work together to address the expectations for writing and research. Like reading, writing is explicitly targeted in the CCSS, and its reach extends beyond the English classroom to all content areas. Writing has long been the "foster child" of literacy, but the Standards have given it new prominence among the quintessential proficiencies of the 21st century. In Chapter 8, we offer specific suggestions concerning how teachers can link text-based writing activities to their objectives. Our focus is on form and content rather than on mechanics, with particular emphasis on summary and argumentative writing, both central to the CCSS. In Chapter 9, we examine how traditional notions of research projects have changed, both to meet the Standards and to reflect the digital world. Here we bring to bear the approaches described in Chapter 8 to real-world questions requiring data analysis and interpretation.

Throughout the book, our discussion of instructional approaches is motivated by two guiding principles: Every approach we describe must have a solid foundation in research *and* be reasonable for teachers to implement with a diverse group of students. We resisted the temptation to include techniques that were appealing on the basis of an instinct or a hunch. Had we included them, this book would have been much longer and its message diluted. We believe that by emphasizing a short menu of effective approaches, we have provided the tools that teachers will need to help their students attain the new Standards.

Contents

CHAPTER 1. Embracing the Common Core   1

A Brief Description of the CCSS Initiative   3
Why Embrace the Standards?   5
Necessary Changes Related to the Standards   7
The CCSS: Their Format and Implications for Instruction   8

CHAPTER 2. Understanding Adolescent Readers   14

The Scope of the Challenge   14
Defining Adolescent Literacy   16
A Time of Change   17
Motivating Adolescents to Read   20
Take-Away Suggestions   26

CHAPTER 3. Understanding Challenging Texts   28

Seminal Works in the Disciplines   28
Quantitative Measures of Text Difficulty   31
Qualitative Measures of Text Difficulty   33
Readers and Texts   35
A Possible Process for Choosing and Using Texts   36
Final Thoughts   38

CHAPTER 4. Designing Challenging Text Sets   39

An Expanded Understanding of Content-Area Texts   40
A Word about "Texts"   40
Text Representation Theory   41
Building Background Knowledge through Intertextual
    Connections   48
The Quad Text Set in Action: An Example from ELA   50
The Quad Text Set in Action: An Example
    from History/Social Studies   53
The Quad Text Set in Action: An Example from Science   54
Final Thoughts   56

CHAPTER 5. Building Background Knowledge   58

What Is Background Knowledge and How Do We Get It?   60
Moving to Instruction   65
Teaching Technical Vocabulary   65
Strategies for Previewing   74
Incorporating Writing   81
Final Thoughts   85

CHAPTER 6. Supporting Students during Reading   86

Choosing a Stance for Adolescent Readers   87
Recent Large-Scale Efforts   88
Rationale for Collaboration   91
Reading Guides   92
Peer-Assisted Learning Strategies   99
Reciprocal Teaching   103
Jigsawed Text Sets   106
Making Accommodations   109
Final Thoughts   111

CHAPTER 7. Implementing High-Quality Discussions after Reading   112

Common Core Requirements for Discussion   115
Characteristics of an Effective Discussion   116
Who's in Control?   119
Reciprocal Questioning   121
Reciprocal Teaching   122
Questioning the Author   124
Collaborative Reasoning   128
Discussion Web   129
Devil's Advocate   132
Final Thoughts   135

CHAPTER 8. Text-Based Writing to Support Understanding   136

Barriers to Text-Based Writing   137
Why Text-Based Writing—*and Why Me?*   138
Writing Activities That Work   140
Summary Writing   141
Argumentative Writing   152
Final Thoughts   161

CHAPTER 9. Research in the Content Areas   163

A Short History of Research in the Content Areas   165
"Real Research"   166
Data Collection Tools   168
Data Analysis Tools   170
Data Evaluation Tools   173
Data Sharing Tools   176

A Word about Collaboration as a Tool of Inquiry   178
Final Thoughts   179

CHAPTER 10. Leading for Change   180

Changing or Tweaking   180
Barriers   181
Creating a Specific Vision   182
Gathering the Resources Your Vision Demands   184
Final Thoughts: Making It All Make Sense   188

APPENDIX 1. Text Set Examples from English Language Arts   191

APPENDIX 2. Text Set Examples from History/Social Studies   201

APPENDIX 3. Text Set Examples from Science   209

References   217

Index   227

CRACKING THE COMMON CORE

CHAPTER 1

Embracing the Common Core

He ate and drank the precious words.
His spirit grew robust;
He knew no more that he was poor,
Nor that his frame was dust.
He danced along the dingy days,
And this bequest of wings
Was but a book. What liberty
A loosened spirit brings!
    —EMILY DICKINSON
        (in Todd & Higginson, 1890)

Dickinson's depiction of the delights inherent in the reading experience is not unusual in our culture. Readers often speak of "getting lost in a book," "being carried away" by a particularly intriguing plot, or being profoundly changed by the information and ideas they find in their reading. Although we don't agree with Dickinson's claim that reading has *unlimited* power to overcome injustice, poverty, or mortality, Dickinson's poem serves as a powerful reminder of how important literacy is to students' development and independence. It is a process by which they grow the "wings" they need to make their way successfully into college and the workplace, and into their roles as contributing members of their communities. We want to think hard about our students' literacy development because it has a profound impact on their futures and on a democratic system that requires an informed and literate public.

Unfortunately, there are a number of frightening statistics that demonstrate that our children are not developing the literacy skills they need to graduate and be successful in college or their careers (Graham & Hebert, 2010). Although we will be focusing on student proficiency more specifically in Chapter 2, suffice it to say that many fear today's students do not have the literacy skills needed to be successful in college or to compete in an increasingly globalized marketplace. It is also clear that individual states can no longer set their own widely varying standards of proficiency (Rothman, 2012).

Preparing students to compete in the global marketplace is not our only worry. Impoverished literacy skills lead to an estimated 50% of 2-year college students and 20% of 4-year college students having to take remedial courses to prepare them for the rigors of college-level work—close to 1.7 million beginning students every year (Complete College America, 2012)! To deal with this number of unprepared students, we spend an estimated $2 billion annually on remediation (Fulton, 2010), with the effectiveness of these remedial courses and programs described as questionable by some and a "bridge to nowhere" by others. In fact, large numbers of students do not matriculate from remedial courses into regular college coursework (Complete College America, 2012).

The most recent SAT scores also highlight the low literacy levels of American students. For the 2012 test only 43% of high school seniors achieved the "SAT Benchmark" score of 1550, which represents a better-than-average likelihood of achieving a B– or higher in college coursework (College Board, 2012). More troubling are the long-term trends in SAT achievement. Mean scores for critical reading and writing have been lower each year since 2006, reaching an all-time low in both critical reading and writing on the 2012 SAT (College Board, 2012). These figures are admittedly influenced by increasing percentages of seniors taking the test. In *The Manufactured Crisis*, Berliner and Biddle (1995) posit that the decline in SAT performance over several decades is an artifact of greater access to the test for students who do not fall into the traditional "college prep" category. We view greater student access to the SAT and the chance to attend college as positive. However, if more of our students are contemplating postsecondary education, then we need to reevaluate the ways that we prepare students to meet the demands of these programs. High schools cannot be an on-ramp to the "bridge to nowhere."

To address these issues, the National Governors Association and the Council of Chief State School Officers collaborated in the construction of the Common Core State Standards (CCSS). We recognize that they have engendered controversies in the literacy research community, but we welcome the changes to instruction that the standards demand. We believe that the increased rigor of the CCSS has the potential to improve children's literacy by refocusing teachers, schools, and the educational establishment on high levels of reading and thinking, and on developing the skills that students need to understand and communicate about challenging texts. However, because of our ongoing work in schools across the country, we also understand that teachers already inundated with mandates and initiatives might be ready to throw up their hands as government adds yet another initiative to an already full plate. Many schools and teachers might welcome the idea of the robust standards that the CCSS represent, but they might not know how to integrate the new standards into their curriculum and instruction. It is our hope that this book will help to provide a transparent framework for incorporating the CCSS across middle school and high school content-area instruction, and to provide creative and actionable suggestions for helping all teachers contribute to the development of complex literacies in their students.

We begin this chapter with a discussion of the development and composition of the CCSS Initiative. We argue that the new standards require a sea change in the way schools and teachers design curriculum and instruction. In the chapters to come we describe the needs of our adolescent readers and writers, and the demands of the texts that they will be required to read and write. In other chapters we discuss how to support student reading through "before," "during," and "after" instructional strategies. We attend to the importance of text-based writing and discussion to student comprehension and thinking, and we end the book with a chapter on teaching content-area research and inquiry skills. Finally, we speculate about the leadership support that teachers will need as they meet these challenges.

A Brief Description of the CCSS Initiative

To be frank, although we have welcomed the rigor that the CCSS bring, we have also been somewhat surprised at the speed with which the standards were developed and released, and even more surprised by their rapid adoption. State and local control of schools has long been a hallmark of the American educational system, and past initiatives to create national standards have sputtered and failed (Rothman, 2011). However, although the CCSS built on past reform initiatives and the ongoing work of the states on their own educational standards, a number of factors began to make it clear that a common, focused, and rigorous set of standards was finally needed, and that having 50 sets of widely variable educational standards was a significant problem for our nation's future. The demand for higher levels of literacy in college and the workplace, together with our increasingly globalized economy, made the cooperative efforts to develop the CCSS an educational and economic necessity.

Although the genesis of the CCSS Initiative can be found in a number of previous educational reform efforts through which states developed new state standards and standardized tests that measured learning outcomes (see, e.g., Coburn, Pearson, & Woulfin, 2011), Rothman (2011, 2012) argues that the No Child Left Behind Act of 2002 (NCLB) made the need for national standards much more apparent. Because the act required that all states administer the National Assessment of Educational Progress (NAEP), NCLB made it much easier to compare student achievement on state tests with their achievement levels on the NAEP, making disparities in rigor among states' standards much easier to spot. Poor reading scores on the NAEP in the early 1990s led to the perception that there was a national reading crisis that required changes in reading instruction (Coburn et al., 2011). However, with a vast majority of children scoring at a proficient level on state tests, and only a small number of students scoring proficiently on the NAEP, education officials began to see that sweeping reforms were needed to increase the rigor of the state standards (Rothman, 2012).

Figure 1.1 provides a controversial illustration of these differences. In 2005 and 2010 the Thomas Fordham Institute compared the clarity and rigor of state English language arts (ELA) and math standards to that of the Common Core standards and graded each state with an A to F rating. Interestingly, the CCSS were also rated in this report, receiving a B+ score for their overall rigor. We present the 2010 findings from 10 states here—not to endorse them, but to show you that there is evidence that standards vary across states. If your state is not represented, you can investigate for yourself by visiting the Fordham website at *www.edexcellence.net* and checking out the *State of State Standards and the Common Core* report (Carmichael, Wilson, Porter-Magee, & Martino, 2010).

It is clear from looking at Figure 1.1 that individual state literacy standards vary widely, from states like California with standards that exceeded the clarity and rigor of the CCSS to states like Delaware with standards that fell well below the Common Core mark. However, although the figure includes a balance of five states that met or exceeded the rigor and clarity of the CCSS and five that fell below that level, the Fordham evaluation is actually less optimistic. They reported that the CCSS were more rigorous than the literacy standards of 37 states. Although the authors of this study warn that there is not a clear relationship between better standards and higher student achievement, they also warn that the failure to adopt and implement rigorous standards, and to design assessments that can effectively measure student attainment of them, can cause significant proficiency gaps among the states (Carmichael et al., 2010).

State	Grade	Comparison to the Common Core (B+ rating)
California	A	Clearly superior to CCSS
Massachusetts	A–	Too close to call
Colorado	B+	Too close to call
Virginia	B+	Too close to call
Florida	B	Too close to call
Hawaii	C	Clearly inferior to CCSS
Minnesota	C	Clearly inferior to CCSS
Arkansas	D	Clearly inferior to CCSS
Pennsylvania	D	Clearly inferior to CCSS
Delaware	F	Clearly inferior to CCSS

FIGURE 1.1. Rigor of state literacy standards compared to the Common Core.

A report entitled *The Proficiency Illusion* (Cronin, Dahlin, Adkins, & Kingsbury, 2007) addressed these gaps. The study, which used a common metric to compare the proficiency standards among the states, found that although in some states students must score at the 77th percentile rank nationally to be considered proficient, in other states students could be considered proficient by scoring at only the 10th percentile rank! Statistics like these made it clear to educational leaders that a common set of rigorous standards, aggressively implemented, could be an important first step in bridging these proficiency gaps. Furthermore, taking this step could provide much-needed transparency in the educational data on the basis of which states, schools, and teachers must make important instructional and curricular decisions.

However, unlike previous efforts to design rigorous common standards that began at the national level, the CCSS Initiative (CCSSI) began with a distinctly state-level flavor in 2009, with the National Governors Association and the Council of Chief State School Officers in the vanguard of the new initiative (Rothman, 2012). The process of construction is documented in the introductory section of the Standards, available at *www.corestandards.org*, but we will summarize it here. Reaching an agreement where states would be enlisted to help in the development of the new standards but given the option of whether or not to adopt the final product, all states but Texas and Alaska agreed to work together toward a common standards solution. From that initial meeting, individuals representing higher education, state departments of education, teachers, professional organizations, parents, and other stakeholders worked to draft several iterations of the standards and to benchmark them against international standards (National Governors Association [NGA] Center for Best Practices and Council of Chief State School Officers [CCSSO], 2010). Throughout the process, the work group solicited feedback, and the final standards document was released to the public on June 2, 2010. As of this writing, 45 states and the District of Columbia have adopted the CCSS.

Why Embrace the Standards?

The road to the release and adoption of the CCSS has not been an easy one, and a number of organizations and scholars have leveled significant criticism at the standards. Figure 1.2 represents some of the major organizations that are part of the current debate about the CCSSI. Although most scholars and organizations dismiss the Cato Institute's fear that the CCSSI represents a dangerous and unconstitutional move to expand federal control of education, another think tank, the Brookings Institution, has challenged the Standards from the standpoint of effectiveness, predicting that in the long run they will have little impact on achievement (Loveless, 2012). Some professional organizations have also been cautious in their support of the standards. These include the National Education

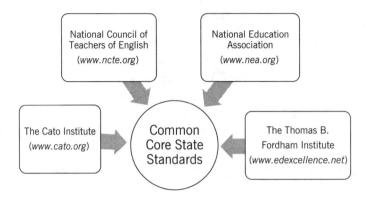

FIGURE 1.2. Key organizations involved in the Common Core debate.

Association (NEA) and the National Council of Teachers of English (NCTE), who are concerned that teacher expertise and decision making could be more limited when the standards are implemented. Furthermore, NCTE argues that students' cultures, interests, and social and emotional needs should be considered in their implementation (NCTE, 2012). The list of representative texts used as illustrations of those meeting the standards is particularly controversial, as is the focus on "close reading" of these texts, which the organization fears might disenfranchise an increasingly diverse population of American students.

Although supportive of the rigor represented in the CCSS, the Thomas B. Fordham institute has expressed concern over the cost of implementation and calls for a strategic and balanced approach to what states and districts pay for teacher training, educational materials, and student assessment as they adopt the core and assess students. We respect these concerns and share in some of them. From our perspective, however, they are outweighed by the CCSS's intense focus on the high-level skills that college and the workplace demand, particularly when it comes to students' ability to read, analyze, and use complex literary and informational texts, proficiencies correlated with post–high school success (ACT, 2006). We believe that the spotlight on these skills is a significant benefit of the new standards, and one that offers educators the opportunity to begin to serve the large number of American students who are unable to critically read challenging texts.

From our work in schools, we know that an invigorated focus on critical reading is needed, because the opportunities for substantive interaction with complex texts *in classrooms* is becoming increasingly limited. In our professional development work, we have been calling this problem the "textless approach" to instruction, a type of instruction that has a number of manifestations. One might be an ELA teacher reading all of *To Kill a Mockingbird* to her students because she feels they will not, or cannot, do the reading on their own. Another might be a biology teacher translating a complex scientific text on DNA replication into a PowerPoint and then having students copy the notes instead of wrestling with the reading themselves. Yet another manifestation might be a history teacher showing the full video of the musical *1776* to her students instead of tackling complicated primary source documents from the American Revolution. Although these instructional choices provide students with exposure to content-area concepts, we argue that these choices cannot lead to the development of independent readers of complex texts, since we only get better at an activity by actually *doing* it. The text-less approach reminds us of one of our children, who wanted to become better at tennis but didn't want to practice tennis, preferring instead to believe that a $275 tennis racket would be enough to improve his game. That he did not get better at tennis from such a "practice" regimen is not surprising (not only because he didn't choose to practice but because we didn't choose to supply the new racket!). So why do we expect a different outcome when it comes to the reading ability of our students?

Necessary Changes Related to the Standards

We embrace the CCSS because they challenge us to make substantive changes to the way we think about student time during school.

The first change that we will have to face is the CCSS focus on complex texts. The standards challenge educators to think more strategically about the texts they use in their instruction, and we believe this is an important change. Research reveals that material that is currently being read in schools is not challenging enough to prepare students for the demands of the texts that they will find when they graduate from high school (ACT, 2006). While the difficulty and cognitive demands of texts found in college and the workplace continue to rise, the textual difficulty of materials found in K–12 schools continues to decline, leading to a significant gap between the reading experiences and skills developed in middle and high school and the texts and skills needed to be successful beyond the walls of those schools (see Figure 1.3).

Second, we are embracing the CCSS because they force schools to think equally hard about how they can include more informational reading and writing in instruction across *all* content areas. Highlighting the importance of shared

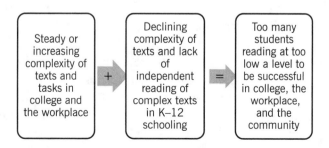

FIGURE 1.3. The text complexity gap.

responsibility for literacy development, the standards make it clear that connected reading, writing, and thinking activities can no longer be the sole purview of the ELA teacher (NGA and CCSSO, 2010). This is surely not a new idea; content-area reading textbooks were available in 1970 (e.g., Herber) and continue to be required reading in most master's and many undergraduate programs (e.g., McKenna & Robinson, 2013). What is different now, though, is the rationale for such approaches.

College and workforce training programs primarily require the ability to read complex *informational* texts independently (NGA and CCSSO, 2010; Pritchard, Wilson, & Yamnitz, 2007), so developing this ability requires the efforts of all teachers. This means that teachers of history, social studies, science, health, and career and technical courses—those teachers whose content areas primarily use informational texts—have a significant opportunity to contribute substantively to the literacy development of their students. Please don't misunderstand us! We know that all content teachers have always contributed to the development of their students. However, because of the CCSS focus on developing the critical reading of complex informational and literary texts, schools across the country must now recognize the equal importance of all teachers in this particular pursuit and not place this burden on ELA teachers alone.

A case in point involves a high school that recently suffered a significant drop in its state reading scores. To address this disappointing performance, the school officials decided that along with their regular course content, every student would read one additional novel per marking period in their ELA classes. Although we understand why the school might make this choice, from the CCSS perspective this response is misguided for a number of reasons, but primarily because it completely ignores the contributions of other content-area teachers to students' critical reading ability. This is particularly true because of the CCSS focus on informational texts, texts that offer very different challenges than the literary works that are a part of this well-intentioned but misguided initiative.

The CCSS: Their Format and Implications for Instruction

So what, specifically, are these new standards and how do they help us to consider approaches other than the "textless" method described above, or approaches that are grounded only in ELA classrooms? For those of you who may be unfamiliar with the CCSS, you may feel daunted by the task of understanding a completely different set of standards from those you are currently using. However, unlike some complicated state and national organization standards that you may have worked with, we believe that one benefit of the CCSS is their simplicity and accessibility. The standards begin with the broad College and Career Readiness Anchors, which complement the more specific grade-level standards. At each grade level, three categories—Reading Literature, Reading Informational Texts, and Writing—contain 10 succinct standards each. An additional two categories contain six standards each: Speaking and Listening, and Language. Technology does not have a category of its own but is suffused throughout the standards. Figure 1.4 depicts the overall structure of the CCSS for ELA. Because they are focused on categories of important skills, we believe these standards are specific enough to guide curricular and instructional decisions, while open enough to allow for professional decision making and differentiation to meet student needs.

Additionally, the CCSS include three important appendices. By "important," we mean that unlike most appendices these are not filled with incidental material of little real significance. On the contrary, these are "must reads" for anyone wishing to gain a full appreciation of the standards and their implementation. Appendix A deals primarily with text difficulty, helping teachers analyze content-area texts in order to guide selection of texts for their students. As we have already discussed, the reading level of K–12 texts has continued to decrease, even though the reading demands of texts in college and the workplace grow. This appendix provides important tools to help teachers analyze the complexity of content-area texts using both quantitative and qualitative means. However, it also encourages teachers to consider how the tasks they assign and the qualities of their readers impact student motivation and their ability to use texts to accomplish content-area goals. The issue of text complexity is such an important component of the standards that we will devote a chapter to it.

To provide further help with the text complexity issues addressed in Appendix A, Appendix B provides teachers with important exemplars of texts that meet the complexity demands of each grade level, as well as performance tasks that meet the robust reading and writing demands of the CCSS. These include suggested stories, drama, poetry, and informational texts that meet complexity demands in ELA, as well as informational texts for history and social studies, science, mathematics, and technical subjects. Appendix C provides teachers with writing samples that meet the demands of the CCSS at each grade level.

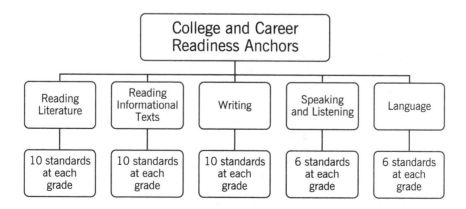

FIGURE 1.4. Structure of the CCSS for ELA.

Although we will be exploring many specific standards in later chapters of the book, we suggest that a good way to begin is by exploring the four categories of skills in which the 10 Anchor Standards for Reading fall. We briefly describe these standards here, and the instructional shifts that they require for schools and educators. The standards' design reflects the belief that flexible, high-level comprehension requires the three proficiencies represented in Figure 1.5: attention to detail, recognition of craft and structure, and integration of knowledge and ideas.

Category 1: Key Ideas and Details

1. Read closely to determine what the text says explicitly and to make logical inferences from it; cite specific textual evidence.
2. Determine central ideas or themes of a text and analyze their development; summarize the key supporting details.
3. Analyze how and why individuals, events, and ideas develop and interact over the course of a text.

The Common Core Anchor Standards related to Key Ideas and Details demonstrate that a textless approach can no longer be an instructional choice. As Figure 1.6 shows, students are going to be expected to read, connect their reading to their background knowledge and previous reading, concisely summarize main textual ideas, and be able to purposefully analyze texts and use textual evidence drawn from that reading to make arguments. In fact, it is the Anchor Standards' focus on text-based argument, what Gerald Graff (2003) calls "the hidden curriculum" of all college-level work, that is one of the primary shifts that we see in the standards, and it is clear that students must be taught how to read and to argue as "disciplinary experts" (Ferretti & Lewis, 2013). This expectation

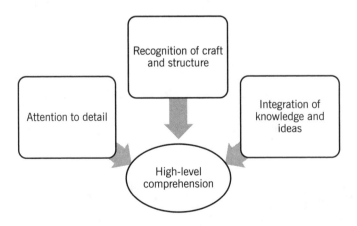

FIGURE 1.5. Structure of Anchor Standards for Reading.

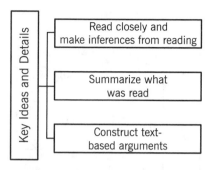

FIGURE 1.6. Key Ideas and Details.

can vary widely across content-areas (Wineburg, 2001) and therefore requires shared responsibility across all content-area specialties. Although analytical and argumentative thinking and writing has not been a focus of content area classes (Applebee & Langer, 2006; Kiuhara, Graham, & Hawken, 2009), this category of the Anchor Standards compels educators to think carefully about what it means to read, think, and argue like a historian, scientist, literary critic, artist, and so forth and to develop instructional activities that support these content-specific ways of thinking.

Category 2: Craft and Structure

4. Interpret words and phrases as they are used in a text, including determining technical, connotative, and figurative meanings, and analyze how specific word choices shape meaning or tone.
5. Analyze the structure of texts, including how specific sentences, paragraphs, and larger portions of the text (e.g., a section, chapter, scene, or stanza) relate to each other and the whole.
6. Assess how point of view or purpose shapes the content and style of a text.

Like the first set of Anchor Standards, the standards related to Craft and Structure focus on the reading and analysis of texts and how textual elements relate to one another. However, this category also encourages us to focus on two other student proficiencies. As you can see in Figure 1.7, Anchor Standard 4 first encourages educators to reevaluate the way they introduce and teach content, academic vocabulary, and word attack skills. If the Common Core standards demand that students be able to interpret words and phrases in challenging texts, then teachers will need to evaluate how they contribute to students' "word consciousness" through contextualized vocabulary activities that encourage students to make multiple connections to content-specific technical words, and through analysis of words based on context and student knowledge of word roots and

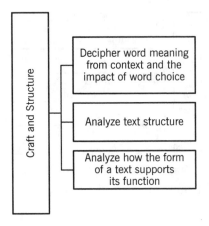

FIGURE 1.7. Craft and Structure.

affixes. Decontextualized vocabulary instruction focusing on rote memorization and testing with lists of SAT words, the modus operandi of many American schools, does not meet this high standard since these lists do not have a clear connection to what is currently being read in any of a student's classes.

Second, this set of Anchor Standards forces us to think specifically about authorial intent in reading, and how the specific word and organizational choices of authors, filmmakers, artists, or speakers impact the meaning and effect of the texts they produce. This is a high-level skill, and one that demands that students think past the basic meaning of the text to how the author's consciously created form serves clear rhetorical purposes. Putting the author front and center in instruction—which is controversial in a number of circles—is an instructional shift that educators must take into account when incorporating these Craft and Structure standards.

Category 3: Integration of Knowledge and Ideas

7. Integrate and evaluate content presented in diverse formats and media, including visually and quantitatively, as well as in words.
8. Delineate and evaluate the argument and specific claims in a text, including the validity of the reasoning as well as the relevance and sufficiency of the evidence.
9. Analyze how two or more texts address similar themes or topics in order to build knowledge or to compare the approaches the authors take.

The Anchor Standards addressing Integration of Knowledge and Ideas broaden the definition of *text* from the previous two categories, which are focused primarily on traditional print text. As Figure 1.8 highlights, this set of Anchor Standards forces educators to use a variety of print, digital, video, and audio

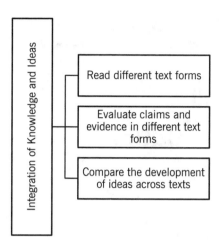

FIGURE 1.8. Integration of Knowledge and Ideas.

materials in their instruction and to teach students to analyze the content that is presented in each. Like our first set of Anchor Standards, this set also focuses on argument, and on the evaluation of authorial claims and the evidence authors use to support these claims. Additionally, although our first two categories focus on student ability to trace the development of ideas, themes, and characters in single texts—and how authorial choices can impact this development—the Integration Anchor Standards focus on student ability to make comparisons and analyses of the development of ideas *across* texts. This set of standards makes it clear that to meet them educators must develop sets of related texts, as well as activities that build the skills needed to synthesize and evaluate texts.

Category 4: Range of Reading and Level of Text Complexity

10. Read and comprehend complex literary and informational texts independently and proficiently.

No figure is needed to address this Anchor Standard! If students are going to learn to read complex texts independently, then we must begin to take seriously how we incorporate more connected reading and writing activities in all of our secondary classrooms, and how we must shelve the "textless" approaches described previously. However, just committing to more reading is not enough. We must help our students build these skills by using a wide variety of texts in our content classes and incorporating instructional strategies that help students acquire the ability, confidence, and stamina needed to read and analyze these texts. In addition, we must take a strategic approach to choosing texts that support both our individual content-area learning goals *and* our students' overall literacy development. These are our goals for this book. Let's get started!

CHAPTER 2

Understanding Adolescent Readers

A teacher who is attempting to teach without inspiring
the pupil with a desire to learn is hammering on cold iron.
—HORACE MANN

While we may know that current levels of student achievement are not accept-able and that new standards demand quite advanced achievement, we can do nothing to bridge that gap without understanding the needs of our students. In this chapter, we hope to extend your awareness of the factors that contribute to adolescent literacy development. This is not merely an academic exercise, for we believe that such awareness is key to providing instruction that is ultimately more effective.

The Scope of the Challenge

For nearly half a century, the NAEP has provided a widely accepted indicator of the reading proficiency of students at grades 4, 8, and 12. Comprehension scores are categorized at three levels—Basic, Proficient, and Advanced—which we have summarized in Figure 2.1. The criteria defining each comprehension level vary by grade level and are based on the skills needed to comprehend texts encountered at that level. The unpleasant reality is that there is a fourth level, as well, the one that is most concerning to us: below basic.

Figure 2.2 provides the most recent NAEP results in a nutshell. The question is how to interpret them. There are several ways to judge the extent of the challenge that American teachers now face. The most common, and easily the most alarming, is to focus on the percentage of students who fall below the Basic level. Not only are these proportions striking, but what the table does not reflect is that

GRADE 4	
Basic (208)	Fourth-grade students performing at the *Basic* level should be able to locate relevant information, make simple inferences, and use their understanding of the text to identify details that support a given interpretation or conclusion. Students should be able to interpret the meaning of a word as it is used in the text.
Proficient (238)	Fourth-grade students performing at the *Proficient* level should be able to integrate and interpret texts and apply their understanding of the text to draw conclusions and make evaluations.
Advanced (268)	Fourth-grade students performing at the *Advanced* level should be able to make complex inferences and construct and support their inferential understanding of the text. Students should be able to apply their understanding of a text to make and support a judgment.
GRADE 8	
Basic (243)	Eighth-grade students performing at the *Basic* level should be able to locate information; identify statements of main idea, theme, or author's purpose; and make simple inferences from texts. They should be able to interpret the meaning of a word as it is used in the text. Students performing at this level should also be able to state judgments and give some support about content and presentation of content.
Proficient (281)	Eighth-grade students performing at the *Proficient* level should be able to provide relevant information and summarize main ideas and themes. They should be able to make and support inferences about a text, connect parts of a text, and analyze text features. Students performing at this level should also be able to fully substantiate judgments about content and presentation of content.
Advanced (323)	Eighth-grade students performing at the *Advanced* level should be able to make connections within and across texts and to explain causal relations. They should be able to evaluate and justify the strength of supporting evidence and the quality of an author's presentation. Students performing at the Advanced level also should be able to manage the processing demands of analysis and evaluation by stating, explaining, and justifying.
GRADE 12	
Basic (265)	Twelfth-grade students performing at the *Basic* level should be able to identify elements of meaning and form and relate them to the overall meaning of the text. They should be able to make inferences, develop interpretations, make connections between texts, and draw conclusions; and they should be able to provide some support for each. They should be able to interpret the meaning of a word as it is used in the text.
Proficient (302)	Twelfth-grade students performing at the *Proficient* level should be able to locate and integrate information using sophisticated analyses of the meaning and form of the text. These students should be able to provide specific text support for inferences, interpretative statements, and comparisons within and across texts.
Advanced (346)	Twelfth-grade students performing at the *Advanced* level should be able to analyze both the meaning and the form of the text and provide complete, explicit, and precise text support for their analyses with specific examples. They should be able to read across multiple texts for a variety of purposes, analyzing and evaluating them individually and as a set.

FIGURE 2.1. NAEP reading proficiency levels, scale scores, and descriptions, updated in 2009.

NAEP level	Grade 4	Grade 8	Grade 12
Advanced	8	3	5
Proficient	26	31	33
Basic	33	42	36
Below Basic	33	24	26

FIGURE 2.2. NAEP reading percentages at each performance level for grades 4, 8, and 12. Grades 4 and 8 are from 2011; grade 12 is from 2009.

over time they have scarcely budged. Though many describe the situation as a crisis, it more closely resembles an immovable object, one that has resisted reform after reform (McKenna, 2011). In our view, however, the CCSS offer the potential for real change. They represent a comprehensive approach, enlisting content teachers at every grade level and implicitly requiring effective practice and shared responsibility for student literacy development across the content areas.

A second perspective on the NAEP results is the view from the top. The percentage of students scoring at the Proficient and Advanced levels is not likely to arouse alarm. After all, these students are at minimal risk of school failure. In their case too, however, we contend that these percentages present American educators with a second challenge, that of increasing the number of adolescents who excel at reading. Support for this view comes from the Program for International Student Assessment (PISA), which compares the reading proficiency of 15-year-old students in 32 participating countries. In 2009, the United States ranked 14th out of the 32 (Organisation for Economic Co-operation and Development [OECD], 2010), not exactly the world-leading performance we might have hoped for. There has been much conjecture about the causes. Diane Ravitch (2010) argues that we have overfocused on students who struggle, devoting inordinate resources to a problem that is not likely to be solved. In the process, she maintains, we have shortchanged abler students, possibly denying them the chance to realize their potential. Again, we are persuaded that the CCSS can have the effect of supporting strong readers as they explore texts of increasing complexity.

Defining Adolescent Literacy

Given our goals in this book, we also must focus careful attention on the characteristics of older readers. Adolescent literacy is a surprisingly recent concept (Bean & Harper, 2009), dating back only to 1990s and driven by the position statement adopted by the International Reading Association (IRA; Moore, Bean, Birdyshaw, & Rycik, 1999; see also the recent revision [IRA, 2012]). The newness of the idea means that there is little consensus about the meaning of the term, let alone its classroom implications.

To fully frame the challenges of adolescent literacy, Bean and Harper (2009) suggest that we must first grapple with a more basic question: What is adolescence? We all have our own idea, of course, and that may be part of the problem. Our perspectives may be too limited, not accounting for dimensions of adolescence that might inform our understanding of students and their instructional needs. Nancy Lesko (2001) suggested that there are two principal ways of viewing adolescence: as a biological stage through which all of us must pass or as a sociohistorical phenomenon that differs with context.

Bean and Harper (2009) extend this breakdown further. Based on an extensive review of research, they suggest four ways in which literacy experts tend to interpret adolescence. We summarize them here:

1. *Grade level.* Perhaps the simplest way to define adolescence is to identify its onset in terms of traditional grade levels. This approach suggests a demarcation between the primary grades and those that follow, and it ignores the gradual development of literacy over time.
2. *Literacy needs.* Reflected in the CCSS are the demands of gradually increasing text complexity plus literacy requirements unique to each content area. This perspective helps us chart a desired trajectory, and departures from it are viewed as deficits.
3. *Literacy practices.* Every adolescent has grown up in a wired world. The use of digital technologies, both for personal and academic reasons, requires that we reconsider traditional notions of literacy, which originated in a print-only world.
4. *Diversity.* The adolescent experience is influenced by a host of factors that go beyond physical maturation and proficiency. They include "race, ethnicity, social class, sexuality, home language, citizenship," (p. 48) and more, and they contribute to the uniqueness of each adolescent.

We agree with Bean and Harper that once a teacher adopts one of these perspectives, there is a danger of minimizing the rest and ignoring the complexities of adolescent literacy. We also agree that "taking a strictly cognitive stance toward understanding struggling or, indeed, any readers and their needs may be seriously limited" (p. 49). The challenge for teachers lies in fostering cognitive strategy development without losing sight of the other factors that influence that growth, especially social and technological factors.

A Time of Change

Alexander and Fox (2011) attempted to look across these perspectives in their recent review of research. They concluded that it is vital for teachers to keep in mind the physical development of adolescents because of its complex relationship with reading. For example, the rapid rate of physical maturation can influence self-perception. Reading often reinforces cultural norms and pressures. At the same time, adolescents often "use text as part of active exploration of possible/ideal selves" (p. 165). They gradually construct a reading identity, which includes beliefs about their proficiency and also about whether reading is enjoyable or useful. All the while, cognitive development improves markedly, and students are better able to think abstractly, arrive at inferences, and construct more elaborate mental representations of text content. This does not mean that they can always do so without support, however, but brain development provides the tools for this kind of thinking.

These changes are obviously complex—so much so that it is dangerous to generalize. That will not stop us, however, because we believe it is important for teachers to have a general idea of where students are headed as they pass through the often-turbulent phase called adolescence. Although it is true that each student moves along a unique trajectory, the similarities reflect an overall pattern that is characteristic of most.

- Physical changes bring about altered self-perception.
- The need for social interaction and acceptance grows, though this need is felt more strongly by some.
- Puberty becomes a factor influencing reading behavior.
- Cognitive ability improves, including the capacity for abstract and inferential thinking.
- The sense of reading self-efficacy increasingly influences choices about whether and what to read.
- Low self-efficacy often leads to less reading, which in turn limits the growth of proficiency.
- A sense of the value of reading becomes clearer and, when negative, more difficult to alter.
- Reading attitudes and behaviors in and out of school often diverge.
- The ability to monitor comprehension improves, although a student's strategies for troubleshooting may not be adequate.
- The influence of prior knowledge increases dramatically and becomes a major determiner of comprehension, particularly in content subjects.
- Social networking increasingly influences reading activities, in ways that are sometimes positive and sometimes concerning.

You will see that these characteristics of adolescents infuse our thinking about how to work with them effectively in school. Because we see this period as pivotal in reading attitudes, we combine texts and set transparent and engaging purposes for reading and writing. Because adolescents focus on their reading identities and on the perceptions of their peers, for example, we favor approaches that include collaboration. Because they are digital natives, we consider use of technology an integral aspect of literacy. Below we consider other salient findings about reading and adolescents.

The Influence of Gender

NAEP results have consistently documented the fact that girls outperform boys at all three grade levels tested. The most recent results, shown in Figure 2.3, are typical of a long-standing pattern.

Causes of the achievement gap are unclear. Smith and Wilhelm (2009) suggest three possibilities. One is that girls and boys are wired differently, in a way that favors girls. A second theory is that boys are disadvantaged by having too few male teachers serving as role models. Yet another theory is largely sociocultural. It may be that boys sometimes "choose not to engage in the kinds of literate activity privileged in schools" (p. 364), which they view not necessarily as feminine but as "schoolish" (p. 364). Whatever the cause, it is hardly limited to the United States. Of the countries participating in PISA, *all* report a significant advantage in reading for 15-year-old girls over boys the same age (OECD, 2010).

It is no wonder that motivating boys to read is a challenge frequently voiced by middle and high school teachers. A common recommendation is to build on interests commonly associated with boys (technology, sports, war, etc.), but Smith and Wilhelm (2009) warn that doing so involves two dangers. One is that teachers risk "treating boys as a monolithic group"; the other is that they risk reinforcing stereotypes and "hegemonic masculinities" (p. 366). We by no means want you to encourage gender-based stereotyping, masculine or feminine. These authors suggest a more general approach, focusing instead on texts that include situations that have clear goals, involve social interaction, provide a sense of control, offer a range of choices, and pose a degree of challenge. These qualities make sense to us and they are useful guideposts for planning.

But what of girls? Boys are not alone in often requiring attention to motivation. To be sure, the gender gap is good news for girls, but Sprague and Keeling (2009) warn of the danger of overlooking the needs of girls. Although it is true that girls as a group tend to be more proficient than boys, there is nevertheless a significant percentage of girls at grades 4, 8, and 12 who are below the NAEP Basic level. Girls who struggle are just as likely as boys to benefit from efforts to motivate them. However, the approaches likely to be effective in motivating girls may differ from those useful with boys. Sprague and Keeling (2009) remind us that girls contend with a host of social and emotional issues distinct from those faced by boys. They recommend making available titles from Shirleen Dodson's (2011) *100 Books for Girls to Grow On*. These books offer role models of girls

	Grade 4	Grade 8	Grade 12
Females	36	39	44
Males	31	29	33

FIGURE 2.3. Percentage of males and females scoring at or above the Proficient level. Grades 4 and 8 are from 2011; grade 12 is from 2009.

facing the same challenges. Discussing a common book in literature circles or book clubs can help girls connect with characters, obtain insights from the author and one another, and perhaps develop a more positive attitude toward reading in the bargain.

Although Sprague and Keeling also suggest that whole-class novels can lead to differentiated discussions about female characters, we advise caution. A whole-class selection chosen for its potential to guide girls has several drawbacks. Guzzetti (2009) points out that adolescent girls frequently fear ridicule from boys and may not be forthcoming during whole-class discussions. Another problem is that the issues girls might like to examine are of less importance to boys, and, as much as we would like to broaden the developing male perspective, we must also be mindful of what is likely to motivate boys. Finally, the canon itself may lead girls to "perceive that they are marginalized by their lack of representation in texts" (p. 373). This is not to say that canonical texts are unimportant, only that they may convey an unintended message and one that it's important to counter. We believe that one way of encouraging girls to interact openly is to establish discussion blogs, some of which could be set up with limited membership.

Motivating Adolescents to Read

The word *motivation*—from the Latin *movere*, to move—indicates the decision to act. A motivated student is one who *decides* to read. The question for any teacher is how to encourage students to make that decision. A good way to frame the challenge is to consider the source of motivation. It may have an intrinsic origin, within the student, or it may originate outside the student in the form of an external, or extrinsic, goal. Intrinsic motivation involves "behavior that is motivated by internal needs, desires, or feelings" (Dunston & Gambrell, 2009, p. 272). In contrast, extrinsic motivation occurs when a student views reading as a means to an end: to earn grades, rewards, recognition, and so forth. This distinction suggests two pathways to motivation. Both are susceptible to teacher influence, and both depend on what a student has come to believe about reading.

Making the decision to read is always based on the student's belief about what will happen (McKenna, 2001). They may not be as deliberative as Prince Hamlet (Figure 2.4), but by the time students reach adolescence they have formed definite ideas about the result of reading. Students who harbor negative attitudes believe that reading is likely to result in frustration, failure, boredom, social alienation, or some combination of these. Changing a student's belief structure may not be easy, but that's really what all teaching is about.

Let's consider the two paths to motivation from the standpoint of altering beliefs. We might succeed in motivating students extrinsically through the use of incentives. And in the short term that might constitute a victory. However, it

FIGURE 2.4. The decision to read is based on a prediction of what will occur.

might also reaffirm the student's belief that reading is, after all, boring or frustrating. If we take the intrinsic path, we must challenge the student's beliefs about reading and try to create a bit of cognitive dissonance that will cause the student to reconsider his or her beliefs about reading.

Consider a student who is reasonably proficient but who believes reading to be boring. If we successfully match that student to texts that reflect a preexisting interest, we may provoke some degree of reconsideration. Over time, the student may move from the belief that "reading is boring" to "reading is usually, but not always, boring." That is a fundamentally different outcome than using rewards to prompt the reading of a particular text.

Challenge Beliefs through Choice

Motivation depends on the situation in which reading may occur, including what is to be read, for what purpose, and in what social context. For this reason, it may be inappropriate to label a particular student "reluctant." If as teachers we were to alter the situation—by providing different options for reading, for example—the reluctance might disappear (O'Brien, Stewart, & Beach, 2009). For this reason, it is important for teachers to provide a range of choices with the goal of helping students connect texts with preexisting interests. Equally important in motivating students who appear to struggle is establishing purposes for reading that are relevant. "Students who see no value in doing well on high stakes assessments or don't value traditional academic pursuits are neither motivated nor engaged, because they perceive little social purpose tied to simply passing the test or completing assignments" (p. 88).

The goal should be to afford purposes with relevance and immediacy. For many teachers, accomplishing this goal will involve expanding the boundaries of what counts as an acceptable text. Alexander and Fox (2011) have observed that the "keys to reading motivation for adolescents might be found in nontraditional or alternative texts processed in out-of-school settings" (p. 171). In other words, in sources other than books. They might include articles, op-ed pieces, ads, maps, and an array of emerging possibilities such as graphic novels, videos, websites, and social media.

Providing choices casts the teacher in the role of broker. The object is to match students with texts that are likely to have appeal, which means not only acquiring a range of texts but finding out about students' interests. McKenna and Robinson (2013) recommend creating an inventory of interests and then asking students to "grade" each one from A to F. Interests receiving A's are "pure gold" (p. 228). Such inventories will differ considerably from subject to subject. An ELA interest inventory will be broad and is likely to include types of literature. A science inventory will be narrower and will include mostly nonfiction selections. Figure 2.5 shows how the beginning of two such inventories might look, one for literature and one for biology. In each case the teacher has exploited the common research finding that students (like nearly everyone else) find the unusual aspects of a topic inherently interesting.

Not by chance, each of the topics in these inventories can be linked to a web source, so the match between an interest and a text is nearly automatic. And in fact it could become completely automatic if a teacher were to present the topics not as an inventory but as a hyperlinked list. A student could browse the choices and proceed immediately to the source. Figure 2.6 summarizes strategies that include choice.

Think about how interesting these topics are. Then grade each one from A to F.

Language Arts

_____ 12 things you didn't know about Charles Dickens

_____ Charles Dickens's secret door

_____ Why no one knows when Ambrose Bierce died

_____ Why the first day of first grade was so unusual for Toni Morrison

_____ How Herbert Spencer decided not to marry George Eliot

Biology

_____ Why the first man to climb Mt. Everest didn't believe in yetis

_____ Why Jane Goodall does believe in yetis

_____ Animals you can see through

_____ The world's most venomous snake

_____ Carnivorous plants

FIGURE 2.5. Samples from interest inventories in language arts and biology.

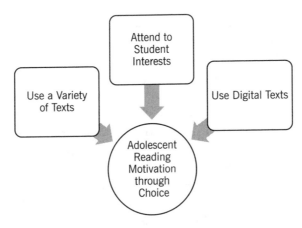

FIGURE 2.6. Using choice to motivate adolescents.

Challenge Beliefs through Challenge

We have been speaking about providing a range of choices in the hope that students will connect with an author, theme, topic, or genre. A smorgasbord of texts may help to achieve this goal, but what about the student who has experienced frustration? Shouldn't the range of choices include texts that were once described as "hi-lo" (high interest, low readability)? These questions are more complicated than they seem. On the one hand, matching readability to reading ability has instinctive appeal as a means of motivating students by removing the element of frustration. We agree that the texts available to students should reflect different levels of complexity, and in Chapter 4 we will suggest ways for including them in organized sets.

At the same, we warn against routinely matching students with easy texts. Although they may successfully comprehend them, there may be unintended consequences. One is failure to fulfill the CCSS requirement that students encounter texts of steadily increasing complexity. This expectation does not mean that every text needs to be potentially frustrating, but it does suggest that a steady diet of easy texts is unlikely to move students in the right direction. A second consequence concerns adolescents' beliefs about themselves as readers. Dunston and Gambrell (2009) point out "that students' perceptions of themselves as less capable learners are often reinforced when they are given literacy tasks that are 'easy' and less challenging than those assigned to peers" (p. 276). In other words, well-intentioned teachers may actually do their students a disservice by assigning them exclusively to low-level texts. A similar judgment may account for the failure of many intervention programs for adolescents. "Limited or narrowly conceived literacy programs or interventions," Alexander and Fox have observed, "may exacerbate rather than ameliorate reading problems for adolescents" (2011, p. 170).

One reason that routine placement in low-level texts is problematic is that it overlooks a number of contributing factors. O'Brien et al. (2009) maintain that many adolescents who are categorized as "struggling" are the victims of simplistic large-scale assessments that "fail to take into account that adolescents read particular texts for specific reasons, related to the completion of certain tasks; that they approach these texts with various stances, motivations, and expectations; and that they harbor a range of perceptions about themselves as readers before, during, and after tackling a particular text" (p. 81). They argue that adolescents are often matched to texts purely on the basis of comprehension and readability measures, "regardless of other crucial factors such as interest, motivation, and purpose" (p. 85).

Evidence of what can be accomplished when these factors are considered comes from the work of Samuel Miller (2003), who found that students were successful with challenging literacy activities when they possessed an interest in them. Even poor readers were motivated by activities that were creative and challenging, and they generally rose to the occasion when the opportunity presented itself. Miller describes a high-challenge language arts activity as having these characteristics:

- It lasts more than a single day.
- It involves writing one or more paragraphs aimed at higher-order thinking (e.g., character analysis, science research, letters to real people).
- Students work collaboratively to share ideas and give one another feedback.
- Teachers monitor closely and provide support where needed.

Tasks having these features bolster students' ability to regulate their own efforts and to work collaboratively in social settings. Just as important is what a high-challenge activity lacks. It will not include tasks found in many worksheets, such as matching, underlining, and bubbling in answers. Nor will it target low-level word recognition and grammatical skills. Miller found that all of the students he studied (high and low achievers alike) preferred the high-challenge activities, although low achievers lacked self-confidence *unless* such assignments were frequent enough to prove to them that they could succeed. He also found that none of the teachers with whom he worked experienced a decline in achievement test scores after committing to this approach. In fact, the scores for several teachers' classes rose significantly.

It seems to us that the notion of motivating students by presenting them with challenging tasks, although admittedly counterintuitive, is well aligned with the CCSS. It is therefore important to revisit the idea that texts must always be carefully matched with students in order to facilitate comprehension and prevent frustration. Under the right circumstances, challenging and complex texts can be engaging. These circumstances include adequate support, social interaction,

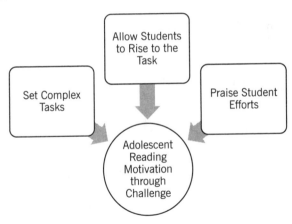

FIGURE 2.7. The role of challenge in increasing adolescent motivation.

and a relevant purpose for reading. Figure 2.7 illustrates the role of challenge in motivation.

Challenge Beliefs through Communication

How we interact with students is just as important as creating opportunities for them to succeed and engage, perhaps even more so. Teachers who see their students as individuals are more likely to move them toward the goal of becoming readers. Above all, they should avoid "the view of adolescents as less than adults" (Guzzetti, 2009, p. 382); they should challenge them to think maturely and encourage them in their day-to-day efforts. Dan Willingham (2009) offers this advice for how teachers can constructively communicate with students in order to motivate them to progress:

- Praise effort, not ability.
- Tell them hard work pays off.
- Treat failure as a natural part of learning.
- Don't take study skills for granted.
- View catching up as a *long-term* goal.
- Show students that you have confidence in them. (pp. 142–144)

This perspective is far removed from the one that many middle and high school teachers tend to adopt. It has been our experience that too many view instruction as more about content than students. When asked about their stance, they are likely to reply that it's a matter of standards and test scores. We find it ironic that the best way to help students achieve standards and perform well on tests is to attend to them as individuals, support their efforts, seek out their interests, and encourage them continually.

The work of Carol Dweck (2007) has important lessons for communicating with students in ways that motivate them to take risks. She describes two mindsets useful in characterizing adolescents. A *fixed* mindset results from the belief that one's abilities and talents are constant and unchanging. Individuals with fixed mindsets believe they possess "only a certain amount of intelligence, a certain personality, a certain moral character" (p. 7). Struggling adolescent readers with a fixed mindset accept as fact the idea that reading will, for them, always be a source of frustration and failure. They are just not cut out to be good readers. In contrast, a *growth* mindset is one through which individuals view themselves as malleable, capable of learning new things and acquiring new proficiencies. Such individuals are more willing to take part in new activities, and they feel confident that though they may fail at first, they will eventually succeed.

We suggest that one key to motivating poor readers is to nudge them from a fixed toward a growth mindset. Doing so requires encouragement and understanding, qualities that translate into the six suggestions offered by Dan Willingham. It also requires posing challenges that they may initially believe are beyond their reach. When, with support, these challenges are met, they are in a position to reevaluate how they view themselves and to realize that growth is possible after all.

Take-Away Suggestions

We summarize this chapter by listing key points to consider in your efforts to motivate adolescents to read. You will find no magic bullet among them, but together they will serve you well if you take them to heart and apply them in practice.

1. Use a simple inventory to learn about student interests and recommend texts.
2. Make a variety of texts available, varied by difficulty, topic, genre, and source.
3. Use your knowledge of gender preferences, but do not assume they apply to all students.
4. Avoid the trap of stereotyping girls as superior readers. It's all relative.
5. Remember that the term *struggle* is specific to the tasks you require of students.
6. Look for ways to link in-school and out-of-school literacies.
7. Work hard to build prior knowledge for any text you expect students to comprehend.

8. Do not forget your abler readers who may choose not to read. Nudge them through challenge and interest.

9. Challenge negative beliefs about reading by providing positive experiences.

10. Avoid consistently placing struggling readers in low-level texts. Challenge them.

11. Arrange for students to collaborate on projects that require reading.

12. Work to establish a growth mindset by praising effort and accepting failure as natural.

CHAPTER 3

Understanding Challenging Texts

What is easy is seldom excellent.
    —SAMUEL JOHNSON

When we first started to study the CCSS, we were struck by their rigor. In fact, as former high school teachers all, we viewed that rigor as a move to provide the Advanced Placement curriculum for all students. That type of performance for all students strikes many as unrealistic. As we continued to consider the implications of the standards, though, we realized that that was their intent—if students are college and career ready, they can do college work; the Advanced Placement curriculum *is* college work. We also began to think about the vastly different life choices that students would have, particularly students raised in poverty, if their academic skills and dispositions were geared toward such advanced achievement. That is why we have chosen to embrace the possibilities offered by the standards. In this chapter, we will tackle the question of what makes a text hard to understand to undergird our stance on the instructional strategies that teachers will need to embrace. We will start by describing the approach to text selection required by the standards. Then we will begin to unpack the challenges that those texts will pose and that must be met with instructional actions on the part of teachers if students are to be successful. Finally, we will make some recommendations to guide your text selection.

Seminal Works in the Disciplines

Think about your own college reading. In your first 2 years, taking a broad range of required courses in science, math, English, history, the arts, and language, you purchased expensive textbooks that may have presented the most difficult (and perhaps boring) technical reading you had yet experienced. You accomplished all of this reading on your own, with little, if any, assistance from your professors.

Depending on the class, this reading was more or less connected to the lectures you attended, and more or less required on the midterm and final. Likely, you figured this out as quickly as possible so that you would read only what was actually required. Many of you had both the academic skills to accomplish this and the study skills to strategize. Many of you had learned these skills in high school. However, some of you learned these things in an uncomfortable trial by fire during your college experience. Not all high school graduates are successful at the routine college requirement to read independently from challenging text. As we mentioned in Chapter 1, many entering students have to take remedial reading, writing, and math classes in community college before being admitted to credit-bearing courses. Many more drop out without earning the skills or credentials required for a career. In our own careers as university professors, we have had students in our classes who could not perform at the level we required and could not earn the degrees they wanted.

Whether you agree with it or not, the solution to this problem adopted by the CCSS authors was to demand that students have more experience with more challenging texts across their K–12 experience. They planned backwards, assuming that in order for all students to have the chance to succeed in college, they would have to be ready to read typical college textbooks independently. It is difficult to fault this logic in general, but it remains to be seen whether shifts in text type and text difficulty across time will yield the type of student the standards describe, poised for the literacies required in the modern college and workplace. The CCSS draw attention to the fact that students must be able to read seminal texts across different domains, and that those texts present specific challenges and opportunities.

One of the most controversial aspects of the CCSS is found in the appendices. Appendix A defines attention to text complexity as one of the requirements of the standards. After considering issues of text complexity, quality, and range, the standards work group chose a set of exemplar texts as illustrations and listed and/or excerpted them in Appendix B. These texts were selected from a longer set proposed by education professionals. They are presented in grade-level bands (K–1, 2–3, 4–5, 6–8, 9–10, and 11–12) and categorized by type. A look at the categories (see Figure 3.1) provides a window into the logic of the standards.

In the primary grades, stories, poetry, and informational texts are read by students and also read aloud to them. In the upper elementary grades, those same three types of texts are read by students. Beginning in middle school, though, drama is added to the narratives, and informational texts are included in three more specific lists: ELA, history and social science, and science, math, and technical subjects. The work group made this decision to highlight and specialize its presentation of informational text because most reading done in college is informational in nature and highly specialized. They also referenced the 2008 NAEP reading framework, in which passages are 50% informational in fourth grade, 55% informational in eighth grade, and 70% informational in twelfth grade.

Grade-Level Bands		
K–1, 2–3	4–5	6–8, 9–10, 11–12
Stories Read-aloud stories	Stories	Stories
Poetry Read-aloud poetry	Poetry	Poetry Drama
Informational texts Read-aloud informational texts	Informational texts	Informational texts: • ELA • History/social science • Science, math, and technical subjects

FIGURE 3.1. Categories for text exemplars in CCSS Appendix B.

The call for more reading and for more reading of complex nonfiction is certainly not without merit. Reading achievement requires reading practice and instruction, and students may not be getting enough of either. In fact, a seminal study of first-grade classrooms revealed that students spent only 3.6 minutes per day reading informational text (Duke, 2000). Things don't get much better later. A recent analysis of the amount of time that students spend actually reading during ELA in third grade revealed that teachers' editions of core reading programs recommended only 15 minutes per day of actual reading (Brenner & Hiebert, 2010). This is a shockingly small amount of attention given to reading breadth and volume in these early grades! However, as children enter adolescence, the time when common sense would tell us that students should be required to read more, there is even less time for reading. English becomes a content area, and content-area teachers are disinclined to focus in-class time on student reading (e.g., Ivy & Broaddus, 2000). The call for more reading in general and for more reading of informational text should not be surprising, especially if we want more proficient readers.

Who decides what students read is a complicated and politically charged issue traditionally left to states and localities. Therefore, the specificity of the "list" of text exemplars in the CCSS is problematic. States have adopted the Standards before any coherent sets of curriculum resources are available. Because of this, they may view the list as a full curriculum rather than as an illustration, although the Standards document cautions against doing so. The list of narratives includes classics from American and world literature (e.g., Shakespeare, Steinbeck, Kafka) and from classical literature (e.g., Homer, Ovid) and relatively few pieces of adolescent or multicultural literature. When we consider the motivational and identity-forming needs of adolescents that we reviewed in Chapter 2, young adult literature, written specifically for them, becomes even more essential. The informational text exemplars include specific primary source documents in history, as well as books and articles about a variety of topics that could never actually constitute a full curriculum. Because of our shared commitment to supporting teachers in the real world, we are not inclined to enter this debate. Instead, we will consider any texts as opportunities to build knowledge and skills. Rather than endorsing it, we will provide you with our best advice about how to understand the CCSS approach to text difficulty.

Quantitative Measures of Text Difficulty

One of the key components of any approach to curriculum is vertical articulation. Each successive grade level has to aim for more challenging work. It may be that the shock of the text difficulty requirements contained in the Standards is heightened because previous standards documents from states and from professional organizations were silent on this very important fact (Hiebert, 2012). They may have said that an eighth grader should read eighth-grade text with comprehension, but they failed to define what eighth-grade text is or how it is different from seventh-grade or ninth-grade text. That is not true now.

We will start with the simplest notion of text difficulty from the Standards. We have long had quantitative measures for estimating it. In fact, there are more than 200 available. These are mathematical formulas that use an algorithm to rank-order texts from easier to harder. These scores are then interpreted to define a grade-level range. It is important to know that deciding what constitutes a grade-level range is necessarily arbitrary. And the Standards document has redefined the process.

We recently helped a district choose trade books for reading instruction to meet the requirements of these new standards, and we quickly realized that our own previous shared sense of what level of difficulty is associated with particular grade levels was inconsistent with the rubric for text difficulty presented in the Standards. Our own realization is shared by many; a survey of educational leaders indicated that more than half believe that the new standards are more rigorous than the standards that they have been using, and many are experiencing frustration and confusion about how to implement them (Center on Education Policy, 2011). Prominent reading educators have taken a strong stance against "pushing" increases in text difficulty until after grade 3, instead making sure to build the basic skills and stamina necessary for tackling those texts at later grades while also building knowledge and habits through careful coordination of instruction, support, scaffolding, and practice (Hiebert & Pearson, 2012). We cannot take the call for increased text difficulty lightly. If we are to choose reading materials consistent with the requirements of the Standards, we must understand the definition of text difficulty adopted for the document and apply it thoughtfully.

The easiest place to see the change is in the Lexile table in Appendix A of the CCSS. It is summarized in Figure 3.2. Even without a full understanding of what a Lexile is, inspection of the figure makes it clear that the CCSS have set

Grade-Level Band	Previous Lexile Range	CCSS Lexile Range
4–5	645–845	770–980
6–8	860–1010	955–1155
9–10	960–1155	1080–1305
11–12	1070–1220	1215–1355

FIGURE 3.2. Lexile requirements of CCSS.

new Lexile standards. The previous range for grades 9 and 10 is now the range for grades 6–8. Since Lexiles are featured so prominently in the Standards document, it makes sense to spend some time understanding what they (and other quantitative measures) are.

Part of what makes a text simple or hard to understand is whether you know what the individual words that the author has chosen actually mean. While which words you know is entirely based on your personal experience with language, you are more likely to know the meanings of words that are used more frequently in written text. The sentence structures that the author has used also contribute to text difficulty. Generally, shorter sentences have simpler structures and are easier to understand.

Lexiles are numbers derived from a formula that considers sentence length and word frequency (Schnick & Knickelbine, 2000). They are widely available at *www.lexile.com* for most currently available books. Shakespeare's *Macbeth* measures 1350 Lexiles; Abraham Lincoln's *Gettysburg Address* measures 1340; Suzanne Collins's *Hunger Games* registers 810; Ray Bradbury's *Fahrenheit 451* measures 890. What these numbers mean is that the first two texts contain a greater number of rare words and longer sentences than the last two, and this fact provides us a partial understanding of which two are more difficult to understand.

If you have read the books we have listed above, you can probably generate a reasonable list of other reasons that Shakespeare's and Lincoln's texts are "harder" than Collins's and Bradbury's. There simply is more to it than that. Currently, researchers are trying to improve the number of language variables accounted for in quantitative measures (Benjamin, 2012), but for now, there is relatively little difference among the available measures. If your school already uses a quantitative system as part of its approach to tracking text difficulty, it may not make sense to change over to Lexiles. In Figure 3.3, we present grade-band ranges for additional traditional quantitative systems generated in a recent study (Nelson, Perfetti, Liben, & Liben, 2012). These measures include ATOS, developed by Renaissance Learning and used in the Accelerated Reader program; Degrees of Reading Power (DRP) from Questar Learning; SourceRater (SR), developed by the Educational Testing Service; and Pearson's Reading Maturity Metric (RM). Again, to underscore the differences in the CCSS definitions of grade level, look

Grade-Level Band	ATOS	DRP	SR	RM
4–5	4.97–7.03	52–60	.84–5.75	5.42–7.92
6–8	7.00–9.98	57–67	4.11–10.66	7.04–9.57
9–10	9.67–12.01	62–72	9.02–13.93	8.41–10.81
11–12	11.20–14.10	67–74	12.30–14.50	9.57–12.00

FIGURE 3.3. Grade-level bands for additional quantitative measures.

at the ATOS. What Accelerated Reader previously defined as grade-level text for grades 7–9 now corresponds to grades 6–8.

There is another issue that researchers are exploring with respect to the CCSS mandate for increasing text complexity at all grade levels. The approach resembles a simple, linear progression. It is possible that students' reading and writing development would be best accelerated through different routes to increased complexity—particularly those based on nonlinear growth (Williamson, Fitzgerald, & Stenner, 2013). We do expect that a shift in text complexity alone, absent radically different types and amounts of teacher support, is unlikely to produce the outcome we want—knowledgeable citizens with the reading and writing skills to be successful in college and careers.

Qualitative Measures of Text Difficulty

Common sense tells us that computer-generated numbers alone cannot capture text difficulty. Elie Wiesel's *Night*, a classic depiction of the horrors of the Nazi Holocaust, at 590 Lexiles does not belong in a third-grade curriculum. Hemingway's *A Farewell to Arms* (730 Lexiles) or *For Whom the Bell Tolls* (840 Lexiles) will not be understood by many upper-elementary students regardless of their reading proficiency. There is more to text difficulty than what can be counted electronically.

Quantitative measures may be necessary but are certainly not sufficient for understanding what makes a text challenging or helping us plan instruction using these texts. It will be up to educational leaders and teachers to resist the easy solution of using only simple, quantitative measures. In fact, even the text exemplars in the CCSS document are not assigned to grade-level bands strictly by their Lexiles; there are texts on the list with Lexiles of 660–720 in the 2–3 band, the 4–5 band, and the 6–8 band (Hiebert, 2012). We found a recent call to distinguish between text difficulty (which can be easily measured quantitatively but which fails to account for many variables) and text complexity (which is still an important and poorly understood part of the reading equation) to be very useful (Mesmer, Cunningham, & Hiebert, 2012). This is similar to the distinction that the late Edward Fry, himself an author of a widely used readability formula, made between using readability systems and leveling systems to organize text; leveling takes more into account than just the words and sentences (Fry, 2002). In addition, we are mindful that what makes a text difficult for nonnative speakers of English might be different than what makes it difficult for native speakers (Crossley, Greenfield, & McNamara, 2008).

Qualitative analysis of text difficulty is specifically described in the CCSS (see Appendix A) as a process that can be accomplished only by a mature and informed reader—not by a computer. As we move to selection of more complex texts and to planning the instruction that will be essential to scaffold student understanding, we must also become more skilled in qualitative analysis. Luckily, though, skilled qualitative analysis of what makes a particular text potentially difficult has immediate implications for instruction. If we are to use more text, a wider variety of text, and more complex text, we must orient ourselves to conducting qualitative analyses as a regular part of instructional planning.

Think again of your own college reading. What made your survey-level biology textbook hard? How is that different from what made specific poems you read in literature classes hard? You will find some overlap, but you will also find areas of difficulty that are discipline specific. That is, interpreting diagrams and other visual information is much more a part of literacy in the sciences than in the humanities; understanding figurative or archaic language is much more essential in the humanities than the sciences. In both cases, though, specific readers (including yourself) had the knowledge and skills to read both widely and deeply across disciplines. Creating more readers with those skills is the overarching mandate of the standards. Teachers of English, with their specialized knowledge of literature, are in the best position to conduct qualitative analyses of literary texts. Teachers in other subject areas will also have to become expert at analyzing the texts that they use. Not every middle and high school teacher must be a literary critic, but every teacher must become a text critic for the texts in his or her discipline.

Figure 3.4 presents our interpretation of the areas of qualitative analysis that are included in Appendix A of the CCSS. As we improve our skills in defining what makes a particular text difficult, we will know better how to make it more accessible. As an added benefit, we will have a better understanding of what it will take to teach students how to write well about what they read.

We recognize that qualitative analysis of text difficulty is a time-consuming business. It requires that we view what we read through a specific lens. As we have begun to plan CCSS lessons, we have had to engage in multiple readings of the same text for different purposes. For example, we read to consider the levels of meaning or purpose. Then we read to consider the structure. Then we read to consider the language and knowledge demands. We also recognize that individual teachers are likely to vary widely in the extent to which they are skilled in this type of text analysis. However, there will be no substitute for committing to

Domain	Considerations
Level of meaning	Mature readers must be able to understand what a text says and what it means. Some texts, like allegories, are specifically designed to contrast the two. More than one level of meaning is more difficult to understand.
Purpose	Texts that are designed to provide information have a clear purpose. Other texts, like political speeches, are designed to make biased arguments. The author's intent, when not explicit, may make a text more difficult to understand.
Text structure	Texts that are structured as a sequence of events, in order, are easier to understand than those structured more ambiguously or those including multiple structures.
Visual representations	Interpretation and integration of the multiple visual representations of meaning with the verbal information may make a particular text difficult.
Language demands	Complex texts by great writers use language that is original and very different from conversational English. The primary source documents so essential in the humanities may use language that is no longer familiar. Texts in all disciplines may be challenging because they contain sophisticated grammatical structures.
Knowledge demands	All texts make knowledge demands. Knowledge takes many forms. It can be cultural, linguistic, or textual. Understanding the knowledge demands of text requires that a mature reader recognize what is *not* in the text—the knowledge that the author believed the reader to have.

FIGURE 3.4. Considerations in the qualitative evaluation of text.

it if you are to plan instruction aligned with the standards. You will see below that we recommend you not do this alone.

Readers and Texts

Quantitative and qualitative analyses make no sense without knowledge of what particular students know and can do. This notion is an old one. In fact, Zakaluk and Samuels (1988) proposed that any measure of text difficulty should include a measure of reader skill. Put another way, it doesn't make sense to know how difficult a text is in the abstract; we have to know how difficult it is for a specific reader. That is part of the rationale for the Lexile framework that we described above. Lexiles can be produced for individual students, either through the *Scholastic Reading Inventory* (Scholastic & MetaMetrics, 1999) or through correlations with other standardized tests. A student-level Lexile predicts that a student can read a text with that same Lexile independently with 75% comprehension. The same thing is true of ATOS. Alternatively, these measures can provide a teacher with an estimate of how much teaching and support might be necessary to bridge the gap between a reader and a text.

This reader–text consideration provides a foundation for understanding comprehension in general. The RAND Reading Study Group (2002) advanced a widely cited heuristic for understanding comprehension as a product influenced by characteristics of the reader, the text, and the activity within a sociocultural context. Similarly, Appendix A of the CCSS recommends that text selection be guided by quantitative, qualitative, and reader and task considerations. Reader considerations go beyond knowledge and skill levels to include social and emotional development. As we change our thinking about what constitutes grade-level text, particularly narratives, we will have to realize that some texts that are "hard enough" for a particular grade level when evaluated quantitatively are, in realistic terms, socially or thematically inappropriate at those grade levels.

A Possible Process for Choosing and Using Texts

Now that we have unpacked the text complexity requirement of the CCSS for you, what do we actually think you should do? Because of our intense work in real schools, we think about such issues very pragmatically. In Chapter 4, in fact, we present an approach to the problem that involves selection of multiple texts, and subsequent chapters recommend very specific instructional routines. But you really do have to start by establishing instructional objectives and deciding what texts you will actually use to achieve them.

First, work schoolwide. To truly enact the CCSS in middle schools and high schools will require the full participation of every teacher in every discipline. We know that some states and districts are simply requiring that English departments move to the use of 70% informational texts. This simply does not make sense. We cannot teach literary analysis without literature. While informational texts have an important role to play in ELA classrooms, the important lesson here is that we will not be able to go on avoiding actual student reading in science, math, social studies, arts, and career classrooms. Given our recent work in middle schools and high schools, current practices are totally inconsistent with the CCSS call to use extensive connected reading and writing as the major tool for learning—in ELA or in the other content areas.

Second, read Appendix B of the CCSS in full and ensure that at least one of the exemplars listed there is used in each discipline at each grade level. While we know that these specific texts are not required, they do provide a variety of choices that may be very different from the texts currently used. They will also help you make the case that CCSS is not an "English thing." It's for everyone. While only the English teachers can use the canonical texts suggested, social studies teachers can use the literary nonfiction and the informational texts.

Third, use the text recommendations as an estimate of the distance between the CCSS and current practice. When specific selections are already in use at the grade level recommended, discuss student work with those texts. To what extent can students read them independently? What reading and writing tasks are currently associated with them? How have past students performed on those tasks? What instructional changes should be made? When specific texts are currently used at a higher grade level than recommended, should they be moved?

Fourth, do not ignore the quantitative measures of text difficulty. In our experience, they represent a sea change; they move specific texts up at least 1 year in a student's educational career. This means that assessments designed to measure the CCSS will assume students have extensive experience with texts identified for use in their current grade level. But don't be too strict. Use your current grading period structure as a guide. As you choose texts, make sure that during each grading period students read at least one full-length text in each discipline within the quantitative band for that grade level.

Fifth, do not forgo traditional textbooks and informational articles, especially in science and social studies. They are important text types, and they can be analyzed in the very same way as trade books. Publishers can provide quantitative measures and you will find that Lexiles are now routinely available for nearly all textbooks.

Finally, use qualitative analysis of text difficulty as the foundation of instructional planning. Teaching with text requires this. Enacting the CCSS requires this. We must collectively move from instructional planning that is based on scheduling and then covering core content through lecture and structured note taking to engaging students in reading and writing to learn. Since this will be very new for many, many teachers, Figure 3.5 outlines a possible process.

Three reads is a lot to ask, but it will be necessary as you start to rethink the role of text in instruction. If you work with colleagues, you can divide the responsibilities, each taking on one specific text or unit. When you read for structure, create a graphic representation of the author's organization. Making the structure visible will go a long way toward deepening your understanding, and

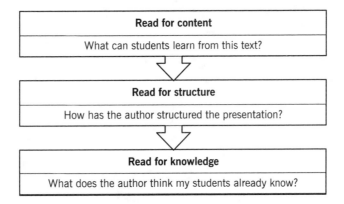

FIGURE 3.5. Procedure for qualitative analysis of text.

we hope you will learn to make that structure visible to your students. It may be that over time your skills will improve, and you will learn to read for content and knowledge at the same time. But even if you don't, this procedure will get you ready to teach.

Final Thoughts

We have heard states' and districts' messages to teachers that the CCSS are very similar to what they are already doing. We could not disagree more strenuously. Along with the truly bold focus on writing, the issue of text complexity stands out to us as the clearest indication that these standards are different. If you are lucky enough to work in college towns, as we three do, it may be helpful to you to go to the bookstore and browse the textbook section. There you can see what freshmen are expected to be able to read—totally on their own—to learn. The CCSS are an attempt to plan backwards from this somewhat harsh reality. As you will see in subsequent chapters, though, we believe that there is much we can do together to improve their chances.

CHAPTER 4

Designing Challenging Text Sets

Books, like friends, should be few and well-chosen.
—SAMUEL JOHNSON

As individuals we may accept Dr. Johnson's simple advice about the importance of a few well-chosen friends; however, as teachers, we cannot take his advice when it comes to books: Books and other instructional texts *do* need to be well chosen, but as we argue in this chapter, in order for us to meet the robust demands of the Common Core standards and to prepare our students for the demands of college and the workplace, those texts cannot be few in number. In fact, they must be numerous and they must be complex. Not only must we include many difficult texts in our curriculum, we believe that we can no longer think of instructional texts as stand-alone entities. Instead, we propose that content-area teachers must use well-organized *text sets* that provide students both the background knowledge and the opportunities to apply the strategies and skills needed to comprehend, analyze, and connect with difficult content-area material.

We know that the reality of trying to include more texts into our instruction will be a difficult pill to swallow. The curriculum is already full, you might say. However, we are here to help. In this chapter we will be providing a framework for designing integrated text sets for content-area instruction, sets that can help you to build both student content knowledge and the skills necessary for acquiring content knowledge independently. We will start with a discussion of comprehension theory and the amazing processes by which readers come to understand a text. We will then describe a process for planning backwards from the most challenging content-area texts by choosing other texts that prepare students for the comprehension challenges they will face. We will advocate for multimedia texts to build student background knowledge and then shorter informational texts to deepen background knowledge and give opportunities for differentiation. In this chapter we will also discuss how to use young adult (YA) literature, websites, and blogs in these sets to provide both motivation for reading and the opportunity

for making creative connections. Finally, we will discuss ways to carve out important space for our classroom textbooks within the text set framework.

An Expanded Understanding of Content-Area Texts

Not long ago, when reviewing a high school summer reading list for incoming
freshmen, we found a number of works that would certainly meet the CCSS
demands for challenging literary texts. Among the independent reading suggestions for the new freshman class was *A Doll's House* by Henrik Ibsen. The play,
which details a woman's struggle to define herself against an oppressive male-
dominated Victorian society, is a significant literary work that pushes readers to
confront the impact of society on individuals, and on the most basic of human
relationships. However, independent reading of a 19th-century Norwegian parlor
drama provides 14-year-olds neither the context nor the motivation necessary to
engage this complex work. Nor does reading this work independently help students develop the analytic skills to make creative connections between this text
and others they have already read or may encounter in the future. It is not that
texts like this are not worth teaching—in fact, the CCSS demand the use of difficult literary works such as this—it is rather that we believe that this text must
be used in concert with others if we are to realize its full potential as a vehicle for
achieving the Standards. Unfortunately, if we think back to our own freshman
year experiences, many of us would have probably read the *Cliffs Notes* for this
work rather than attempting to tackle this isolated reading experience.

A Word about "Texts"

Since we will use the word *text* so often in this chapter, we want to begin by telling you what we mean by it. Although many educators' minds move immediately
to their classroom textbook when they hear "text," we think more broadly. Certainly, classroom textbooks must be part of our instructional mix. However, it is
also important that we understand how a copy of a speech, a map of the American colonies in 1670, or a World War I army uniform can serve as important
"texts" for history instruction. Or how videos of cell division, a hand-cranked
model of the solar system, a data table, or selections from *Scientific American* can
be equally important "texts" to science teachers. There is an increasing number
and variety of sources from which we can gain information, and stretching our
own definition of *text* acknowledges this reality.

There are several reasons that we need to think more broadly about the texts
we use in our instruction, and why we need to think more about sets of *related*
texts. First, the demands for integrated literacy experiences in the CCSS make it
clear that we must think creatively about how we organize our content material.

If we are going to help students to "integrate and evaluate content presented in diverse formats and media" (NGA and CCSSO, 2010, p. 35) and "analyze how two or more texts address similar themes or topics" (NGA and CCSSO, 2010, p. 35), we can no longer hold on to the notion that one textbook, primary source, or multimedia piece can accomplish all of these goals. Instead, we must think strategically about how to build integrated reading and writing experiences that push our students to make creative and analytic connections that break the boundaries of a single work.

There is also an important second reason for thinking in terms of *sets* of texts instead of individual texts. In our previous chapter we spoke of the qualitative and reader-text issues we must take into account when choosing challenging texts that are aligned with our instructional goals, and the very real comprehension challenges that difficult content-area texts pose for our students. If students are going to be able to "read and comprehend complex literary and informational text independently and proficiently" (NGA and CCSS, 2010, p. 35), we must not only think about the instructional strategies that we use to build these independent reading skills; we must also think strategically about how to combine related texts in ways that can both help students make the text-to-text connections we spoke of above, and to overcome the comprehension challenges that our most demanding content-area texts pose to them.

This issue is important for teachers to consider because we know that those who are successful in school and the workplace can understand and use complex texts. Understanding text complexity issues can help us support our students' reading in ways that can lead to greater reading stamina, engagement, and comprehension. At the same time, we also need to understand what readers bring to the comprehension process, particularly how they actively construct meaning from texts. So, before we begin to address how to build sets of texts to accomplish our instructional goals, we need to think a bit more about what it means to actually comprehend a text. Understanding this process can help us think more clearly about the instruction we design to support student understanding and about how we can combine texts creatively to help our students become independent readers, thinkers, and citizens.

Text Representation Theory

As content-area teachers we might think of comprehension as pretty straight-forward—it is the process by which we come to understand a text. However, as the psychologist Walter Kintsch (1994) points out, this commonsense notion of comprehension is actually too general to be helpful to most of us when trying to understand what happens when our students engage with a text. This is because comprehending a text comprises multiple processes, operating at several different cognitive levels. Therefore, although this chapter will be primarily focused on developing text sets for content-area instruction, we do need to spend a little bit of time unpacking the term *comprehension*.

When students read a text, they begin to construct a complex mental model of what they read—a cognitive *representation* of the text. This mental model is built when the reader "encodes" the information on the page (or on the screen) into his or her working memory. Once this basic mental model is created, it is combined with the reader's rich personal experiences and previously read or viewed texts—his or her background knowledge. This process creates an "inner text" of what has been read (Lenski, 1998, p. 74), or, as Roland Barthes proposes, a "rewriting [of] the text of the work within the text of our lives" (1985, p. 101). This view of text representation reinforces the important notion that readers must actively construct meaning from texts. We would like to spend some additional time breaking down the steps of this representational process in order to explain the role that text sets can play in enhancing student comprehension. Figure 4.1 represents the general process of meaning making.

A good place to start in understanding this process is with the representational theory of van Dijk and Kintsch (1983). Their model of text representation allows us a more comprehensive understanding of how text is represented in a reader's memory because they break the representation process into three distinct stages, represented in Figure 4.2. You will see that the three stages are progressively more complex.

Think of text comprehension moving up from the bottom to the top of the figure. The first level is what they call the *surface code*. At this level the words and phrases are encoded in memory (Graesser, Millis, & Zwann, 1997). The second level of representation is the *text base*, where the reader is able to grasp the full

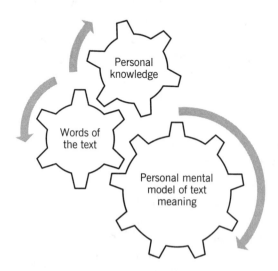

FIGURE 4.1. Creating a mental model of text meaning.

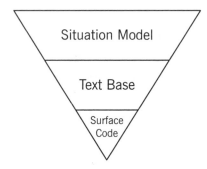

FIGURE 4.2. The representational theory of van Dijk and Kintsch.

structure of the text by organizing the words and phrases into meaningful units that help make larger text units become clear (van Dijk & Kintsch, 1983). This is a representation of the text at what some researchers have called the "gist" level or, as Mackey (1997) describes it, the "good-enough" reading level. The most comprehensive level of representation is what van Dijk and Kintsch call the *situation model*. This stage is where the text becomes more than just a "gist" representation and becomes an "inner text" (Lenski, 1998), elaborated by and integrated with a reader's prior knowledge. In van Dijk and Kintsch's model, text is encoded at increasingly abstract levels as a reader moves from the *surface code* to a coherent *text base* to a more fully integrated *situation model* where the text is fully integrated with the background knowledge and experiences of a reader.

To illustrate this complex process, let's look at a selection from a work that we mentioned at the beginning of this chapter, *A Doll's House* by Henrik Ibsen. We have chosen this sample text as an illustration because it is a challenging text included in Appendix B of the CCSS as a text suitable for use with 9th and 10th graders. Remember that the play is about a woman's struggle to define herself against an oppressive male-dominated society around the turn of the last century. Here is a passage that shows an interaction between Nora and her husband, Torvald Helmer, after Nora has come home from a shopping excursion:

TORVALD: (*in his room*) Is that my lark twittering there?

NORA: (*busy opening some of her parcels*) Yes, it is.

TORVALD: Is it the squirrel frisking around?

NORA: Yes!

TORVALD: When did the squirrel get home?

NORA: Just this minute. (*Hides the bag of macaroons in her pocket and wipes her mouth.*) Come here, Torvald, and see what I've been buying.

TORVALD: Don't interrupt me. (*A little later he opens the door and looks in, pen in hand.*) Buying, did you say? What!

NORA: Why, Torvald, surely we can afford to launch out a little now. It's the first Christmas we haven't had to pinch.

TORVALD: Come, come; we can't afford to squander money.

NORA: Oh yes, Torvald, do let us squander a little, now—just the least little bit! You know you'll soon be earning heaps of money.

TORVALD: Yes, from New Year's Day. But there's a whole quarter before my first salary is due.

NORA: Never mind; we can borrow in the meantime.

TORVALD: Nora! (*He goes up to her and takes her playfully by the ear.*) Still my little featherbrain! Supposing I borrowed a thousand crowns today, and you made ducks and drakes of them during Christmas week, and then on New Year's Eve a tile blew off the roof and knocked my brains out.

NORA: (*laying her hand on his mouth*) Hush! How can you talk so horridly?

According to van Dijk and Kintsch's model, you first processed the words and created the *surface code* in your mind, a representation firmly based on the text itself (see Figure 4.3). From this basic level of representation, you began to form

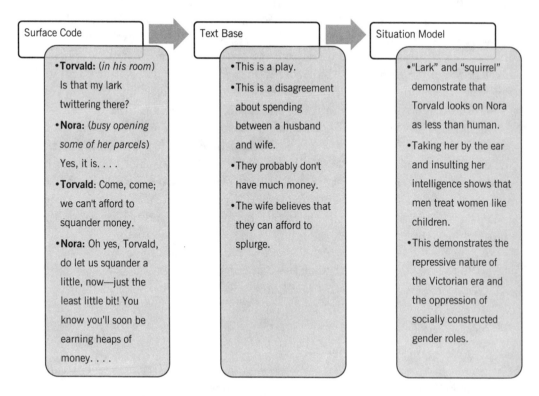

FIGURE 4.3. Illustration of the comprehension process.

the *text base*. Here you were able to encode the individual grammatical structures of the text by combining these structures with enough basic background knowledge to form a coherent representation at the "gist," or "good-enough," level. At this stage in the representational process you were able to form a solid working mental model of the text. In this case you understood that the text is a play, that it takes place in the home of a married couple, and that the couple is having a disagreement over the amount of spending that the wife is doing. However, in order to create a robust *situation model*, you need much more background knowledge.

In the case of the construction of meaning represented in Figure 4.3, you bring to bear critical background knowledge of figurative language, imagery, and history—knowledge that enriches the *text base* to form a comprehensive mental model of a woman oppressed by her husband and her society. For instance, if you have knowledge about the manners and gender roles of the Victorian era, you can quickly bring that knowledge to bear to make inferences about Nora and Torvald's relationship and why these characters act the way they do. These inferences are strengthened if you have experience with figurative language and imagery and you determine that Torvald's use of animal "pet" terms like "lark" and "squirrel" suggest that Nora is considered by the men around her as something less than a fully functional human being, imagery that is reinforced later in the passage when Torvald "playfully" takes her by the ear and admonishes her like a child. Therefore, in order to move from a "good-enough" understanding of a text (this is a play about a couple that disagrees) to a comprehensive understanding (this work is about the way that society can repress and dehumanize), we must have critical background knowledge and practice using it to construct robust situation models of the texts we read. As Umberto Eco (1979) reminds us, "Texts are lazy machineries that ask someone to do part of their job" (p. 214).

It is clear that developing the "situation model" of this drama requires a good deal of student background knowledge. To fully represent this text, a student must have knowledge of the Victorian values that drive this relationship, and it would be helpful to have a working knowledge of feminist criticism. (Don't worry. We include a full unit design for this text in Appendix 1 at the end of this book.) The representational process is similar with informational texts. Let's look at another example—a text that could be used in an earth science class to explore geothermal activity and the formation of geysers in Yellowstone National Park. This open-access text is reprinted in Figure 4.4.

Similar to the way that you engaged *A Doll's House*, you first processed the words of this informational text, creating the *surface code* in your mind, and from this surface code processed its "gist," or *text base*. At this level of representation, you understood that the authors are describing the geothermal activity that leads to the production of geysers and hydrothermal explosions, and that the text includes specific examples of this activity. However, in order to form a

Because the boiling point of water increases with increasing pressure and pressure increases with depth, deep water can be hotter than boiling water near the surface. If the pressure that confines this deep water is reduced quickly, pockets of water may suddenly boil, causing an explosion as the water is converted to steam. Such activity drives the eruptions of geysers, like Old Faithful, which are repetitive releases of plumes of steam and water. Rarely, steam explosions are more violent and can hurl water and rock thousands of feet. In Yellowstone's geologic past, such violent events, called "hydrothermal explosions," have occurred countless times, creating new landscapes of hills and craters.

A recent and notable hydrothermal explosion occurred in 1989 at Porkchop Geyser in Norris Geyser Basin. The remains of this explosion are still clearly visible today as an apron of rock debris 15 feet (5 m) across surrounding Porkchop's central spring. In the 1880s and early 1890s, a series of powerful hydrothermal explosions and geyser eruptions occurred at Excelsior Geyser in the Midway Geyser Basin. Some of the explosions hurled large rocks as far as 50 feet (15 m).

U.S. Geological Survey
Fact Sheet 2005

FIGURE 4.4. Earth science text sample.

more robust situation model, you have to combine the gist of the text with your background knowledge. Perhaps you have visited Yellowstone, so the background knowledge gained from this visit will enhance the mental model you form of the text. You might recall the bowl-shaped valley that would collect the water needed for these fabulous displays, and you might remember the intense heat and power of individual geysers you visited during your trip. You might also combine your knowledge of water pressure in order to form a more comprehensive mental model. Remembering the effect on your ears of swimming to the bottom of a pool could be critical for helping you understand how columns of water can pressurize the deeper water pockets that power geysers. You might be familiar with the broader scientific meanings of key vocabulary in the passage, like *apron* and *pocket*, allowing you to visualize the spread of the debris field and the collections of superheated water that can create aprons. It is the combination of both the *text base* and your own background knowledge that provides the comprehensive understanding of these and other texts, representations that can then be used to make connections with other readings about geothermal activity, to design experiments using water and heat, or to make arguments about the safety of living near Yellowstone National Park. As Kintsch (1988) points out, constructing representations of text is heavily reliant on background knowledge, and there are substantive differences between "remembering a text and learning from it" (Kintsch, 1994, p. 294). By helping students build background knowledge and then connect it with content-specific textual information, teachers can make it possible for them to "own" texts in ways that go beyond basic understanding. Such instruction will also better prepare them to remember and use the information.

To illustrate how important background knowledge is to student engagement in the comprehension process, let's look at an interesting experiment conducted by McNamara, Kintsch, Butler-Songer, and Kintsch (1996). The experiment used two different texts and two different types of readers. The texts were about the same subject, but one was called "low coherence" because it provided few explanations and the other "high coherence" because it provided more. The students in this experiment were categorized as either high-knowledge readers or low-knowledge readers. Not surprisingly, on free-recall questions, which tapped the readers' understanding of the text at the gist level (the *text base*), both high- and low-knowledge readers did better with the high-coherence text, because the representation of the *text base* is firmly grounded in the text itself. However, on inferencing and problem-solving questions, which require a more fully developed situation model, an interesting result occurred. Whereas low-knowledge readers on average performed better on inferencing and problem-solving questions when they read the high-coherence text, the high-knowledge readers actually performed worse with the high-coherence text! (The findings of the experiment are represented in Figure 4.5.) Although this finding seems counterintuitive, it supports the arguments we have made about how critical background knowledge is to our students' ability to make sense of complex texts. Difficult texts have gaps in meaning that must be filled by the creative and constructive participation of the reader. This is why Kintsch (1994) argues that "a text that spells everything out and explains everything to the last detail does not leave enough room for constructive activities on the part of the learner. . . . We need texts that . . . leave gaps for the reader to fill" (p. 301). Luckily for us, those are just the types of text that the CCSS demand!

Low-Knowledge Readers	
Low-Coherence Text	**High-Coherence Text**
Poorer recall scores	Poorer inferencing/ problem-solving-scores
High-Knowledge Readers	
Low-Coherence Text	**High-Coherence Text**
Better recall scores	Worse inferencing/ problem-solving scores

FIGURE 4.5. Experimenting with background knowledge.

Building Background Knowledge through Intertextual Connections

You may well ask how you can go about building the background knowledge that is most critical to your students' understanding of your content-area material, and how you can help them learn to "fill in the gaps." Many teachers begin this process through the use of before-reading activities that are directed at specific classroom texts (Lenski, 1998). For instance, before having students read *The Declaration of Independence*, a history teacher might highlight key vocabulary from the document and provide a preview of the text's structure: It begins with a preamble, then lists citizens' natural rights, then lists the colonists' grievances, and finally declares the colonies' break from England. Through these activities students are better prepared to engage this CCSS-recommended text because they have the vocabulary needed to understand the complicated language and the text structure knowledge needed to meaningfully chunk the work into more understandable sections.

In another classroom, a literature teacher's lesson on the poem "Annabelle Lee," by Edgar Allan Poe, might begin with anecdotes about Poe's love for Virginia Clemm and her untimely death from tuberculosis that inspired this macabre work, the biographical information serving as the critical background knowledge students need to explore both the mood and theme of the piece. In another classroom, a science teacher who is using the text on geothermal activity that we discussed previously might place students into small groups to design a prereading diagram of a geyser. This before-reading activity activates prior knowledge, helps students make predictions about the geothermal processes at work, and guides their reading as they check the accuracy of those predictions.

These are all effective instructional strategies to build or activate the background knowledge needed to engage these texts. However, these strategies—effective as they might be—still focus only on preparing students to read a *single* content-area text. We would argue that a more efficient and effective means of building the critical background knowledge needed to engage the complex texts that the Common Core standards demand would be to build prior knowledge using *sets* of texts. Each text in the set would have to be engaging in its own right, but each would also include critical information that is important to understanding a complex content-area *target* text. We believe that these sets of related texts will not only help students understand the most challenging of our content-area texts but will also prepare them to make the connections between texts that are critical to their success in college and beyond. We believe our ability to help students make these connections can be the difference between their understanding at the gist, or *text base*, level and their ability to form a more comprehensive situation model (Van Dijk & Kintsch, 1983).

Researchers have been writing about the importance of text-to-text connections for some time. Some argue that students *must* make intertextual links if they are to comprehend texts at a deeper level (e.g., Lenski, 1998). Referencing the work of Bakhtin, other researchers argue that teachers have to help students make textual connections because texts never exist in isolation. Instead, they exist in relation to texts that have been read in the past, and to those that will be read in the future (e.g., Bloome & Egan-Robertson, 1993). Like these researchers, we believe that content-area teachers are uniquely positioned to help students make these critical connections through strategically constructed text sets. These can provide students with the opportunity to practice the intertextual processes needed to build meaning across texts and meet the knowledge and comprehension demands of our most challenging content-area material.

In order to build effective text sets, then, we have to take into account two important considerations. First, we have to think hard about what challenging target texts we want students to read. This means we want to identify content-area texts that both meet the CCSS text difficulty demands *and* serve as important vehicles for our own content-area learning objectives. Additionally, we want to analyze these target texts for the comprehension challenges they present to our students—the vocabulary they contain, the structure of the texts, and the critical background knowledge we believe our students need to engage them. Then after we consider these issues we can move on to thinking about the related texts in the set. Here we want to be sure to include a wide variety of text formats that will both build the missing background knowledge and serve as effective vehicles for making the cross-textual connections. We would like you to think of this as a process of "planning backwards." By this we mean that we need to begin our instructional planning with our objectives firmly in mind and then choose challenging content-area texts that will help us to achieve those objectives. However, we then need to "plan backwards" from those texts by strategically choosing additional ones that provide the critical background knowledge necessary.

Although there are a number of ways to design these sets, we begin with a simple framework that we call the *quad text set*. This collection of four related texts begins with our target text, which in many of our content areas will be a challenging traditional print text (see Figure 4.6). Because we want to stretch our students' definition of what counts as "text," we then choose a visual such as a still image or a short video to immediately engage students in the topic and to provide important background knowledge they can utilize to construct meaning from the target text. We suggest that the third text be either a single informational text or set of differentiated informational texts, which could include selections from the classroom textbook. These texts are not only used to meet the CCSS demands for the use of more informational texts in classrooms, but also to continue to build critical background knowledge needed to tackle the target text. For the fourth text in the set, we recommend exploring selections from contemporary YA fiction and nonfiction or material from websites, blogs, or even suitable fan fiction sites. These highly engaging contemporary texts encourage students to read because of their relevance to our students and their perspectives. However, they also help students build intertextual connections and find "the common spaces"

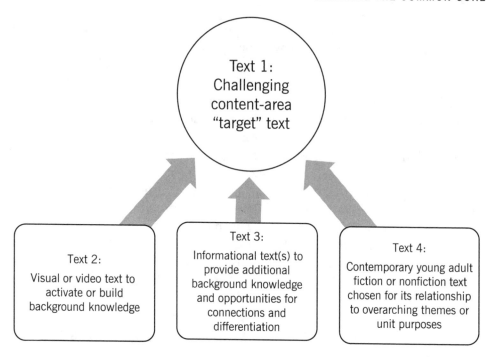

FIGURE 4.6. Illustration of backwards planning using a quad text set approach.

(Bright, 2011, p. 39) between highly engaging texts and the overarching themes and purposes in our target texts.

The Quad Text Set in Action: An Example from ELA

As an example, consider an ELA teacher who would like his students to be able to use a feminist critical lens to analyze a literary text. In order to accomplish that objective the teacher might look into Appendix A of the CCSS to find that *A Doll's House* (the text we sampled at the beginning of this chapter) is a recommended literary work because of its complexity. It is also a perfect vehicle for achieving his objectives because of its depiction of a male-dominated society and how the sensitive heroine suffers because of it. Knowing that students are going to need a lot of background knowledge to form the situation model, he begins to plan backwards from this challenging text, first determining the background knowledge that students will need and then choosing a set of texts that will fill that knowledge gap with information. After thinking about his target text, he determines that students will have very little background knowledge about the Victorian society in which this play is set, that they will be unaware of the tenets of feminist criticism, and that they may not have thought very much about the way society reinforces gender-specific roles. The rest of the text set will have to fill these gaps.

A helpful framework for planning this instruction is represented in Figure 4.7. Planning backwards from his objectives and the target text, our ELA teacher now begins to build the set he needs to accomplish his goals. He begins by choosing two short video selections from the 1950s, which he captured and saved from YouTube using freely available software (e.g., see Firefox's Downloadhelper add-on). They included a family scene from *Leave It to Beaver* and a very funny interaction between Ricky and Lucy from the *I Love Lucy* program. Not only does he feel that these short video texts will be fun and engaging for students, but he also knows that they are full of the gender-specific stereotypes of midcentury America, a more contemporary time period that has many analogues with the Victorian attitudes of the previous century. Nevertheless, he also knows these videos cannot provide the important background knowledge students need about the Victorian era itself. For this, our ELA teacher chooses three informational texts about different aspects of the Victorian Age: an Internet text on the manners of the age, a provocative text on Victorian corsets and their relationship to the oppression of women, and a magazine article on Victorian entertainment. Because he has limited time, he is going to divide these texts among different groups of students, with all groups "reporting out" at the end of their reading. Additionally, this teacher chose the texts for their reading difficulty as well as

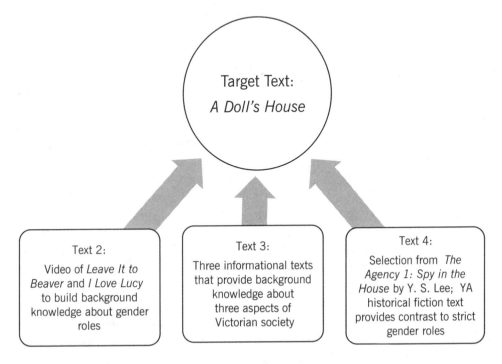

FIGURE 4.7. Text set to build background knowledge for *A Doll's House*.

their content, with the Internet text being the most accessible of the three, and the text on Victorian corsets the most difficult. In this way the teacher not only provides his students with background-knowledge-building informational texts but also differentiates instruction by providing texts at different reading levels to meet the needs of individual learners.

The last text in the set is a three-page selection from a contemporary YA historical fiction piece set during the Victorian era in London. *The Agency 1: Spy in the House* by Y. S. Lee is a thoroughly researched historical fiction piece that depicts Victorian society, including the often horrific lives of the poor. However, our ELA teacher chose this text not only because it reinforces the background knowledge gained from the other texts in the set, but because it also presents an unconventional female character, in this case a young woman who becomes actively employed as a spy in order to solve the mystery of a missing cargo ship. Although you may find yourselves putting *our* text down to pick up Lee's text, this YA novel represents a unique opportunity for cross-textual connections because it contains accessible information about traditional Victorian gender roles, while also featuring a character who stands in opposition to this portrayal—a key motif in Ibsen's play. This text set, therefore, accomplishes a few strategic goals. First, it provides the background knowledge needed to form a robust situation model of the target Ibsen text, and it includes information about the social context of the work and the thematic focus on feminist criticism, information that is critical to fully understanding the work and to achieving the teacher's instructional objectives. However, it also provides students the opportunity to read a diverse selection of texts, a key goal of the CCSS.

Furthermore, this text set includes two methods for arranging texts to promote critical connections. The teacher chose both *complementary texts* and *conflicting texts* (Hartman & Allison, 1996) for his set. The short 1950s video texts and the differentiated informational texts are *complementary* because they provide students with multiple opportunities to see different aspects of past gender norms, which are critical to their understanding of the Ibsen play. However, along with these complementary selections, the teacher also chose a selection from a contemporary YA text. Although this text is in many ways complementary because of its realistic depiction of the time period, it can also be considered a *conflicting text* because of its alternative and "disruptive" use of a strong female character working outside the gender-specific boundaries of her age. This element of conflict is not only helpful for developing students' critical thinking habits as they are forced to entertain competing viewpoints (Lenski, 1998), but it can also can serve as an opportunity for thinking more deeply about the main female character in Ibsen's play. We are not advocating for any particular mix of complementary or conflicting text choices in your instructional text sets. We do, however, encourage you to think hard about how your choices both build key background knowledge and accomplish your instructional objectives.

The Quad Text Set in Action: An Example from History/Social Studies

Quad text sets work equally well to prepare students to read difficult texts in other content areas. Let's look again at the history teacher who wanted to prepare her students to read *The Declaration of Independence*. Our teacher is using this text because it is a seminal document of the Revolutionary era and it serves as an important vehicle for demonstrating the democratic ideals of the Age of Reason. However, planning backwards from this text, she knows that students lack both the vocabulary and the contextual knowledge to understand how "revolutionary" this document really is. Therefore, now that she has determined her objectives, the target text that will serve as a vehicle for those objectives, and the critical background knowledge needed to access this text, she can begin to build her text set (see Figure 4.8).

She begins her set with three short selections from the high-spirited musical *1776*, each selection focusing on either the creation or signing of *The Declaration of Independence*. Knowing that setting purposes for texts is important, our teacher focuses student attention on three things: the personal and political conflicts surrounding the creation of the document, the variety of emotions expressed by the delegates to the Continental Congress, and the reactions of Thomas Jefferson. Although she knows that these texts are not historically accurate (and maybe a little corny!), she believes that the musical's focus on the personalities of the delegates will provide students with important contextual knowledge. Then, acknowledging that a singing John Adams, Benjamin Franklin, and Thomas Jefferson

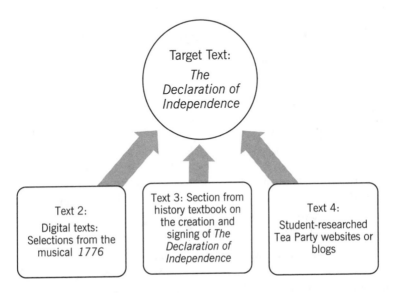

FIGURE 4.8. Text set to build background knowledge for *The Declaration of Independence*.

might provide some context but no systematic method for understanding the key vocabulary and structure of the document, she chooses a four-page selection from her textbook on the creation and signing of the *Declaration*. Although this section of her text is somewhat dry, she feels that her textbook's presentation of key vocabulary, its succinct overview of the events leading up to the *Declaration*, and its description of the elements of the document will help her students actually read the full primary source. Although she knows that the *Declaration* will still need to be strategically "chunked" for students through the use of a reading guide, she now feels confident that students can read it and assigns the text in small reciprocal teaching groups.

At this point you might be asking, "Where is the fourth text?" In this teacher's case, she decides to use the fourth text in a different way from our ELA teacher. Instead of using the last part of the set to build background knowledge, she decides to extend students' understanding of the *Declaration* by having them find texts on their own that will connect the *Declaration* with contemporary society. To accomplish this she divides students into teams and provides each with a list of websites and blogs from state Tea Party groups. Armed with the reading guides they completed for the *Declaration*, and focusing on the list of colonists' complaints, students search their assigned websites with the purpose of finding similarities. Students collect the information, choosing their 10 best connections, and then make PowerPoint slides that are shared with the class. Although arranged differently from our ELA set, our history teacher's set does many of the same things. It provides multiple exposures to different texts, affords the opportunity to create multiple intertextual links, and includes a complex, foundational U.S. document.

The Quad Text Set in Action: An Example from Science

The complex nature of science concepts and texts also lends itself to the use of strategic text sets that move students beyond the gist. Let's take the case of a biology teacher who is beginning to plan a unit on cell division. This teacher faces some challenges. Not only is cell division a complicated process to comprehend, but our teacher also understands the limitations of her content-area textbook to convey it. From her recent reading of science journals focused on instruction, she understands that there is a disconnect between the texts that are used in secondary school and the more complicated discipline-specific textbooks and journal articles that students read at the university level. These differences include the complexity and distribution of the visuals in those texts (diagrams of biological processes, data tables, photographs, graphs, etc.). The discipline-specific scientific journal articles and textbooks contain significantly more complicated visuals that must be interpreted (Rybarczyk, 2011). Indeed, she generally sees her textbook as some of her colleagues nationwide do: as an authoritative work that stifles critical thinking (Lemke, 2011).

In order to overcome the limitations of her content-area textbook and to prepare her students to read more complicated science texts that build critical thinking skills, our biology teacher begins to plan backwards. She starts with her unit objectives. Not only does she want students to have knowledge about the structures and processes involved in cell division, but she also wants them to be able to understand how cell division might be impacted by changes in environment. She begins with a target text, in this case a complex journal article that describes how environmental factors spark mutations in cell division. She begins her instruction with her classroom textbook (see Figure 4.9) and a very specific purpose. She needs an overview of the process of mitosis, the "gist" of the steps in the asexual reproduction of cells. She divides her students into groups, each with graphic organizers that organize information about the six phases of cell division. From this text, students build a coherent *text base* of the chapter and acquire a general cognitive representation of the process of mitosis.

Now the teacher brings in some video texts. Understanding how important analogies can be to student understanding of biological processes, she finds four different student-created analogies that she captures from YouTube. All of the videos compare the process of mitosis to something easier for students to understand: a soccer team tryout, a house, a 1970s-style athletic tube sock, and a synchronized swimming contest. Using a six-section graphic organizer, students view the videos as a full class, each student responsible for identifying the elements of the analogies that are related to the six steps in the process of mitosis. Then, in groups, students discuss the analogies and decide which of the four videos they believe is the most comprehensive depiction of the process given their reading of the biology text. Following this discussion, students write an argument that supports their opinion, referencing both the videos and the biology textbook. In this way, the teacher is able to reinforce critical thinking in her

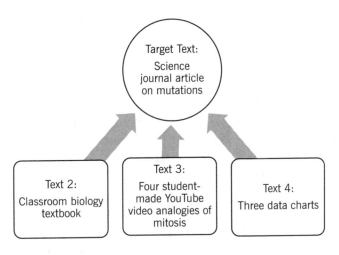

FIGURE 4.9. Text set to build background knowledge for science journal article.

students by encouraging them to form arguments based on these digital texts. In doing so, she also provides multiple textual exposures to the concept of cell division and the technical vocabulary that is used to describe the process. These lesson components together produce a much more comprehensive representation of the text for students at the situation-model level, and the activities clearly address the Common Core standards related to evaluating and creating arguments that use relevant and sufficient evidence.

Now that the students have a more robust representation of the cell division process, our teacher can tackle the lack of complexity of visual representations of data in her textbook compared with the more specialized materials that students are required to read in college (Rybarczyk, 2011). The teacher chooses a complex data table that represents findings from a series of experiments charting the effects of environmental factors on the likelihood of cell mutation. Distributing this text to students, she encourages them to interpret the data in the table and to determine which factors would be most likely to lead to mutation and to possible cancers. Now that they have the critical background knowledge, they are ready to tackle the target text—a complex science journal article on the causes of skin cancer.

Final Thoughts

As you can see from these three strategically created text sets, we believe that no single text or textbook can serve as an effective vehicle for deep understanding. This is especially true for typical content-area textbooks. As the authors of the Common Core standards point out, over the last 50 years the complexity and sophistication of K–12 texts have declined, while the demands for reading complex and diverse texts in college, training programs, and the workforce have increased. Our biology teacher clearly understood all of this when she planned her text set. Consequently, if we continue using only our current K–12 textbooks, many students will enter their postsecondary work unprepared in the skills they need to engage with the increasingly complex texts they will encounter. In fact, statistics on the literacy development of high school graduates demonstrate that there is a gap between what students need to know after graduation and what they do know: remember that 20% of incoming freshmen must take a remedial reading course in college (Southern Regional Education Board, 2006), and 40% of high school graduates lack the literacy skills employers are looking for (National Governors Association, 2005).

Although textbooks do have their drawbacks, they can and should be included in our instruction. It may sound strange for us to say at this point, but we believe that classroom texts should be a very important part of content-area instruction because of their iconic role in the American classroom. For those of you who use a single classroom textbook, this may seem a given. However, although many of us hand them out at the beginning of the year, have our students cover them, scold students when texts are lost or forgotten, and collect them (once all offending marks are erased) at the end of the school year, we believe that because of teacher choice, text quality, or institutional factors, textbooks are often "lost and forgotten" in current content instruction. We find this troubling because a foundational classroom textbook should be viewed as an important instructional tool. When used in concert with other texts, the textbook can build the contextual and vocabulary knowledge needed to tackle the complicated target texts that the CCSS demand, can help students learn to use text features to guide their own comprehension, and can be particularly good for guiding students in summary writing, an activity that improves not only writing quality but comprehension as well (Graham & Hebert, 2010).

And so, if we are going to teach to the demands of the CCSS, then one of our most important jobs is to choose challenging texts that work together in sets. We hope this chapter helped you think about how these sets can be arranged to achieve your instructional goals.

CHAPTER 5

Building Background Knowledge

Knowledge is the true organ of sight, not the eyes.
—*THE PANCHATANTRA*

As we read to prepare for this chapter, we noticed surprisingly similar findings in a large and very diverse set of research studies: Background knowledge explains a huge amount of variance in all kinds of learning. The more you know, the easier it is to learn. We read studies of reading comprehension, surely, but we also read studies of mathematical problem solving, computer modeling, and interpretation of all sorts of visual information, especially in science. We read studies of young children and studies of college students. Nearly all learning processes are facilitated when background knowledge is stronger. If we want students to learn from reading, then, it makes sense to build background knowledge before they read.

To be fair from the beginning, we are taking a very limited stance on what background knowledge is. All individuals have background knowledge that is generated from their experiences. The problem is that specific, academic background knowledge, generated only through academic experiences, is what is necessary for success in the challenging readings of the CCSS. Student access to the academic experiences that build this knowledge should not be determined by their parents' income; it should come as one of the benefits of schooling (Marzano, 2004). We will define background knowledge in this chapter as the specific knowledge that enables a reader to understand the intentions of an author in a particular text.

Reading comprehension is one of the domains in which researchers have described the relationship between academic background knowledge and success. Here is the conundrum again: The more you know in advance, the easier it is to read to learn more. Students who read more generate more background knowledge from their reading and that makes new reading easier. The challenging texts that are required by the CCSS, whether in English, history, science, or technical subjects, are not chosen for their accessibility or their link to what students already know. In fact, at least in the first years of implementation of the CCSS, the texts will be both harder in general and also more central to success in school. For teachers, then, the million-dollar questions include:

- How do we manage both teacher-directed building of knowledge and the use of reading to build knowledge?
- How do we make good use of time so that students of diverse backgrounds (and knowledge) can engage in extensive, productive reading of challenging texts?

We think that part of the answer to these questions lies in understanding why, when, and how to build background knowledge before reading. We also think the answers lie in our ability to embrace some facts about reading comprehension.

Comprehension is a *personal* cognitive construction. Since our students will bring individual types and amounts of background knowledge to the literacy tasks we plan, we must acknowledge that those initial differences will mean that they will reap differential gains. They will experience the Matthew effect (Stanovich, 1986) as readers with greater initial knowledge will read more easily and build more complex understandings while those with more limited initial knowledge will acquire more basic information. In the terms we introduced in Chapter 4, those with stronger knowledge before reading will build richer, more coherent situation models. Make no mistake: we champion the strides made by the ablest readers. We take the stance that it is not the goal of education to decrease the knowledge gap among students, but rather to decrease the gap between students with initially low achievement and the knowledge and skills required for success in college and careers. Expert building of background knowledge by teachers will allow students to spend more time reading more complex texts. Though the benefits will not be the same for all students, all students will benefit.

In this chapter, we begin by defining background knowledge and providing you some insights into researchers' exploration of the role of background knowledge in text comprehension. That will help you to understand why we have selected a relatively short list of instructional strategies you can use to develop students' background knowledge before they read. You will also see why we are taking the stance that you have to preteach both central concepts from the text and the structure of ideas in the text. As is the case with every strategy we recommend in this book, these meet our test criteria. They are theoretically sound and reasonable to implement across time and content areas. They are also tools you can use to bridge the distance between what your students know and what you want them to learn when they read.

What Is Background Knowledge and How Do We Get It?

Here is the short answer: Background knowledge is everything you know, and you get it in all of the ways that you learn—including by reading. Background knowledge is an umbrella term for all of the knowledge you bring to learning. And as we illustrate in Figure 5.1, that umbrella covers several sources. Vocabulary knowledge is the understanding of word meanings. To return to our example of *A Doll's House* from Chapter 4, readers must know or be able to infer the meanings of nearly all the words Ibsen chose to use, from *pinch* to *squander*. The reader's prior knowledge will also be brought to bear, such as knowledge of Ibsen's work and the Victorian era, bolstered by the teacher's choice of factual texts to group together in a set. Experiential knowledge will likewise be helpful, including personal familiarity with the nature of marital relationships. Finally, structural knowledge will help in a seamless way as the reader uses grammatical knowledge to interpret clauses and sentences and, at a higher level, relies on genre knowledge about how dialogue is formatted in a play, how the action is partitioned into scenes, and so forth. These sources of knowledge, complex as they are, work in concert during proficient reading, but deficiencies in one or more of them can jeopardize comprehension.

The big idea is that readers bring knowledge to text, and that knowledge takes many forms. Building knowledge specifically and deliberately before reading increases the chances that reading will be productive, not only in terms of successful comprehension but in new knowledge acquired. Picture the process as a spiral. Each experience of productive reading will generate additional background knowledge for the next reading, and so forth. Let's examine the components of background knowledge in more detail.

The "parts" of background knowledge represented in Figure 5.1 are related. One of the reasons that those with stronger background knowledge learn more easily is that they have more ways to store new information. Rupley and Slough

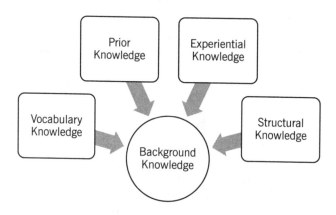

FIGURE 5.1. Types of background knowledge.

(2010) describe vocabulary knowledge as the specific hooks on which learners hang new learnings and prior knowledge as the larger "promulgation" of these hooks. Vocabulary knowledge, then, is each individual word meaning that you have stored while prior knowledge is the sum total of those words and their interconnections.

Experiential knowledge helps individuals refine and specify their word knowledge over time. One of the reasons this is so important is that words have different, very specific meanings in different content areas. Rupley and Slough use the word *parent* as an example—it has an everyday meaning, but also very different meanings in biology, chemistry, and physics. We looked it up. In biology, a parent is the nucleus of a cell that divides into two or more daughter nuclei. In chemistry, a parent is a chain of connected carbon atoms in a hydrocarbon. In physics, a parent is the nucleus of an atom that undergoes radioactive decay. While each of these definitions has some connection to the concept of parent in everyday language, knowing what a father and mother is will not replace the specific science knowledge required here.

Part of building background knowledge, then, is building the specific vocabulary (either specialized words or new meanings of old words) associated with each content area. As students get older, their accumulation of background knowledge has a larger and larger effect on text comprehension (Alexander, Kulikowich, & Jetton, 1994). This may be, in part, because the texts they read are more specialized and difficult. They read deeply within the domains of literature, of history and social science, and of the sciences, and they must understand the specialized language of each domain.

Word meanings, no matter how broad or deep or interconnected, are not all there is to background knowledge. We described the relevance of Walter Kintsch's text representation theory as an explanation of the process of comprehension in Chapter 4. Remember that readers are responsible for processing the words and phrases in a text at the surface level. Then they build a model of text meaning (the situation model) by filling in what the author has not provided. Background knowledge plays a central role in this process; it facilitates this meaning construction. In a content-area text, then, comprehension involves "building a conceptual knowledge structure that includes the main concepts and essential relationships among the concepts in the text" (Taboada & Guthrie, 2006, p. 5).

Background knowledge helps provide us with the structure to understand ideas. The most complex background knowledge touches the structure of knowledge in each domain. In history, background knowledge of the structure of historical thinking guides a reader to look for causes, courses, and consequences of events, and to expect that texts will provide cultural, political, and economic explanations for these events. In science, background knowledge guides us to see how living and nonliving things are classified and related. In literature, we analyze an author's selections of conflicts and themes within historical periods. Slightly less complex is our recognition of text structures. We expect narratives to contain sequences of events; we expect scientific texts to contain procedures; we expect historical texts to contain causes and effects.

Because it is both consequential and complicated, two stances underlie our treatment of background knowledge in this chapter:

1. Reading comprehension requires domain-specific background knowledge.
2. One of the ways to develop domain-specific background knowledge is through extensive reading.

As we showed you in Chapter 4, the design of text sets allows you to use texts (and student time spent reading and writing them) to build background knowledge for more complex texts.

The study of the effects of background knowledge on reading comprehension has a long history. Initially, researchers identified three components of background knowledge. The first component is the reader's expectation that the text is actually about a particular content area—the context of the text. *When you picked up this book, you did so fully cognizant that it would be about how the CCSS change our goals for teaching with text.* The second is the extent to which the actual words of the text provide concrete associations with that content—the transparency of the text. *Unless you were forced, you kept reading this book because its style was accessible to you and you were able to learn reasonable strategies for addressing the CCSS.* The third is the extent to which a reader already knows that content area—the familiarity of the text (Carrell, 1983). *If you are reading the book together with colleagues or classmates, each of you has a different understanding of the ideas here, based on what you already know about reading and writing in content areas.* Without diluting our treatment, we may be able to narrow our definition to two components of background knowledge—content knowledge, which might be conceived as vocabulary knowledge, and structural or genre knowledge, which is a measure of the way knowledge is organized in a domain (Valencia, Stallman, Commeyras, Pearson, & Hartman, 1991).

If we look at background knowledge as content and structure, it may be that we need to think of an individual developing expertise as a reader (and then a writer!) in each content area by initially developing content knowledge and then seeing the broader structure of knowledge in the domain. At first, a reader has only generic comprehension strategies, such as looking for structural cues (e.g., headings, topic sentences, summaries). After employing those more generic skills to read successfully about a topic, the reader adds what was learned about the topic to these generic strategies, making the reading of a new text easier. Over time, with wide successful reading, the reader brings domain knowledge to each new reading, and that expertise makes reading comprehension in that domain much easier (Surber & Schroeder, 2007). Figure 5.2 depicts this movement from

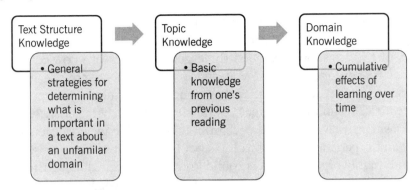

FIGURE 5.2. Movement toward domain knowledge.

the general comprehension strategies that students learn and use as more novice readers in elementary school to the knowledge that they gain through employing these strategies. During the course of adolescence, we want students to move from simple topic knowledge to more structured domain knowledge.

Think of the way you read in the content area you teach. You have both content knowledge and structural knowledge. If you teach history, you look for causes and consequences of historical events. They might be political, social, or economic. You know much about individuals and events, but you also know how historians interpret trends and describe eras. If you teach literature, you look for themes and conflicts, and you notice language choices. If you teach science or mathematics or a technical subject, you look for processes and procedures and causes and effects. Also think about times when you have to read outside your own content area. You may be a voracious, wide reader, flexibly moving from one domain to another. More likely, though, you are like us—when we choose what we read, we read what we know. We earned this comfort level over time by investing time; we reap the benefits by experiencing this type of reading over and over again.

What teachers do to support movement from text structure strategies to topic knowledge to domain knowledge matters. General discussions meant to spark interest in a topic do not improve comprehension of a complex text. There are simply too many extraneous ideas. Because basic knowledge is most likely developed (and stored) as vocabulary knowledge, deliberate preteaching of concepts and vocabulary central to text understanding is what improves comprehension. For this reason, we will take the stance that direct instruction of specific word meanings before reading is necessary but not sufficient for building background knowledge (Stahl & Jacobson, 1986; Stahl, Jacobson, Davis, & Davis, 1989).

The movement from basic vocabulary to domain knowledge requires that knowledge become structured. Langer (1984) documented this movement by interviewing a cross-section of increasingly older students. She collected evidence of background knowledge before reading by listing key concepts from a text and asking students to "free associate," writing what they knew about those terms. Analysis of these responses yielded three general stores of knowledge. Highly organized background knowledge included the ability to provide hierarchical descriptions, precise definitions, analogies, and links among concepts. Partially organized background knowledge contained examples, characteristics, and some definitions. Diffusely organized background knowledge included personal associations and experiences as well as low-level links by word parts or sound. Students with highly organized background knowledge recalled more after reading.

This finding, that more coherent background knowledge increases reading comprehension, has been replicated many times and with different populations of students. Background knowledge influences comprehension directly and through its influence on a reader's inference generation (Tarchi, 2010). Students with learning disabilities perform better on inferential reading comprehension tasks when they have higher prior knowledge. All students, with and without learning disabilities, benefit from adult-directed activation of relevant prior knowledge when topics are unfamiliar. The benefit extends to both reading and writing tasks. Students need both knowledge and strategies to be successful in reading comprehension tasks (Carr & Thompson, 1996). Likewise, prior knowledge has an effect on both quantity and quality of writing for high school students (Chesky & Hiebert, 1987). Taken together, these findings suggest that time spent building background knowledge before reading or writing is time well spent.

We believe that the most important route to academic background knowledge is wide and deep reading. The strategies we present below are meant to make that reading time productive. Figure 5.3 presents the cycle that you can initiate for your students. You can begin by using instructional strategies to make text accessible. In this way students can read to build academic background knowledge and then bring the knowledge gained to their next reading. Over time, both across grade levels and within specific courses, students who engage in extensive, challenging reading will build the structured domain knowledge that makes all learning so much easier.

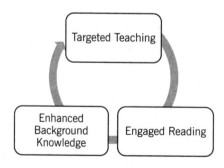

FIGURE 5.3. Cycle of building academic background knowledge.

Moving to Instruction

As this is the first time we are actually presenting instructional strategies, we want to set you up for success. We will always provide a brief description of the history, or derivation, of a strategy. Then we provide some contextualized information—application examples within different content areas. We will have to be selective here, so if your content area is not represented in the examples for a particular strategy, don't assume that it isn't useful. After the examples, we will provide a procedure for planning. Finally, we will provide a coaching form, so that you can work with teammates or instructional coaches to provide one another feedback during your implementation trials. You can use the coaching forms to prompt personal reflections (especially if you collect video), guide peer observations, or invite a coach into your classroom to watch you implement strategies.

Teaching Technical Vocabulary

As you read a complex text from the perspective of your students, you might be overwhelmed by the number of words you could choose to teach. Don't be. In this case, more is not better. If you choose words wisely, your initial teaching will not be the only chance that students have to learn those words. We know students need multiple *meaningful* exposures to words to really learn them—initial teaching provides one exposure, but then the reading itself provides another. A rich discussion and writing after reading provide additional exposures. When you choose words, look for those that are essential in your domain and that will be repeated many times in future readings and discussions, eventually yielding the 12 encounters that researchers have estimated to be required for truly learning new concepts (McKeown, Beck, Omanson, & Pople, 1985).

We don't want you to go overboard here. When you read the text that your students will read, you know the meaning of every word. You are an expert in the domain, with rich background knowledge. As novices read, they need not understand the meaning of every word. In fact, word learning itself is not an all-or-nothing phenomenon. Perhaps the reason we need many meaningful encounters with a word to truly own it is that each encounter adds incrementally to our understanding. Word learning progresses over multiple encounters (see Figure 5.4), from no knowledge to the rich, decontextualized knowledge that allows us to easily define and contextualize a word we know well (Beck, McKeown, & Omanson, 1987).

Since you need not teach every word in advance of reading, you must learn to choose the words that are absolutely essential to understanding the text. Based on the background reading we did to better understand the role of background knowledge in comprehension, we have a recommendation. Make a visual representation of the text. You can use whatever seems best matched to the author's

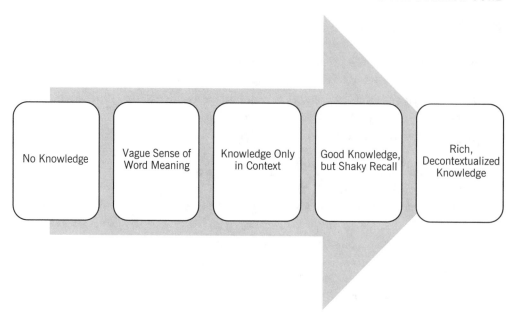

FIGURE 5.4. Continuum of word learning.

organization and easiest to generate—a story map for a narrative, a concept map for an information text. In completing your visual, you will have had to identify essential concepts and depict their linkages—that will provide you a strong rationale for choosing which words to teach in advance. You should teach the words that are essential to the text's skeleton, or structure. Once you have your list of words, choosing an instructional strategy is much easier.

Concept of Definition

If your text is about one central concept that must be developed in advance, concept of definition (Schwartz & Raphael, 1985) may be the best choice for you. It has the added bonus of forcing you to include all of the hallmarks of effective vocabulary instruction—definition, examples, and nonexamples. It also has a structural component, providing a visual representation for how students should store a word in their memory in relation to other words they already know. Figure 5.5 shows a concept of definition map for the economic concept of scarcity.

You read (and write!) a concept of definition map very specifically. That is, it's not enough to present the diagram. You must talk the students through it as you construct it. Here is what the teacher might say while constructing the diagram in Figure 5.5:

"Scarcity is an economic problem characterized by limited goods and services, high demand, and high prices. Oil prices are high because of scarcity. Some

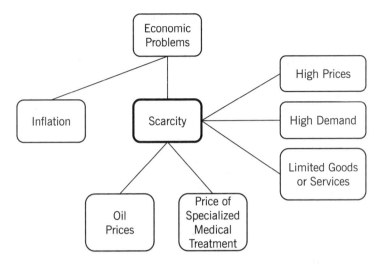

FIGURE 5.5. Concept of definition example.

medical treatments are expensive because of scarcity. Inflation is also an economic problem, but it is not the same as scarcity because it is a general rise in all prices, rather than prices of goods and services whose supply is limited and whose demand is high. Scarcity only applies to certain goods and services meeting these conditions: limited supply and high demand."

If you read this script and draw the map at the same time, you will see that the structure of the map shows the relationships among ideas. The target term is central, connected upwards to a superordinate category. To the left of that superordinate category is another member of that category. It is included as a nonexample to show that the category also contains members other than your target term. To the right are characteristics of your term; below are examples. Figure 5.6 provides both a blank template and a coaching form; you will find concept of definition very easy to use when you are teaching central concepts.

Semantic Feature Analysis

More often, you will find yourself teaching groups of related words—that is how most content-area materials are structured. An earth science reading might compare and contrast igneous, metamorphic, and sedimentary rocks. An introductory government class might read a piece about the relative merits and drawbacks of representative democracy, republicanism, and totalitarianism. Ancient Egypt can be described in terms of the Old, Middle, and New Kingdoms. Eukaryotic cell division involves both mitosis and meiosis. Earthquakes tend to happen along normal, reverse, thrust, or strike-slip faults. Welders uses six different energy sources, depending on the situation. Historically, artists have used perspectives

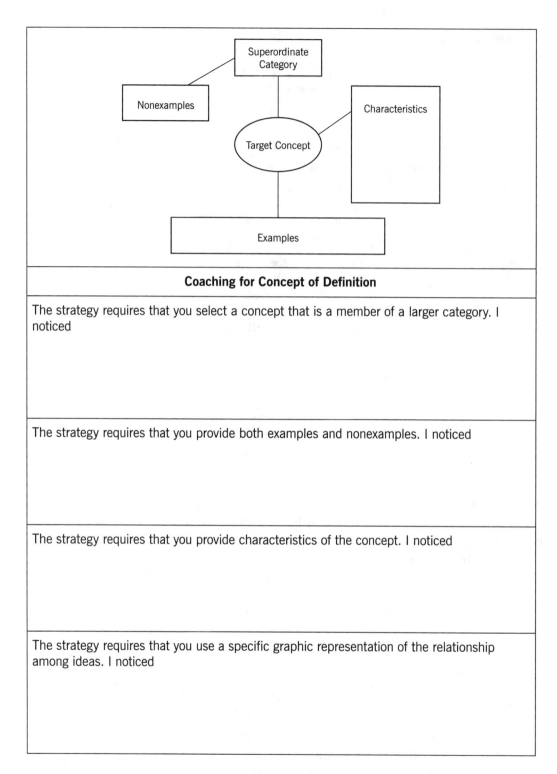

FIGURE 5.6. Planning and coaching template for concept of definition.

varying from zero-point to four-point. If you remember that domain knowledge is the cumulative, structured knowledge of the specialized vocabulary associated with the domain, the possibilities for generating these lists of related words are nearly endless. We might add that an economics text might focus on a range of economic problems, rather than just scarcity (inflation, debt, etc.). So presenting them together as members of the same category would be a logical way to plan. Luckily, you are not required to come up with the lists from your head—you will find them in the readings that you assign.

A semantic feature analysis (Johnson & Pearson, 1984) is a grid that allows us to compare and contrast members of the same category along a set of attributes, or features, that a member may or may not possess. To make a semantic feature analysis chart, follow these steps:

1. Place the category name at the top of the left-hand column. (It helps if it's plural.)
2. List your target terms below the category name so that each term has its own row.
3. Write a feature at the top of each of the columns to the right.

For each entry, then, an individual feature is either present or absent (or sometimes present). You can either mark them before students read or have the students read to fill in the chart.

In Figure 5.7, constructed for a text about the process of developing a vaccine, the chart allows students to compare and contrast the phases of vaccine development in terms of their attributes. To read the completed chart, you can begin at the left-hand column and read across for the attributes of each stage in development, or you can read down any column to see which stages include this attribute. You may notice, for example, that only the exploratory stage includes a

Phases of Vaccine Development	Search for antigens	Test in tissue cultures	Test in animals	Test for immune response	Test in adults	Test in children	Blind	Randomized	Large numbers
Exploratory Stage	Y	N	N	N	N	N	N	N	N
Preclinical Stage	N	Y	Y	Y	N	N	N	N	S
Phase I Trial	N	N	N	Y	Y	S	N	N	N
Phase II Trial	N	N	N	Y	S	S	Y	Y	N
Phase III Trial	N	N	N	Y	S	S	Y	Y	Y

FIGURE 5.7. Semantic feature analysis example.

search for the possible antigens that a vaccine will comprise, and only the Phase I, II, and III trials include human subjects. Notice also that Phase I trials always include adults, and sometimes children. A completed semantic feature analysis contains a lot of information about a set of terms in a very small space. Notice too that the process of filling in the grid is quick.

To create and use a semantic feature analysis chart, first identify the set of concepts that your text compares and contrasts. Then fill in their attributes one at a time, proceeding from left to right across the row until all attributes of all concepts are included. Once you have that information in hand, decide whether to display a filled-in organizer, talking through the comparison of features before your students read, or to have your students look for the attributes themselves during reading. Either way, you will be scaffolding student understanding of the nuanced differences between your target terms and also directing their attention to the most important information in the text you have chosen. Figure 5.8 presents a blank template and also a coaching form.

Using Visuals

Often a picture is worth a thousand words. If the text you have chosen is about a scientific process, a geographic location, a cultural practice, or a period in history, chances are you can build background knowledge through visual information more quickly than through verbal information. This strategy is more general than the previous two, because it depends on the visual that you have chosen. If you are having students read about the circulatory system, for example, beginning with a labeled diagram that shows the organs is an efficient way to introduce the specialized vocabulary in a context that students can easily process. The same is true for a text about the Industrial Revolution—showing a few pictures of key technologies from that period (the cotton gin, the steam engine) will help students to generate an initial context for their reading. The best thing about using visuals is that they are often already provided in your text—there is nothing wrong with using a part of the author's work to give students a jump-start. And doing so sends the message that the visuals in a text are not fluff and that attending to them can be central to understanding.

The accessibility of video opens a whole new world of visual background knowledge. If you need convincing, visit *www.ted.com*, home of the TED (technology, entertainment, design) talks—short video lectures on a wide variety of topics. Think about how much you can learn personally in the few minutes you spend there. Then spend a few minutes exploring some high-utility sites (*www. schooltube.com, www.youtube.com*) for topics central to your content area. Think about these from the perspective of students: to what extent would five minutes of video make a text chapter easier to understand? Depending on your school's firewalls, you might have to save the videos rather than play them live, but there are many sources of free software to capture and save video. (We mentioned

Topic									

Coaching for Semantic Feature Analysis
The strategy requires that you select a group of related terms to compare and contrast. I noticed
The strategy requires that you develop a comprehensive list of attributes. I noticed
The strategy requires that you indicate the presence or absence of each attribute for each target concept. I noticed
The strategy allows you to finish the map for students before they read or allow them to do it during reading. I noticed

FIGURE 5.8. Planning and coaching template for semantic feature analysis.

Firefox's Downloadhelper in Chapter 4, but that's just one.) The key to using video to build background knowledge is that you have to choose video that is *directly* related to the content in the text that you want students to read. Tangentially related video, like a broad discussion, is not specific enough to build knowledge. Figure 5.9 presents a coaching template.

The Special Case of Literature

Those of you who teach ELA may be shaking your heads. A single sonnet by Keats or even one soliloquy in a Shakespearean play may contain so many difficult words that none of these strategies is reasonable. Remember that this section is "Teaching *Technical* Vocabulary." In English classrooms, the technical vocabulary includes the words *sonnet* and *soliloquy.* The technical vocabulary consists of the words *about* literature rather than the words *in* literature. For teaching that technical vocabulary, these techniques work perfectly. Think about a semantic feature analysis that compares and contrasts various poetic forms or types of figurative language. What about a concept of definition map for the third-person omniscient point of view? The superordinate category would be points of view, a nonexample would be first person, and characteristics would include narrator knowledge of the thoughts, feelings, and history of all characters. Examples could be built across time as you read more stories and novels.

There is more to understanding complex literature than having background knowledge of literary terms, of course. Often it is the author's choice of rare words and rare meanings of more common words that makes literature worth reading—or very hard to read, depending on your background knowledge. It may be that to make a text accessible you must preteach some of these unrelated words, but only those residing closest to the work's skeleton, or structure, and theme. For a narrative, if you think about the setting, characters, conflicts, and resolution using only words from the text, you will be able to identify those words that readers really must know. We recommend that you teach them directly and quickly, telling what they mean and how they are used in the text. Don't make the mistake of preteaching all of the words that are rare or interesting to you—if they are not central, calling attention to them in advance will actually distract your students.

Images can play a central role in building background knowledge for literature. Try a Google image search for Victorian England. Accompanied by your narration, a selection of these images can help to orient students as they read Dickens for the first time. Sometimes a brief video on the historical period in which a piece is set makes the selection more accessible. Narrowing that same Google search to video provides a strong set of choices, most of which are fewer than 5 minutes long.

Many canonical works have high-quality film versions. A good example is the 1973 movie *A Doll's House,* starring Claire Bloom and Anthony Hopkins.

Coaching for Using Visuals
The strategy requires that you choose specific visuals from the text or directly related to text information. I noticed
The strategy requires that you provide access to all students. I noticed
The strategy requires that you directly explain the vocabulary represented in the visuals. I noticed

FIGURE 5.9. Coaching template for using visuals.

We support the use of excepts from films before reading to provide readers with visual images that make their own reading easier, rather than as "treats" after reading. High-quality images can guide the reader toward a construction of meaning more in line with the author's intent—a key element of the CCSS—and also contextualize a large portion of what might be challenging vocabulary in pieces set in distant places and times. This use of visuals for literature provides a bridge between building technical vocabulary and previewing a text.

Strategies for Previewing

Since what an individual already knows makes it easier for that individual to learn, and since comprehension requires a *structured* set of concepts and ideas, previewing a text is perhaps the most straightforward way to build background knowledge. A preview is not a general knowledge-building session. It is a specific session designed for a specific text on a specific day. Done well, previewing is a clear reference to the CCSS skill categories of key ideas and details, craft and structure, and integration of knowledge and ideas. Done well, and combined with targeted teaching of technical terms, a preview can make a previously inaccessible text accessible to students. Below we present two instructional approaches to previewing. The first is teacher directed; the second is student directed and collaborative. Both use oral language to preview reading content, going further than teaching technical terms to include a focus on how concepts are related to one another in a particular content area.

Listen–Read–Discuss

One of the qualities that make Listen–Read–Discuss (LRD) especially attractive to us is that its designers describe it as a heuristic that is perfect for novice and skeptical teachers in content areas (Manzo & Casale, 1985). The concept is elegant. Build background knowledge for a specific text by presenting it in a fast-paced lecture first. Introduce your lecture by saying that you want your students to be successful in engaging with a really interesting text that you have chosen for the day. Your lecture can contain and explain the difficult concepts in the order they are found in the text, and it can end with a focus question. That is the "listen" part. Then invite students to read. Even a very complex text will be made easier by the fact that you have just pronounced and explained the difficult words and concepts and also presented the author's structure. After the students have listened and read, you discuss the text, first identifying ideas that are clear and then those that are still confusing and need more attention. Students get three passes at the important text ideas—your preview, their reading, and the group discussion.

It is easier to show this strategy than to tell about it. (And you will find that it is very easy to plan for and deliver.) One of the mandates of the CCSS is that we engage students in extensive reading of primary source documents. In many cases, these documents are written in a style that is inaccessible. This is a perfect place for LRD. We chose one of these documents, Patrick Henry's "Give Me Liberty or Give Me Death" speech, a document listed in the CCSS sample texts. The Colonial Williamsburg Foundation reprints this speech on its website (*www.history.org/almanack/life/politics/giveme.cfm*). Read the speech from the website first, and then read it again after reading the preview we have prepared below.

"I have chosen a fantastic speech for you to read today, which combines a compelling argument with well-crafted rhetoric. The setting is 1775, in the Virginia Colony, in the days before the Revolutionary War. Delegates are gathered in a church in Richmond to consider the relationship between the colonies and Great Britain. Remember that those who favor independence from Great Britain are called Patriots and those who like the colonial system are called Loyalists. Very specifically, things are getting so tense that the Royal Governor of Virginia has taken the gunpowder that belongs to the Virginia militia and stored it in a British ship. Patrick Henry is a colonel in the Virginia militia, and he has forced the governor to give the gunpowder back. Patrick Henry is clearly a Patriot. Now leaders are gathered to consider their next moves. It is important to know that Patrick Henry wants to set up a volunteer militia in every county in Virginia and prepare for war, while others think that they should use more diplomatic routes.

"Before you start to read, I want to give you a modern 'translation' that traces the argument that Patrick Henry makes. That will help you to appreciate his really fantastic language choices. The setting is very formal, so he addresses the president of the convention, Peyton Randolph. He compliments the others who have spoken in favor of diplomacy, and you will see that he calls them worthy, able, and patriotic. Then he says that disagreeing with their ideas is not disrespectful to them. He says that he is going to speak his mind because the issue that they are discussing is of 'awful moment' to the country—meaning that it is too important for him to focus on politeness. To him, they are choosing between freedom from Great Britain and slavery, and since that is such an important issue, they should all debate it as aggressively as possible. In fact, this is so important that he thinks not arguing as hard as he can would be an example of treason. So the opening section is an argument about why Patrick Henry is not going to worry about offending the folks who don't agree with him.

"The first section of his argument claims that people tend to look on the bright side. He talks about how nice it is to engage the 'illusions of hope' or to ignore 'painful truths.' He also makes a reference to Greek mythology by talking about the sirens who sang to sailors and distracted them so that their boats crashed into rocks. He says that the issues that they are facing are so important that each one of them has to open his eyes and ears, even if what he finds is very painful. He talks about temporal salvation, which means their physical safety. He says that he is going to face the truth and plan for it.

"The next section is about why Patrick Henry doesn't trust the British. He says that there is no reason to trust them based on past experience. He says that they are acting friendly, but they are actually preparing for war. He says that fleets of ships and armies of men are not evidence of peaceful intentions. He says that the only use of a martial array (which is a grouping of military forces) is to force the colonies into submission (which means obedience). He also reminds everyone that all of this military force means the colonies are the enemy of Great Britain, and that they have to fight against it. He says that they cannot argue against an army. And they have already tried to use petitions and treaties, but haven't gotten anywhere. He says that they cannot hope for peace anymore. They have to get ready to fight to keep the freedoms they have worked for. So this whole section is about why they can't trust the British and keep using diplomatic strategies.

"In the next section he counters the argument that the colonies are too weak. Patrick Henry says that if they wait they will only get weaker. They will lose their guns and ammunition. They need to act now and use what they have. He says that the people of the colonies are its great strength, especially if they are fighting for what is right. He says that God will support them as they do the right thing, and that God will compel allies to help. He says they have no choice. They must be ready for war unless they want to stay slaves to Britain. He says that the war will come, it has to come, and that he is glad.

"The final section is about action. He says that people might want peace, but peace is really not an option. The people are ready to fight, and their leaders should stop stalling. He knows that men will die, but he thinks accepting slavery is not a choice. That's why he ends with 'Give me liberty or give me death.'

"Now I am going to give you 10 minutes to consider the actual language Patrick Henry used. When you are done, we will discuss what parts of Henry's language are clear to you and what language you still want to discuss."

To plan an LRD preview, prepare a monologue that includes the major text ideas. If it is a text you are very familiar with, you may be able to use an outline. For a more complex text (or for your first efforts), consider writing it out as we did above. Be sure your preview follows the text chronologically. Then deliver your preview quickly and in an engaging way. When you ask your students to read, provide a time limit and a purpose that you will revisit in the discussion. As you will see in Chapter 7, a few minutes spent planning good questions will go a long way toward motivating your students to wrestle with text ideas. Figure 5.10 presents a coaching template for LRD.

Coaching for Listen–Read–Discuss
The strategy requires that you prepare a preview that includes and explains difficult concepts. I noticed
The strategy requires that you prepare a preview that follows the author's text structure. I noticed
The strategy requires that you present the preview in an engaging way. I noticed
The strategy requires that you next invite students to read for a purpose. I noticed
The strategy requires that you revisit your purpose in a targeted discussion. I noticed

FIGURE 5.10. Coaching template for Listen–Read–Discuss (LRD).

Prereading Plan

The Prereading Plan (PreP) developed by Judith Langer (Langer, 1981; Langer & Nicholich, 1981) allows students to evaluate and restructure their existing background knowledge by combining it with that of their peers. To prepare for a PreP lesson, the teacher chooses a set of words that represent the main topics in an upcoming text. The words are presented in order, but one at a time. Students engage in a three-step process for each concept: association, reflection, and reformulation. Guiding questions for the three steps of PreP include:

> "What are your initial ideas about this? Tell me anything that comes to mind."
> "What made you think of this?"
> "Based on our discussion, do you have new ideas?"

A sample science text in the CCSS Appendix B text exemplars, Gordon Kane's *The Mysteries of Mass*, is an engaging article from *Scientific American* about the use of standard and string theories, along with experiments in superconductors, to understand the nature of mass. For a group of physics students preparing to read this text, a PreP discussion could center on the terms *mass, particles, quantum physics*, and *dark matter*. While all students could contribute to the first step, stronger physics students would likely be able to provide more elaboration during step two, and weaker physics students could be the target in the third step. All students would be better prepared to read the text productively once their knowledge was activated, shared, and structured through the discussion. Figure 5.11 provides a coaching template.

By the end of the PreP discussion, students are ready to encounter the target concepts in the text. This relatively simple structure for development and restructuring of background knowledge was more effective than motivation techniques to increase student content learning from reading. Unfortunately, though, positive effects were found only for average and above-average readers; struggling readers may require more extensive work to build background knowledge before they can really learn from reading (Langer, 1984).

Designing and Using Graphic Organizers

Graphic organizers can provide an additional level of support for students with weaker academic background knowledge or make especially challenging texts manageable for all. The best graphic organizers combine support for specific concepts and for the structured nature of strong comprehension and domain knowledge. Presented before reading, they preview both content and structure; used during reading, they guide readers to what you really want them to learn.

Coaching for Prereading Plan
The strategy requires that you choose specific concepts central to text understanding. I noticed
The strategy requires that you introduce them one at a time. I noticed
The strategy requires that you first gather associations for each concept. I noticed
The strategy requires that you next invite students to explain the source of their associations. I noticed
The strategy requires that you ask students whether the discussion has created new ideas. I noticed

FIGURE 5.11. Coaching template for Prereading Plan (PreP).

A graphic organizer is a visual model of the relationship of ideas. Semantic feature analyses and concept of definition maps are graphic organizers, but organizers can go beyond these simple forms to contain any combination of pictures, words, and shapes. Graphic organizers help us to show complex ideas and structures in a small space, with relatively little writing. To pique your interest, we have listed in Figure 5.12 the major instructional purposes for graphic organizers along with descriptions and examples (Gallavan & Kottler, 2007). Pay special attention to the last type of organizer. We think that it is most important.

A picture is worth a thousand words, but sometimes we have to make our own pictures to show the relationship among ideas in complex text. If we make graphic organizers that "combine and create," we are presenting students with a representation of the relationship among ideas in the text that they are about to read. We can also go beyond simple shapes to include important information and terms. This provides supportive background knowledge that is both conceptual and structural. It is no surprise, then, that graphic organizers support vocabulary learning, comprehension, and inferential thinking, even for students with learning disabilities (Dexter & Hughes, 2011).

Figure 5.13 is a simple graphic organizer that we created for a middle school science textbook passage about the discovery of radiation. Notice that it shows how portions of the text are related. Notice, too, that we filled in the final box to help students see that their goal during reading would be to find out how Becquerel's hypothesis led to his procedure, and then how his procedure yielded both an expected and an unexpected result. The graphic organizer provides structural support and also content support. The fact that we made it for our students communicates our goal of having their reading be directed, purposeful, and essential

Type	Description	Example
Assume and anticipate	Check and organize prior knowledge or opinions before reading	KWL chart
Position and pattern	Show a sequence or pattern, especially one that repeats, or a cause and effect	Timeline, map, cycle
Group and organize	Classify ideas by type or category	Semantic feature analysis, other charts
Compare and contrast	Show similarities, differences, and relationships	Venn diagram
Relate and reason	Show part-to-whole and whole-to-part relationships	Tree diagram
Identify and imagine	Name, describe, or brainstorm	Semantic map
Estimate and evaluate	Explain or examine a concept	Sociogram, flowchart
Combine and create	Use parts of different graphic organizers in a unique way to represent a set of ideas	

FIGURE 5.12. General types of graphic organizers.

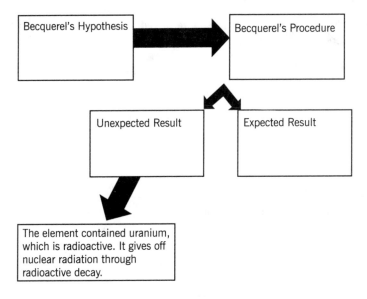

FIGURE 5.13. Sample graphic organizer for a textbook segment.

for meeting the day's objectives. A coaching template for graphic organizers is provided in Figure 5.14.

Incorporating Writing

Many of the instructional strategies we have described above include writing, but we want to highlight its power to generate and organize background knowledge before we close this chapter. For example, the process of cowriting this book on strategic instruction and the CCSS revealed the strengths and weaknesses of our own background knowledge and the inquiry we needed to carry out to fill the gaps in our own understanding. E. M. Forster's famous tidbit, "How do I know what I think until I see what I say?" applies here. We write, in essence, to direct our reading; our writing shows us what research we need to investigate. As you develop expertise, the use of writing to access and organize your existing knowledge becomes more and more helpful.

Concept Mapping

Concept mapping is one form of writing that is easy to incorporate into lessons. It is widely touted in university classes as a cooperative activity or as an assessment (e.g., Bentley, Kennedy, & Semsar, 2011). It can be used before reading to help students share and structure their background knowledge. Preparation is simple. The teacher selects a set of key terms (between 10 and 20 is reasonable) and sets

Coaching for Graphic Organizers
The strategy requires that you create a visual representation of text ideas. You can use words, pictures, and shapes. I noticed
The strategy requires that you introduce and explain the organizer before reading. I noticed
The strategy requires that you provide students direction during reading. I noticed
The strategy requires that you invite some writing during or after reading. I noticed

FIGURE 5.14. Coaching template for graphic organizers.

students the task of creating a graphical representation of their relationships. In essence, students work to construct a graphic organizer. Then they defend their work, sharing with another group and evaluating that group's decisions. Here are 10 terms from this chapter:

background knowledge	semantic mapping
graphic organizers	PreP
previews	concepts
vocabulary instruction	structure
concept of definition	domain knowledge

You can construct your own concept map now, but if these terms were all unfamiliar to you before you read this chapter, this would not have been a good use of your time. Concept mapping is useful before reading only when students have fairly broad concept knowledge that needs to be structured. Figure 5.15 presents one possible map and also a coaching template.

Student-Generated Questions

Interesting, high-level conceptual questions presented before reading can enable a richer reading experience. This is because they set cognitive expectations that help the reader to set up a possible structure for understanding. Using conceptual questions, therefore, links prior knowledge with new knowledge in a productive way. Taboada and Guthrie (2006) found evidence that both prior knowledge of science and student-generated higher-order questions before reading were independently associated with better reading comprehension across multiple texts. As with our concept map example, though, students cannot generate higher-order questions in unfamiliar domains. Figure 5.16 presents their rubric for rating student questions. As we move students from learning from single texts to learning from text sets and from their own research, opportunities for engaging them in meaningful, self-directed purpose setting through the writing of questions

Level 1 Facts	• Simple questions with simple, factual answers. • *How many types of sharks are there?*
Level 2 Descriptions	• Questions that require a simple description or a global statement. • *How do fish swim?*
Level 3 Explanations	• Questions that require a complex explanation with evidence. • *How do predators choose their prey?*
Level 4 Patterns	• Questions require coherent understanding of interrelated concepts. • *How are animal behaviors related to the characteristics of their environment?*

FIGURE 5.16. Rubric for evaluating the complexity of student-generated questions.

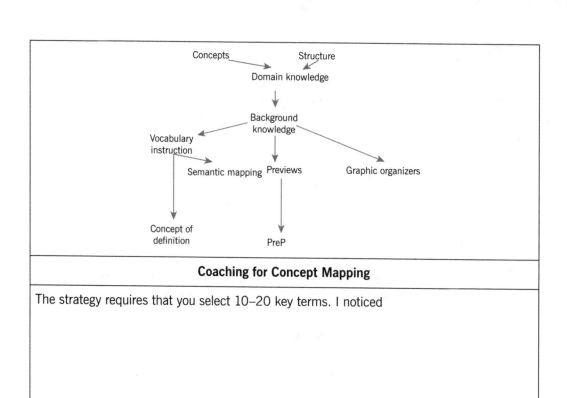

Coaching for Concept Mapping
The strategy requires that you select 10–20 key terms. I noticed
The strategy requires that you ask students to work in groups to construct maps that show how the terms are related. I noticed
The strategy requires that you allow students to share maps across groups. I noticed

FIGURE 5.15. Concept map example and coaching template.

before reading will be an important strategy for linking their background knowledge with their purposes and processes during reading, a topic to which we turn in Chapter 6.

Final Thoughts

The instructional strategies we have related to you in this chapter have much in common. They are all relatively brief, to save time for reading. They are all targeted to a specific day's text, to make reading productive. They all tackle ideas head on and make relationships among ideas transparent, to begin to structure student knowledge and to build real domain knowledge. They all require that you read text carefully and specify your teaching and learning goals in advance. There is no magic to the building of background knowledge before reading. The task places the teacher squarely between students and text. As you know your students (and their background knowledge) better, and know your texts (and their knowledge demands) better, you will be able to make more expert choices in the building of background knowledge. Your success will be measured in the extent to which your students can learn while reading challenging texts.

CHAPTER 6

Supporting Students during Reading

Alone we can do so little; together we can do so much.
—HELEN KELLER

We have spent the last several years choosing strategies to include in this book by working directly in middle schools and high schools. We have worked in several states, and we have worked in both high-performing and struggling schools. We have worked in comprehensive schools and in vocational–technical schools. When we have worked directly with teachers, we have seen radical changes in the way they use text. Generally, we have seen teachers release control (and the opportunity for learning) to students. We have seen teachers move from dramatic *teacher* read-alouds, with students following along, to engaged *student* reading in pairs and in groups. We have seen deadening round-robin oral reading (with individual students called on to read selections aloud while others listen) give way to engaged silent reading and student discussion. The bottom line is this: If you want your students to read better, you have to plan instruction that allows them to read more.

Along the way, we asked teachers why they didn't engage their students in more reading. We expected them to say that the students couldn't read well enough. The answer we actually got surprised us. Teachers told us they didn't ask students to read very much because they could not motivate them. Eventually we saw the reason: they lacked viable lesson frames for organizing their students' time so that they could actually engage in tasks that required reading and writing. In addition, they did not have strategies for connecting reading to integrated

and interesting goals to build units of reading and writing and learning that connected individual lessons to one another and to students.

Like you, we want our classes to be active but orderly, busy but focused, and
responsive but goal directed. We believe that structures for how to read (individually and with others) can advance these goals. As we chose instructional strategies, or frames, for this chapter, we did so with several goals in mind. We wanted
strategies that were adaptable to nearly any text, relatively easy to teach and learn,
and that could be used interchangeably. That is, we wanted to provide you with
a menu of structures for reading during class time that you could choose from
based on your students, your day's text, and your teaching and learning goals.
In this chapter, we will show you four very general ways to maximize student
engagement in reading.

We imagine that few teachers will balk at the suggestions we made in Chapter 5. After all, it makes good sense that if students are to benefit from reading,
we should set them up for success by taking action in advance. We expect more
push-back in this chapter. Many teachers will need to try the techniques we introduce here before they believe that their students can be more personally involved
in their own acquisition of content-area knowledge. What you will have to come
to grips with is the fact that hearing a lecture is one way to "cover" content. Providing time and opportunity to read and think and talk is another. In fact, we
believe that if you don't rethink your use of time and replace lecturing with quick
and targeted building of background knowledge followed by real reading and
discussion and real writing, you will not be preparing your students to meet the
CCSS or for the reading they will do in college and the workplace.

To get you ready to rethink some of your instructional time to include
engaged reading *during school*, we will begin by making a plea for cooperative
groupings by describing recent large-scale attempts to boost the comprehension
of adolescents and by reviewing research on the effects of cooperative groups. We
will then move you through three possibilities, arranged from least intrusive on
typical instruction to more, to most—inviting you to cede some control by creating reading guides, then more control by using a paired reading technique, then
even more control by engaging your students in cooperative text-based discussions. We suspect you may see many contrasts with your present approaches to
planning and instruction. All we ask is that you read with an open mind!

Choosing a Stance for Adolescent Readers

Interestingly, researchers who address the difficult problem of improving the
reading comprehension of adolescents use two very different literatures to design
their work—cognitive psychology as it relates to reading (e.g., van Dijk & Kintsch,
1983) *and* sociocultural theory (e.g., Vaughn et al., 2011). The cognitive psychology stance informs our understanding of how individuals think during reading.

The science of reading typically comes from a cognitive psychology stance; we want to use instructional methods that increase the ability of students to think and learn while they read and write. Sociocultural stances are about the broader context of this thinking. These stances reveal the real need that adolescents have for collaborative, peer-oriented problem solving. As you will see, our efforts to advise you to choose among several during-reading strategies juggle these two real-world goals.

There is yet another tension more recently engaged by researchers (but perhaps always engaged by teachers). When we are using text to teach in the content areas, should we err on the side of content or strategies? We, like many others, are choosing to favor content, or specific attention to the information in the texts teachers choose, over comprehension strategies (McKeown, Beck, & Blake, 2009; Vaughn et al., 2013). You will see, then, that although some of the instructional procedures we describe in this chapter do include the use of comprehension strategies, we simply see them as frames for students to use while reading together. In other words, we do not see your role as teaching comprehension strategies for their own sake. In fact, we are not suggesting that you teach them at all. Instead, we will suggest ways you can quickly model a few strategies so that your students will be better able to engage in solving real comprehension problems by talking about text. We don't think of you as a reading teacher, and we therefore move right to student engagement with your text and your content. We make this choice because we believe that building your students' content knowledge through reading will be a more productive use of your instructional time than either teaching comprehension strategies or lecturing about content-area concepts.

Recent Large-Scale Efforts

Research teams have not ignored the real-life need to understand how to support adolescent reading achievement. Collaborative Strategic Reading (CSR), for example, is a procedure with roots in the service of struggling readers and students with disabilities. It was developed and tested in the upper elementary grades. Recently, though, it was tested in middle schools. A rigorous experiment revealed that it was reasonable to implement in heterogeneous ELA classes and that it was associated with small improvements in reading comprehension proficiency when implemented just twice a week for 18 weeks (Vaughn et al., 2011). As we describe it, you will see that there is no reason it could not be used in other content areas and in high school classes. You will also see that many of the core design elements in CSR are also contained in the relatively simpler strategies we describe later.

A CSR classroom is a noisy place. Students work collaboratively in mixed-ability groups of four to six. They read texts that are segmented by teachers in advance and they talk, using a structured protocol. Learning logs document their work. Figure 6.1 provides an example. Before reading, they preview. During

	Brainstorm	Predict
Before Reading		
	Get the Gist	
During Reading		
	Questions	
After Reading	Right There Think and Search Author and You	

FIGURE 6.1. A CSR learning log.

reading, they engage in reflection on whether specific word meanings are difficult, and they employ strategies (called "click" and "clunk") to help themselves. They also stop periodically to summarize ("get the gist"). After reading, they compose and answer questions, sorted by type as explicit (questions where the answer is "right there") or inferential ("think and search" and "author and you"). To manage the discussion, individual students take on the roles of leader, clunk expert, gist expert, and questioner, with a timekeeper and encourager used if needed.

You may notice here that we are including CSR as part of the rationale for our selection of during-reading strategies rather than as one we describe in depth. That is because we have never actually used CSR ourselves in a middle school or a high school. We believe it has excellent potential, though, and there are supports available to those of you who would like to try it. A comprehensive website documenting a long-term CSR project in middle schools in Colorado provides descriptions, video, and materials (*www.csrcolorado.org/en*). You will see that there are scripts available for discussion leaders and cards to help students learn the click and clunk procedures.

Many of the members of this same research team recently published a study conducted in middle school social studies classrooms. The new intervention they devised built upon what they had learned in CSR over time and embraced the priority for content-area classes to build content knowledge. They call the intervention PACT (Promoting Acceleration of Comprehension and Content through Text). Three 10-day PACT social studies units yielded increases in both content knowledge and reading comprehension ability (Vaughn et al., 2013).

To our eyes, PACT moves beyond a repetitive strategic during-reading framework into thoughtful curriculum design. PACT includes a higher-level content question to anchor the unit, direct instruction in the meanings of key content terms, a video to enhance motivation and activate relevant background knowledge, time spent learning from text, and cooperative learning. As we read about this work, we saw direct parallels with our quad text sets, described in Chapter 4. This synergy across research teams results when individuals with access to the same research try to solve the same problems in schools. Since we, like they, have been helping schools identify instructional routines that build content knowledge while engaging students in reading, it makes sense that our approaches would have similarities.

PACT is brand new in the research literature, so we have not tried it in schools. However, we describe it here because it includes a very specific type of cooperative learning, team-based learning (TBL), which could inform your cooperative learning efforts. In PACT, TBL is used twice, first as an assessment. Individuals take a brief quiz and hand it in. Then they immediately engage in answering the same questions as a group, referring to text as needed to justify their group answers. Both the individual and group grades are counted. Since they engage in these TBL comprehension check activities three times in each unit, the groups build capacity for working together with text. Toward the end of the unit, the cooperative groups complete a higher-level TBL text activity, called a knowledge application. This time, teachers present a complex prompt, and the team has to address it by identifying, synthesizing, and presenting textual evidence from the unit. As in CSR, team members take on roles: lead facilitator, text source facilitator, synthesizer, and product manager. Again, structured, meaningful cooperative work is reasonable to implement and can be associated with better content learning and increased reading comprehension (Vaughn et al., 2013).

Rationale for Collaboration

Regardless of its research pedigree for adolescents, we realize that we will have to sell many of you on collaborative work. Chances are, you engaged in some "group work" in high school and college. Chances are, too, that you did not like it. You found that members of your group were difficult to pin down, that you had to work around their schedules, and that they did not always deliver on their part of the bargain. We regularly hear from teachers that their very strongest students (and their families) resent any group work, thinking that it unfairly burdens them while letting their peers off the hook. We view all of these concerns as legitimate, which is why we are not going to recommend this type of unstructured group work.

We *are* going to recommend cooperative learning. Cooperative learning is much more than just putting students in groups. As in the TBL procedures in PACT, good cooperative learning typically has two very specific requirements: (1) an incentive for the group as a whole and (2) an incentive for each individual. When your goal is using time during school to engage students in more reading and writing, those requirements are easy to meet. The group incentive comes from the structures you establish and use. The individual incentive comes from the enhanced content learning that individual members realize. As you will see, we go well beyond "group work" to provide you with a set of *structured* protocols for engaging students in cooperative work with texts.

One of the best-known champions of cooperative learning, Robert Slavin, has studied its effects on achievement and developed strategies for organizing it. He describes cooperative learning as part of a broader cognitive apprenticeship. In any apprenticeship, a master and a novice are engaged together in real-world tasks. The master demonstrates for the novice, the two share responsibility, and eventually the novice is allowed to work independently, first with feedback and then without. Cooperative learning activities can be structured as cognitive apprenticeships. First, the teacher can provide background knowledge before reading, creating an initial scaffold. Then, during reading, students can discuss text ideas. They can hear their peers pose and solve questions. They can consider multiple interpretations. Slavin's own work attests to the fact that cooperative learning can be implemented on a fairly large scale and that it yields increased comprehension compared with traditional instruction (e.g., Stevens & Slavin, 1995). Cooperative work meets two standards important to us: efficacy and feasibility.

More recent school-based design research conducted by a very productive research team in California (Diane Lapp, Nancy Frey, Doug Fisher, and the late Jim Flood) has nested cooperative learning, which they call "productive group work," inside a larger gradual release of responsibility model. This team structures the cognitive apprenticeship to include purpose setting and modeling, guided instruction, productive group work, and independent tasks. They use the model across the adolescent years and across content areas, encouraging teachers to change the order of tasks as their goals change (e.g., Grant, Lapp, Fisher, Johnson, & Frey, 2012). For cooperative learning to work, it must be structured and nested in meaningful lessons.

Reading Guides

We are going to urge you gently into releasing responsibility to your students by first recommending that you make reading guides. By "reading guides," we do not mean "comprehension questions at the end of the chapter." Those are not reading guides; they are assessments. Reading guides are written directions from you to your students to direct their efforts during reading. Their purpose is "to focus students' attention, to help them process content, and to model strategic reading" (McKenna, Franks, & Lovette, 2011, pp. 207–208). Guides help to ensure that students are actively thinking *during* reading. If you write your own reading guides, they are both an apprenticeship and a collaboration. You are personally *with* your students while they read, acting as a "guide on the side."

When Sharon Walpole's son Kevin (now a medical school student) was in fourth grade, Harry Potter was all the rage. She had read aloud to him the first two books. But when the third came out, Kevin wanted to read it on his own. Sharon knew that he could read the words and that he knew the characters. But she doubted that he could actually hold the complexity of the story in his head. She made a reading guide, which consisted of folded Post-it notes actually stuck on the pages with questions and hints and reminders about character traits and important events. As he read, Kevin's reading was interrupted by the notes, which he unfolded and read. Sharon could allow him to read what was for him complex text, at his own rate, with her direct assistance. That is the purpose of a reading guide, and that is why it can take nearly any form.

Guides are effective in all content areas. A recent study of calculus instruction included the creation of reading guides. The course instructors were faced with the problem that their students had traditionally struggled with the reading demands of their mathematics textbook; the dense and technical writing was overwhelming. The authors called their guides "Note Launchers." They created them personally, taking approximately 1 hour to create a Note Launcher for 10 pages of text. While such a time commitment may seem daunting, think about how many semesters you may use the same textbook; putting in this time to support student work would be well worth it. Since they wanted to build their students' skills, they began with very directive language, even including fill-in blanks to help the students know whether they were understanding the text. At the end of the semester, they were using Note Launchers that were less directive and more conceptually open, hoping that by then students would not need them. What they learned from the students was that the students (1) felt more confident reading with the help of the Note Launchers, (2) believed that all students reading in math should have these comprehension aids, and (3) found the least directive launchers least helpful. Based on this feedback, the instructors reworked the more conceptually open launchers and continue to use them to guide students during reading (Helms & Helms, 2010).

If you keep the idea in mind that a reading guide is any support that you create in advance of students' reading, you can embrace a wider view of text. Helms and Helms were helping students navigate the complexities of traditional mathematics chapters, but the same principles apply when you combine texts, or combine print and digital texts. Karen Wood (2011) describes a reading road map (RRM) that moves (and supports) students back and forth from specific portions of a textbook chapter to websites that are selected in advance to student self-selected websites. We very much like Wood's imagery. The road map for a specific journey includes locations, routes, indications of speed and time, and purposes or missions. For example, you might first want students to read a particular page of text quickly, to get an overview. Then you might want them to read another text portion slowly and carefully, or to write something very specific. Then a detour to a specific website can provide additional support (again, guided by directions). Stop signs can signal the need to stop and write. Forks in the road can indicate that students should do a quick Internet search, choosing their own destination. This sort of creative, personal direction is what will make your reading guides effective supports during student reading. Figure 6.2 is an RRM that we constructed for the first 27 pages of Al Gore's (2006) *An Inconvenient Truth*, itself organized as a journey of sorts.

A second example was used by Bill Lewis when he taught a canonical short story, Edgar Allan Poe's "The Pit and the Pendulum," to high school juniors. After the students miserably failed a reading quiz on the story, a student somberly approached and admitted, "The first paragraph was so confusing I couldn't get past it. After that, I just gave up." This comment forced us to reconsider the challenges that this text posed to students, and a reading road map provided a strategic scaffold and motivation to continue through the difficult reading. Analyzing the story more closely, we saw that the first four paragraphs were extraordinarily difficult. They contained long sentences with multiple embedded clauses. To make matters worse, they are told from the standpoint of a terrified, confused,

Destination	Speed	Mission
Introduction	Fast!	Get a sense of who the author is as a person and how and why he wrote the book.
⬍ (up-down arrows symbol)	You decide.	Look up some movie reviews of Gore's movie.
p. 12 (STOP sign) www.youtube.com/ watch?v=Xvq58AHR6nM	A quick minute.	Listen to Borman's actual voice and think about how people must have felt to see the image and hear him.
pp. 16–19	Moderate.	Orient yourself to these images of the Earth. How does the image on page 14 differ from the images on pp. 18 and 19?
pp. 20–25	Fast!	Why is it important to see that the atmosphere is thin?
pp. 26–27	Slow down.	The text and illustrations work together here. Be sure that you can explain the ideas contained in the two illustrations.
(STOP sign)		Get ready for our discussion. Based on what he has shared about his life story and how he has chosen to begin this book, Al Gore is revealing much about his purpose in writing. What is his purpose? How have his choices so far served his purpose?

FIGURE 6.2. Reading road map example for *An Inconvenient Truth*.

and semiconscious narrator. It's no wonder the students couldn't read it! However, looking past these opening paragraphs, the story becomes easier to understand. There is more action and less interior monologue, and the plot becomes more interesting and comprehensible. Therefore, we knew that we didn't have to complete a guide for the full story. We needed a reading road map to get students over the first comprehension bumps of those introductory paragraphs. The road map we created appears in Figure 6.3.

Remember that we want you to embrace collaboration as an essential part of the learning process of adolescents and that the CCSS (and common sense!) require that we consider text broadly to include oral and visual texts. Wood's (2011) suggestion that we create guides to accompany listening and viewing opportunities are consistent with these goals. We might want students to watch or listen to video podcasts, learn from guest lectures, or watch traditional video presentations as essential "texts" for building their content knowledge. If we have specific purposes for including these opportunities in our curriculum, it makes sense to create Listening or Viewing Guides. Wood suggests a simple process for listening or viewing, which we have represented in Figure 6.4. Within that general process, a traditional guide could provide even more direction and support.

Destination	Speed	Mission
First paragraph, line 10: The courtroom ⚠	Proceed with caution.	Get a sense of the narrator's mental state after he is sentenced to death. What are the things that he hears and sees? Why would his senses be so affected by this death sentence?
First paragraph, line 20: The courtroom ◇SLOW◇	Slow.	The narrator begins to focus on the candle flames in the courtroom. How might candle flames be symbolic of the narrator?
End of first paragraph 🛑STOP	A quick minute.	Think about how you might react knowing that you were about to face imprisonment, torture, and death. How might your reaction be similar to the narrator's?
End of second paragraph	Fast!	The narrator describes going in and out of consciousness. Skim this passage.
End of third paragraph	Fast!	The narrator is being carried down to a dungeon and regains consciousness. Skim this passage.
End of fourth paragraph: The dungeon ◇SLOW◇	Slow down.	The narrator is in the dungeon in the pitch darkness. Choose a sentence that you think best describes the feelings people would have in this situation.
🛑STOP		Based on what you have read so far, what do you think is going to happen to the narrator in the next few pages given his mental state right now?

FIGURE 6.3. Reading road map for "The Pit and the Pendulum."

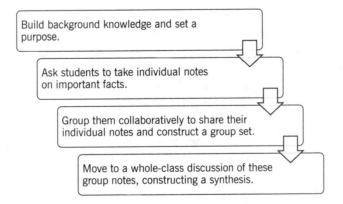

FIGURE 6.4. Procedure for engaging students in listening to or viewing a "text."

Because we believe that reading guides are personal, customized collaborations between you and your students, we hesitate to dictate their characteristics. However, we can provide you with support in how to create one.

1. Read the entire text that you want students to read to identify specific places where you anticipate they will have difficulty. Mark them.
2. Return to each spot you chose. Decide exactly why each is difficult.
3. Create a support for each potential textual roadblock. Here are some possibilities:
   ■ Write a brief bit of explanation.
   ■ Help students make a very specific connection.
   ■ Write a guiding question that can direct their attention.
   ■ Create a table or graphic organizer for students to keep track of how ideas are related.
   ■ Find and include a visual image that can help.
4. Compile your supports and include very specific directions for students to move from your guide to the text and back.

The guide you create this way will always be chronological (unless, of course, you want students to read the text out of order!). We want to highlight here that our purpose is to guide students while they read, not to assess their reading comprehension. This is not the end of their work with this content. You will engage in after-reading work as well, perhaps using the strategies for discussion, writing, or research that we present in later chapters. Reading guides can give you the confidence to yield some control for student learning to the students themselves. Giving them a chance to learn from text is not the same as releasing them into the wild to fend for themselves. This is because you will be there with them, providing support and direction, both indirectly (by providing them with the guide you've created) and directly (by monitoring and troubleshooting as students engage in the selection).

In Figure 6.5, we present a reading guide we created for another canonical short story, "The Interlopers," by Saki. This often-anthologized story is set in the forestland behind a great estate in Eastern Europe. The two characters, heads of two long-feuding families, lay claim to the same tract of hunting land—although the courts have already ruled that one is the land's real owner. They find themselves unexpectedly together, bound by a twist of fate to consider whether the feud is justified or not. We'll not spoil the story for you—you can find it online (e.g., *www.eastoftheweb.com/short-stories/UBooks/Inte.shtml*). Take a look at the guide we made for students. Notice that it really is *not* a set of comprehension questions. It is a personal, self-paced support for reading that was constructed individually by a teacher for a specific purpose and for a specific group of students.

If having students read during class will be a hard transition for you, we suggest that you begin with individually completed reading guides, listening/

viewing guides, or RRM. But then consider moving to pairs. Wood (2011) says that any journey is more enjoyable with a traveling companion; it may be even truer to say that if you get lost, it's great to have someone there to help you find your way. Shouldn't the same be true in reading? Wouldn't it be better for your students if they were working together to think during reading? Simply assigning a guide to a pair is a good start. Figure 6.6 provides a coaching guide for the use of reading guides.

Reading Guide: "The Interlopers" by Saki

Please number your paragraphs before you begin—that will make it easier for you to use this guide while you read. If I have a tip for you, it is numbered by paragraph. Read my tip first. I want you to actually read the story twice—once quickly for the plot, and then again more slowly to help you understand Saki's choices.

First Reading:
  1. Make note of the first character's name.
  2. Make note of the second character's name. Think about how the two are related.
  4. How does Nature intervene in the standoff? What actually happens?
  6. Make sure that you know which of the characters is speaking.
 10. Why is Georg's threat realistic?
 12. Who do you think Georg might be referring to as "cursed interlopers"? Think back about the feud and where things stand.
 19. Make sure you understand the offer Ulrich was making in this paragraph.
 21. What is Georg's answer to Ulrich's offer?
 22. Why does each man want his servants to be first to find the tree?
 25. Why did the men decide to call out together?

Now let's look at Saki's craft. Jot down notes here to prepare for discussion.

Find evidence in the text that proves the type of narrator Saki wanted. How did this choice reveal his goals?

Look back at the first three paragraphs—each has a surprise ending. To what extent does this use of surprise further Saki's goals?

Why does Saki choose to capitalize Nature?

To what extent do the characters evolve? Is this a convincing portrayal? Why?

What does Saki's ending reveal about his views on human nature?

To what extent does the story's title provide a frame for analyzing the story?

FIGURE 6.5. Sample reading guide for "The Interlopers."

Coaching for Reading Guides
The strategy requires that you build background knowledge and set a purpose for reading before students read. I noticed
The strategy requires that you create a guide that uses any combination of text and graphics to support students while they read. I noticed
The strategy requires that students use the guide while they read, moving back and forth from the guide to the text. I noticed
The strategy allows you to have students work individually or in pairs or groups. I noticed

FIGURE 6.6. Coaching guide for reading guides.

To learn more about reading guides, we invite you to visit our open-access professional learning module at *www.comprehensivereadingsolutions.com/reading-guides.*

Peer-Assisted Learning Strategies

Once you have gotten your feet wet by creating reading guides or road maps for individual students, and then by allowing them to collaborate on guides, you may be ready for more structured paired work. Peer-Assisted Learning Strategies (PALS) is a system for reading during class that we have used extensively in middle and high schools in the past few years. PALS comes from the work of Doug and Lynn Fuchs at Vanderbilt University. The PALS website (*http://kc.vanderbilt.edu/pals*) provides video, testimonials, and access to PALS products and training. You will see that PALS is used in reading and in math from kindergarten through high school. You many also visit our open-access professional learning site for additional videos and interviews with teachers (*www.comprehensivereadingsolutions.com/peer-assisted-learning-strategies-2*). While there are fewer research studies of PALS in middle school and high school, it has been used widely with older students.

Our experience is very similar to the description of a PALS experiment in seventh grade, which yielded stronger reading comprehension, understanding of strategies, and self-regulation. In that study, teachers had only two 3-hour training sessions. They chose from a list of trade books. It took three 50-minute class periods to teach students to use the PALS strategies. Students then worked with PALS for 7 weeks, twice each week for 35 minutes. PALS is easy to teach and easy to use and has the potential to increase your students' reading comprehension.

To begin to get your head around PALS, think of it as a way for students to read in pairs for about 35 minutes. The peer-assisted part of PALS is a structured paired grouping. Teachers rank-order students from highest- to lowest-achieving, and then pair them by splitting the list. The highest-achieving student is paired with the middle student. Figure 6.7 provides an example. The teacher has used Lexile scores from a standardized test to rank-order students in a class of 28. The highest-achieving student (number 1) is paired with the middle student (number 15). Know, though, that you can use whatever data are available to you, including your own grades. The goal in pairing is to create a pair with a stronger and weaker partner, but to control the "distance" between them so that your very strongest student is not working with your very weakest.

When PALS is used with younger students, the text is selected with the needs of the lower-achieving student in mind. However, we have actually used PALS in high school with the same text for all. We have used it in middle school with students choosing their own texts. Interestingly, PALS pairs are supposed to

Student	Lexile	Student	Lexile
1	1200	15	950
2	1180	16	950
3	1100	17	940
4	1040	18	940
5	1040	19	900
6	1000	20	890
7	1000	21	860
8	990	22	820
9	990	23	800
10	980	24	800
11	960	25	700
12	960	26	700
13	960	27	700
14	960	28	650

FIGURE 6.7. Sample PALS pairing.

read from the same copy of the text, so each pair only needs one book. We have watched students using the procedure both while sharing a book and while reading their own copies. We have observed that sharing (which is what the authors intended) works better because the students must move closer together. Again, PALS is simply a structure for reading; you have great latitude in choosing what the students will read.

There are four distinct timed activities in PALS: partner reading, retelling, paragraph shrinking, and prediction relay. Figure 6.8 shows the progression and timing of each activity. In partner reading, each reader simply reads orally, while the partner tracks the text, notes errors, and prompts corrections. Note that this simple procedure accomplishes 10 engaged minutes of reading. The retelling activity is a literal turn taking. Partner A looks back in the text and says, "First we read . . . ," Partner B then says "Next we read. . . . " Each pair engages in retelling, taking turns, until 2 minutes have elapsed.

Paragraph shrinking is a bit more complex, integrating oral reading with retelling or summarizing. The pairs pick up reading where they left off. This time, they read in sections. If the text is narrative, the reader reads half a page, again aloud. If it is an informational text, the reader reads one full paragraph (or two if necessary for summarization). The partner then uses a series of prompts to help the reader to summarize:

"Name the 'who' or 'what.'"
"Tell the most important thing about the 'who' or 'what.'"
"Say the main idea in 10 words or less."

The partner actually counts the words in the reader's main idea. If the reader uses more than 10, the partner directs him or her to "shrink it." The same reader continues reading and summarizing for the full 5 minutes. Then the partners switch roles.

Prediction relay adds one additional task. The partner asks the reader to make a prediction about what is going to happen in the next half page or paragraph. Then the reader reads it. The partner evaluates the prediction and then summarizes again, using these prompts:

"Were you right? Why?"
"Name the 'who' or 'what.'"
"Tell the most important thing about the 'who' or 'what.'"
"Say the main idea in 10 words or less."

The role of the teacher during a PALS session is to walk among the pairs, praising students for implementing the protocols and keeping time. We have seen teachers use a digital timer displayed on a SMART board or an automated PowerPoint presentation to keep their PALS pairs engaged together. A PowerPoint has the advantage of not only keeping time but projecting the task. Occasionally, students will ask natural questions during PALS; teachers answer them or help them.

It doesn't really make sense here for us to show you a lesson plan that employs PALS because the order of activities is always the same and PALS is always an appropriate choice when you want students to read connected text. We can tell

Reader	Activity	Time
Partner A	Partner reading	5 minutes
Partner B	Partner reading	5 minutes
Both	Retelling	2 minutes
Partner A	Paragraph shrinking	5 minutes
Partner B	Paragraph shrinking	5 minutes
Partner A	Prediction relay	5 minutes
Partner B	Prediction relay	5 minutes
Total time required:		32 minutes

FIGURE 6.8. PALS activities and time allocations.

you, though, that we have monitored and supported the use of PALS in three distinct settings. First, we worked with a vocational–technical school district to implement PALS as a part of ninth-grade English for students at risk. Students had a 90-minute block for English every day. The school had Lexile scores for students and assigned students with Lexiles of 600–900 to a PALS English class. In that class, teachers used the first 45 minutes of class for intensive reading and writing. They alternated each day between PALS and text-based writing based on prompts devised for the PALS text. Students in this class read *The Hunger Games* (2008) by Suzanne Collins, *The Book Thief* (2006) by Markus Zuzak, and *Autobiography of My Dead Brother* (2010) by Walter Dean Meyers. During the second half of the period, they had a more traditional ninth-grade English lesson. The PALS strategies proved easy to implement for teachers and students, and students increased the time they spent reading in school dramatically.

In a middle school nearby, a principal we know decided to use PALS as a way to begin to engage his teachers in a more targeted and focused selection of instructional strategies and in a more intensive use of text during school. He chose to implement PALS in every classroom at every grade level at a specified time 3 days per week. All content-area teachers were trained in the procedures during preplanning, and all received follow-up coaching and eventually administrative monitoring. In this case, students were paired using the pairing procedure, but the pairs chose their own books from the library. Although PALS is timed, students will read different numbers of pages in each session; if they select their own books, the books will naturally vary in length. In this case, whenever a pair finished a text, they took a pass to the library and engaged with the media specialist in making a new choice together. PALS added 90 minutes a week of engaged reading for these students and also helped teachers to begin to work together to address the challenges of the CCSS.

One of the natural consequences of using PALS as designed is that you will find ways to use pieces of PALS when you want students to read portions of text that would not last 35 minutes. For example, after a brief background-building lesson, you might want students to read just two or three pages. If they know PALS, they could use just paragraph shrinking, ensuring that they are reading, stopping, and summarizing. Or, if the text lends itself to prediction relay, they could use this strategy in the same way. Teachers in the middle school found ways to incorporate PALS procedures seamlessly into their content-area instruction.

One final implementation was similarly motivated, but smaller in scale. After working with us for a year, both face to face and virtually, a group of teachers in a comprehensive high school decided to try PALS (along with nearly every other strategy that we describe in this book). The team included an English teacher, a math teacher, a science teacher, and a social studies teacher. Their principal kept them together as a team and assigned them a cohort of students at risk based on middle school records. The team decided to plan together and to use instructional strategies (including PALS) across content areas as their texts and learning goals provided natural opportunities. All teachers used the strategies; both students and teachers found them natural. Data were promising too, so the principal decided to scale up the strategies to all 9th- and 10th-grade teachers. In short, then, PALS is a feasible and viable strategy for engaging adolescents in reading during school across grade levels and content areas. Figure 6.9 is a coaching template for those of you who want to try PALS.

Reciprocal Teaching

If you can use PALS, you can also use Reciprocal Teaching (RT). RT was first designed in a fifth-grade summer intervention (Palinscar & Brown, 1984). Since then, it has been used in nearly all grade levels and content areas, using narrative text and nonfiction, and it has been studied extensively. You may be skeptical about the appropriateness of a during-reading frame for older students, but RT has also produced strong effects in community college (Hart & Speece, 1998).

RT differs from PALS in several ways. PALS is a timed procedure in which a pair of students reads orally and completes a structured set of activities. RT is an untimed procedure in which a group of students reads silently and engages in a structured discussion anchored in a small set of high-utility comprehension strategies: predicting, questioning, clarifying, and summarizing. Like PALS, RT is collaborative, but instead of pairing students, the teacher assigns them to heterogeneous groups of four to six. Using the same data we used for our PALS pairs, we might create five heterogeneous groups, represented in Figure 6.10, by assigning the students to groups in order. The five highest-achieving students are each assigned to different groups. The process then continues with student number 6 being placed in group 1, student number 7 in group 2, and so on.

The RT procedure is relatively simple, but the type of text analysis it triggers is not. Collaborative groups engage in a cyclical distribution of chunked silent reading and talking about text, with students taking turns as discussion leader. The leader looks at the first chunk of text, first making a prediction based on any available information (e.g., subheadings, illustrations, previous readings). The leader then directs the group to read that chunk of text. After they read, the discussion leader asks some questions, describes a clarification that he or she had to make during reading, and then summarizes before passing the baton to a new leader, who begins the cycle again. The RT procedure is repeated until the group finishes the text assigned. The role of the teacher during an RT discussion is to coach the group leader, making sure that the discussion remains on track. The cycle is depicted in Figure 6.11.

The trick to making RT work with older students is teaching them how to do it. Originators Palincsar and Brown originally recommended 5 consecutive days to teach each of the strategies, but that is not a reasonable amount of time to require in a content-area class. A more recent study of RT (Hacker & Tenent,

Coaching for Peer-Assisted Learning Strategies
The strategy requires that you pair students and that the pairs share a text. I noticed
The strategy requires each student to read aloud for 5 minutes. I noticed
The strategy requires that the students take turns retelling for 2 minutes. I noticed
The strategy requires that each student engage in paragraph shrinking for 5 minutes. I noticed
The strategy requires that each student engage in prediction relay for 5 minutes. I noticed
The strategy requires the teacher to monitor time and circulate to keep pairs on track. I noticed

FIGURE 6.9. Coaching template for Peer-Assisted Learning Strategies (PALS).

Group 1		Group 2		Group 3		Group 4		Group 5	
Student	Lexile	Student	Lexile	Student	Lexile	Student	Lexile	Student	Lexile
1	1200	2	1180	3	1100	4	1040	5	1040
6	1000	7	1000	8	990	9	990	10	980
11	960	12	960	13	960	14	960	15	950
16	950	17	940	18	940	19	900	20	890
21	860	22	820	23	800	24	800	25	700
26	700	27	700	28	650				

FIGURE 6.10. Forming heterogeneous cooperative groups for Reciprocal Teaching.

2002) reveals some useful hints that we believe would make RT easy to begin. Their procedure for introducing RT is outlined in Figure 6.12. It is a relatively simple, one-class-period introduction. Basically, the teacher can form the groups and engage them in a highly teacher-directed version of RT, explaining the strategies very briefly in the context of the entire procedure and using a text that makes sense given the current content focus. After that, groups could use the RT process more independently, with the teacher circulating to provide assistance as needed. Since our goal here is to help you use class time for collaborative student reading, rather than build student comprehension strategies, we think that a quick move to engagement in reading is warranted. Figure 6.13 provides a coaching template for RT.

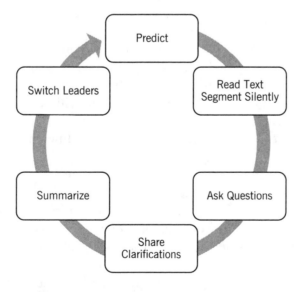

FIGURE 6.11. Reciprocal Teaching cycle.

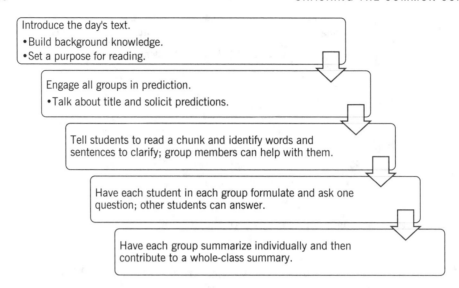

FIGURE 6.12. Strategy for introducing Reciprocal Teaching. Based on Hacker and Tenent (2002).

Jigsawed Text Sets

You may be surprised to see that we have waited to discuss text sets until the very end of this chapter. That is because we don't think that always differentiating your text is a reasonable message for content-area teachers. The first reason is pragmatic: We don't see a clear line from nearly text-free teaching to what will look to some like elementary school reading groups in middle school and high school. Many content-area teachers have very little text to work with at all—let alone sets of texts at different levels of difficulty. The second reason is that we think you can do much through instruction and collaboration to make challenging texts accessible. One of our main goals in writing this book has been to empower you to use challenging text successfully. That said, we do think there are times when changing the text for your readers will be more effective than changing your instruction.

There are several relatively simple ways to bring differentiated text sets into your classroom. The first is to gather a few textbooks designed for earlier grades. A 10th-grade biology teacher might find useful sections in an old 8th-grade biology book, for example, and could take a small set from the district's book room. The same is true for most history and social studies topics. These simpler texts can be used instead of the more difficult ones or as part of a quad text set to build background knowledge; students could read a simple version to warm up for a more complex one.

Web-based sources are even more easily accessible. Remember to keep your view of what constitutes "text" broad. When you know what you want your

Coaching for Reciprocal Teaching
The strategy requires that you group students collaboratively and assign a chunked text. I noticed
The strategy requires that students take turns as discussion leader. I noticed
The strategy requires a repetitive discussion procedure: predict, question, clarify, summarize. I noticed
The strategy requires that students read silently. I noticed
The strategy requires that the teacher monitor and circulate to keep groups on track and coach discussion leaders. I noticed

FIGURE 6.13. Coaching template for Reciprocal Teaching (RT).

students to learn, you can do a quick search to see if there are websites consistent with your goals. Currently, there are several ways you can estimate the difficulty of electronic sources. You can copy and paste text into a word document and use the spelling and grammar tools to get traditional readability statistics; these are helpful when you want to compare the difficulty level of one text to another. You can also use the Lexile Analyzer (*www.lexile.com*). The process is slightly more cumbersome, but it is described clearly on the Lexile web page.

While we don't expect you to match texts directly to each of your students' reading levels, you might be able to choose a set of three texts, ordered by difficulty, and then form homogeneous groups. Making same-size groups doesn't make sense here; if you want groups to be homogeneous, the data will determine their size. Figure 6.14 shows how we might group students with the Lexile data we have been using throughout this chapter. The highest-achieving group has 14 members—too many to function well together. They can be placed in two groups of 7, with the same (most challenging) text. Likewise, groups 2 and 3 can be split, especially if you want to use a jigsaw format after reading.

You will see in the units that we have designed in Appendices 1–3 that we have sometimes incorporated a set of differentiated texts. When we do that, we

Group 1		Group 2		Group 3	
Student	Lexile	Student	Lexile	Student	Lexile
1	1200	11	960	21	860
2	1180	12	960	22	820
3	1100	13	960	23	800
4	1040	14	960	24	800
5	1040	15	950	25	700
6	1000	16	950	26	700
7	1000	17	940	27	700
8	990	18	940	28	650
9	990	19	900		
10	980	20	890		
11	960				
12	960				
13	960				
14	960				

FIGURE 6.14. Homogeneous groups formed from Lexile data.

typically have texts that differ both in their level of difficulty *and in their content*. After students read cooperatively in homogeneous groups (perhaps using the RT structure), they regroup heterogeneously. In the example above, we now have six groups, two reading each of three texts. After reading, we would regroup, combining some members of the "high text" group with some from the "medium text" group and some from the "low text" group. Their goal is to share what they learned from their text with students who did not read it—a reasonable and authentic task. This structure is called a jigsaw because the individual pieces are then fitted together to build something new. It has all the qualities of a good collaborative learning exercise. The homogeneous groups have individual accountability because each member will have to share with others; the heterogeneous groups have individual accountability because individuals must learn information they have not read by listening to one another. You can also create reading guides or use RT for the homogeneous groups and then use a new guide once the students are regrouped in the jigsaw.

The purpose of low-group members reading easier texts with *different but related* content is to prevent their being viewed by other students as inferior. When they move to their heterogeneous groups, which Guthrie and McMann (1996) call "idea circles," they will have unique information to contribute, information that will be useful to even the ablest student. In Figure 6.15, we provide steps in planning a jigsaw and a template for coaching.

Making Accommodations

Some of you are no doubt reading this chapter thinking of a particular student who, regardless of the structure and support you provide, simply cannot read challenging text. We know that student. But we also know that planning around that student to avoid assigning reading in your classroom is wrong for everyone. We live in a world where we have the tools to make texts accessible for all. Assistive technologies, whether full text-to-speech or partial, through hyperlinks, can be easily integrated into any of the during-reading structures we have described here. If we are to realize the potential of the challenging text tasks inherent in the CCSS, we must internalize the difference between equality and fairness. Students who need assistive technologies to allow them to think with text should have them. Period. It may be that some students need assistive technologies permanently, as lifelong "prosthetic" devices that provide them access to experiences they could otherwise not have. In other cases, assistive technologies could function as temporary scaffolds, helping to build student skills over time before being eventually removed (McKenna & Walpole, 2007). Either way, the reality that heterogeneous classrooms contain both readers who struggle and readers with disabilities can no longer be an excuse not to use text in school.

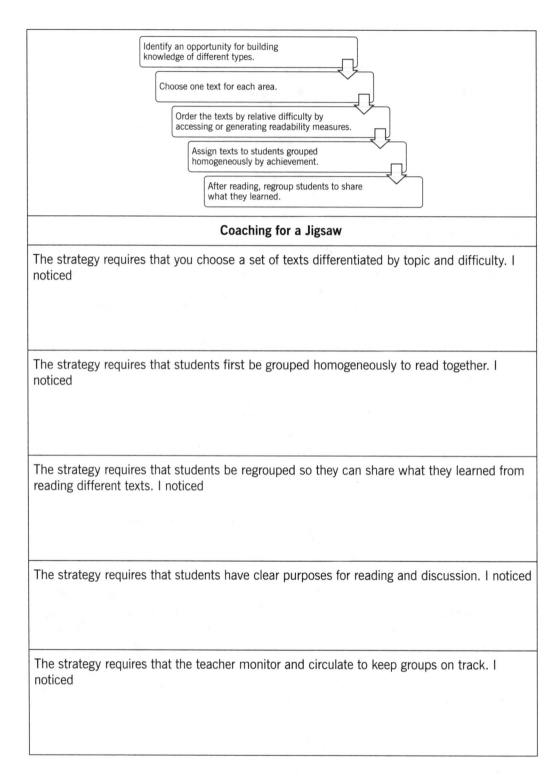

Identify an opportunity for building knowledge of different types.

Choose one text for each area.

Order the texts by relative difficulty by accessing or generating readability measures.

Assign texts to students grouped homogeneously by achievement.

After reading, regroup students to share what they learned.

Coaching for a Jigsaw

The strategy requires that you choose a set of texts differentiated by topic and difficulty. I noticed

The strategy requires that students first be grouped homogeneously to read together. I noticed

The strategy requires that students be regrouped so they can share what they learned from reading different texts. I noticed

The strategy requires that students have clear purposes for reading and discussion. I noticed

The strategy requires that the teacher monitor and circulate to keep groups on track. I noticed

FIGURE 6.15. Planning and coaching a jigsaw.

Final Thoughts

In this chapter, we have asked you to rethink your use of time, to step back from the podium and away from the PowerPoint. We have asked you to set up structures for students to do textual work during school. But we do not do so in a vacuum. We have already explained that the CCSS challenge us to be proactive in building the reading, writing, and thinking skills required after high school. We have considered sources of text complexity. We have thought of texts as sets that synergistically build knowledge. Once you choose your texts, we have described reasonable strategies for building student background knowledge before they read, setting them up for success. And in this chapter, we have provided three relatively simple ways for you to step away and let students read with support—with your support in a reading guide, with a classmate's support in PALS, or with a team's support in RT. If you are to meet the demands of the CCSS, and increase their literacy skills along with their content knowledge, all of your students have to read more.

CHAPTER 7

Implementing High-Quality Discussions after Reading

I always endeavored to listen to what each and every person in
a discussion had to say before venturing my own opinion. . . .
A leader is like a shepherd. He stays behind the flock, letting
the most nimble go out ahead, whereupon the others follow,
not realizing that all along they are being directed from behind.
—NELSON MANDELA

Discussion isn't what it used to be. Time was, whole-class discussion based
on an assigned text served as the primary means by which teachers could
check student understanding and address comprehension problems. Consider an
earth science class that has been studying geothermal processes. The teacher has
assigned a text on geysers, a portion of which you have already encountered in
Figure 4.4. Here is an example of a conventional exchange we might expect to
overhear during a visit to Ms. Morton's classroom:

> MS. MORTON: Let's review what we've learned about geysers. Who can tell
> me what happens to the boiling point of water when pressure increases?
> (*Bill raises his hand*.) Bill?

> BILL: It goes up.

> MS. MORTON: Excellent. That's exactly what would happen. And when that
> happens in a rock cavity below the surface, what happens to the water?
> (*No hands go up*.) Let me put it another way. Bill reminded us that when
> the pressure goes up, it takes a higher temperature for water to boil. The
> pressure rises in a pocket of rock because it's hard for the water to escape.
> So what can we say about the water inside the pocket when it's heated
> beyond 100° Celsius? (*Bill raises his hand. Maria is looking down at the
> text, avoiding eye contact*.) Maria?

MARIA: It gets hotter?

MS. MORTON: (*immediately*) Help her, Bill.

BILL: It stays liquid because there's no room for steam.

MS. MORTON: Yes, and what would happen, Peter, if the pressure on that very hot water suddenly dropped?

PETER: It would turn into steam.

BILL: And explode.

MS. MORTON: I was speaking to Peter, Bill. But you're right.

This example may strike a familiar chord. Teacher-controlled questioning is still very much the staple in the secondary classrooms we've visited. In fact, it has been standard operating procedure for so long that an abundance of research has focused on identifying the most effective questioning strategies. In a postobservation conference, a teacher might understand that this exchange was not actually a discussion. An instructional coach might offer a few suggestions based on research:

"Bill has become a mainstay in your class, hasn't he? You can always rely on him to come up with the right answer. But do you worry that the rest of the class may not be comprehending as well as you'd like? In fact, they may rely on Bill as much as you. One strategy I might suggest is that rather than calling on volunteers, you ask the question first, 'beaming' it out to the whole class. For example, you could say, 'In a minute I am going to ask someone. . . .'"

"Speaking of Bill, when he answered your first question, you told him his response was 'excellent.' Can you tell me what was excellent about it? When I look at the text, I can see that it was a simple, literal-level question. Bill needed to know that he was correct, of course, but praising his answer is something else. Remember that praise is most effective when it's used sparingly and when the teacher specifies exactly what's praiseworthy about the response."

"When Maria's response was off the mark, you called on Bill without hesitation. Next time, you might consider giving a few seconds of wait time to see if she can think it through. If that doesn't work, you might try prompting her with the facts she needs."

"You might get better responses if you posed the questions in advance. What if you were to provide a short reading guide with a few questions about each section? That would let the students focus on what you feel is important.

And having the guide in front of them during a discussion might provide the kind of support Maria needed."

Please understand that we have no problem with any of these suggestions. In fact, we have listed some of the more resilient findings in Figure 7.1. All are based on a solid body of evidence, and they can help teachers fine-tune their questioning techniques. The Common Core, however, has made it clear that these strategies are not enough. In fact, the Standards have redefined the nature and purposes of discussion in striking ways. In this chapter, we will examine what the Standards require and offer practical suggestions about how you can meet the challenges they pose. But take a deep breath because implementing these suggestions

Set students up for success.
• Pose questions in advance, through a listening or reading guide. • Permit students to refer to their written responses as needed.
Find ways to involve everyone.
• Use Every-Pupil-Response approaches to extend participation (handheld digital response systems, show of hands, thumbs up, etc.). • Ask some questions before calling on a particular student to prevent students from tuning out as soon as a classmate's name is mentioned.
Avoid overrelying on volunteers.
• Use a system to ensure that you involve everyone (e.g., placing check marks on the class roster).
Be ready for wrong answers.
• Use constructive criticism. (Find something positive to mention.) • Restate the question, especially for the benefit of English learners. • Ask an easier related question. • Prompt. (Provide a helpful hint.) • Try slicing (asking just part of the question).
Focus on inferential questions.
• Avoid overrelying on literal questions. • When in doubt, start with why. • Look for chances to ask questions that bridge back to earlier content.
Use praise sparingly.
• Acknowledge accurate answers, but keep in mind that not all answers deserve praise. • When praising an answer, tell why. ("That's a great answer because . . ")
Mind your timing.
• Provide wait time, especially when asking higher-order questions. • Provide wait time when a student answers incorrectly. • Provide wait time even when a student answers correctly if the answer can be extended. • Provide feedback promptly.

FIGURE 7.1. A sampler of effective questioning strategies.

may represent a distinct break with your existing practice. (We know because we sometimes struggle to heed our own advice.)

Common Core Requirements for Discussion

The CCSS make clear that it is not enough simply to put "discussion" in your plan book. What actually happens during a discussion must contribute to realizing an aggressive set of expectations. Figure 7.2 presents the Anchor Standards for Speaking and Listening in grades 6–12. Before going further, let's analyze the messages they convey about what our expectations must be.

Even a quick reading of these standards will make it clear that the discussion in Ms. Morton's classroom is far from adequate. The CCSS require that students do far more than respond to a teacher's questions. This is a starting point, to be sure, but they must also be able to speak and listen to their peers and to interpret information not only from text but from what they hear and view. Moreover, their role as interpreters and synthesizers of information from multiple sources is only half the equation. They must also learn to become presenters of information and argument through writing and other media. We have intentionally structured this book to provide ideas to help you plan with these goals in mind. For example, quad text sets, introduced in Chapter 4, not only provide students with the tools necessary for them to access texts of challenging complexity, but they deliberately incorporate media other than print as a means of communicating content.

We must view discussion quite broadly if it is to help us achieve the standards of speaking and listening. But we don't want to get ahead of ourselves. In this

Comprehension and Collaboration
• Prepare for and participate effectively in a range of conversations and collaborations with diverse partners, building on others' ideas and expressing their own clearly and persuasively. • Integrate and evaluate information presented in diverse media and formats, including visually, quantitatively, and orally. • Evaluate a speaker's point of view, reasoning, and use of evidence and rhetoric.
Presentation of Knowledge and Ideas
• Present information, findings, and supporting evidence such that listeners can follow the line of reasoning, and the organization, development, and style are appropriate to task, purpose, and audience. • Make strategic use of digital media and visual displays of data to express information and enhance understanding of presentations. • Adapt speech to a variety of contexts and communicative tasks, demonstrating command of formal English when indicated or appropriate.

FIGURE 7.2. Anchor Standards for Speaking and Listening in grades 6–12.

chapter, we take a close look at the nature of authentic, productive discussions as a starting point from which to build.

Characteristics of an Effective Discussion

In appraising the effectiveness of a discussion, we find it helpful to think in terms of three choices that teachers must make. These choices, or tensions, involve instructional goals. They also involve Common Core expectations, and although we stop short of suggesting that there is a right choice in each case, some choices are more conducive than others to meeting those standards. Figure 7.3 is a preview.

Discussion versus Recitation

We opened this chapter with an exchange between Ms. Morton and her earth science class. She is using the traditional "recitation" model through which the teacher checks and corrects by posing factual questions and responding to the answers. Students are engaged one at a time. To be clear here, a recitation in this context is not an oral presentation of a memorized text or poem; it is a tightly controlled, teacher-led discussion. Mehan (1979) described this kind of interchange as having three parts that are repeated again and again. The teacher first *initiates* the exchange by asking a question addressed to a particular student. The student then *responds*, and the teacher *evaluates* the response. The initiate–respond–evaluate (IRE) model leads to clipped, fast-paced "discussions" that tend to be superficial and focused on the acquisition of factual information. A quarter century ago, Cazden (1988) described IRE as the "default position" of classroom instruction (p. 53). We fear that little has changed. In a recent study

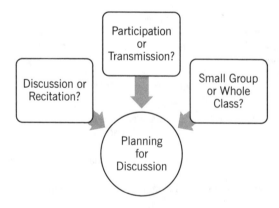

FIGURE 7.3. Tensions in moving to authentic discussion.

of science teachers, for example, Alozie, Moje, and Krajcik (2010) discovered that IRE was standard practice and that it was difficult to alter.

So, what is the alternative? Consider a discussion that involves the following qualities:

- Students are invited to express multiple viewpoints, even views that diverge from the mainstream.
- Students are invited to speak directly to one another rather than to and through the teacher.
- Students are invited to speak in more extended language than that typical of IRE.

Does this sound like some of your own conversations with friends and colleagues? We suspect it does. Certainly friends who wish to remain your friends are not likely to submit you to interrogation by IRE. It's plain that exchanges with these qualities differ markedly from the business-as-usual IRE approach. Alvermann, Dillon, and O'Brien (1987) call this a "true" discussion. Wolsey and Lapp (2009) use the term *authentic*. Either way, such discussion is viewed as a means of consolidating and evaluating content knowledge and as a vehicle for perspective taking. It is a method of learning with a long history. "Good teachers since the time of Socrates," Wolsey and Lapp observe, "have employed discussion as a means of helping students learn" (p. 371).

Resistance to true discussion takes many forms. Chief among them is the fear that the conversation will range too broadly, blurring the focus on learning objectives, especially when multiple perspectives are honored. We acknowledge the danger but believe it can be minimized by communicating the purpose of the discussion in advance, setting clear parameters concerning what will be discussed, and keeping an eye on the clock. Tony Manzo and his colleagues said it well: "Different points of view are welcomed, but there is a soft press to keep them relevant" (Manzo, Manzo, & Thomas, 2009, p. 119). Another objection is that recitation, which teachers view as beneficial, will be sacrificed. We think a helpful distinction lies in the goals of each. Although recitation is primarily a method of assessment, authentic discussion "serves as a tool to construct and negotiate understanding with peers and with the teacher, and offers teachers insights about the additional topical information that should be shared with students" (Wolsey & Lapp, 2009, p. 372). In short, each has a different place.

Participation versus Transmission

Jetton and Alexander (2004) describe a tension between two very different perspectives on secondary instruction and the role played by the teacher in each. A transmission-oriented perspective values teacher talk as the principal route to learning. Because the teacher possesses the expertise and judgment required to know what students need to understand, this perspective champions lecture and demonstration. Discussion is primarily a means of checking understanding, and texts are tools used by students to extract information. In contrast, a participatory perspective emphasizes student interaction, both with the teacher and each other. Where texts are concerned, this interaction is seen as the key to constructing meaning from print and scaffolding student understanding as content is interpreted.

Which perspective is closer to your own view of effective instruction? Each has its arguments. On the side of transmission are traditions dating back centuries, not to mention the present-day press to convey ever-increasing amounts of knowledge. On the side of participation are the sociocognitive theories of Vygotsky and others and the research that supports them. Jetton and Alexander, however, argue that viewing the two perspectives as an either-or choice is wrong. Figure 7.4 depicts the tension between the two approaches in terms of time. As the amount of time devoted to teacher talk (transmission) diminishes, the amount available for participation increases. They argue that the danger lies in the extremes—all transmission versus all participation. Each has its advantages, so the key is to strike a balance between the two. Where discussion is concerned, this means recitation has its place but so does true, participatory dialogue.

Small-Group versus Whole-Class Discussions

Although it is not always feasible, we prefer small groups over the whole class as a format for discussions. There are several reasons.

- Each student has more opportunities to participate in the time available.
- Small-group settings involve fewer risks and invite students to "try on the language and build security" (Wolsey & Lapp, 2009, p. 377).
- There is less need for the teacher to implement formal management strategies.

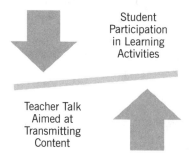

FIGURE 7.4. Transmission versus participatory approaches.

- It is easier, at least in our experience, to maintain a climate of civility and openness.
- The tendency of males to dominate discussions (Sprague & Keeling, 2009) can be managed by configuring groups carefully.
- Small groups afford better opportunities for students to achieve the standards of listening, speaking, and collaborating required by the CCSS.

These advantages come at a cost, however. The teacher must monitor several groups at once, troubleshooting and cheerleading when necessary. Moreover, even after carefully planning the focus of the discussion, the teacher must still surrender control to students. Many teachers find it difficult to do so, and we can only encourage them to judge this practice by its results.

The very different roles assumed by teachers and students is illustrated in Figure 7.5. In a small-group setting, the teacher is typically a facilitator, while in a whole-class discussion the teacher assumes the role of leader. In small groups, students speak to each other rather than to the teacher, and the teacher's position as expert is temporarily placed on hold as group members grapple with issues together.

Who's in Control?

In their recent review of research on classroom discussion, Wilkinson and Son (2011) suggested three useful stances toward discussion, defined in terms of how much control the teacher retains and how closely the discussion is tied to a text.

The *expressive stance* is one that invites students to respond to text in open-ended ways. The focus is on evoking the "reader's affective response" (p. 369). The teacher's job is to set the stage for these expressions to occur, not to dictate how students should feel. This stance is especially well suited to literature, and activities for implementing it include Book Club (Raphael & McMahon,

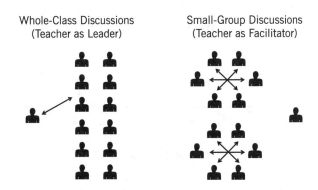

FIGURE 7.5. Student and teacher roles in small-group and whole-class discussions.

1994) and Grand Conversations (Eeds & Wells, 1989; Peterson & Eeds, 2007). These approaches could easily be adapted to shorter nonfiction texts that have the potential to elicit emotion (e.g., *The Gettysburg Address*), and they can also range far beyond any specific text. Because the aim is to promote an expression of feelings in response to what is read, the teacher remains in the background and allows the discussion to takes its own course. Control is in the hands of students.

The *efferent stance*, a term borrowed from Rosenblatt (1978), has a very different goal—that of reading to "acquire and retrieve information" (p. 370). The focus is squarely on the text, and the student's role is to extract and construct meaning from it. This does not mean that different interpretations are discouraged, but judgments must be anchored in an understanding of the text. The intended meaning of the author is central, and determining it may involve considering the author's background and expertise. An example of an activity that reflects efferent thinking is Questioning the Author (QtA), an approach developed by Isabel Beck and her colleagues (Beck & McKeown, 2006; Beck, McKeown, Hamilton, & Kucan, 1997), and one we examine in detail later in the chapter. You will see that in QtA control of the discussion remains with the teacher, a quality you may find appealing.

The *critical-analytic stance* is in between the first two in terms of who controls the discussion. Activities that reflect this stance involve students in "interrogating or querying the text in search of the underlying arguments, assumptions, worldviews, or beliefs" (p. 370). These actions may sound open-ended—and they are to a degree—except that the teacher determines the focus of the discussion and it must be closely connected with a text. For these reasons, control is shared by the teacher and the students. A well-researched approach that takes a critical-analytic stance is Collaborative Reasoning (CR), developed by Richard Anderson and his colleagues (Waggoner, Chinn, Yi, & Anderson, 1995). We take a closer look at CR later in the chapter.

We have depicted these three stances in Figure 7.6 in terms of who controls the discussion. Because this book is focused chiefly on discussions aimed at learning through text, we will describe several well-researched after-reading instructional strategies that are closely linked to text. You will see that we have arranged them from least to most disruptive to what we see as common practice.

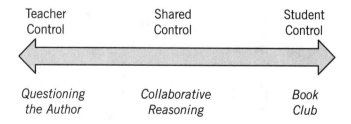

FIGURE 7.6. Three stances toward discussion.

Reciprocal Questioning

Ample research supports the practice of asking students to generate questions pertaining to a text. In fact, the National Reading Panel (National Institute of Child Health and Human Development, 2000) identified it as one of the best-validated instructional approaches available. The rationale is simple. In order to ask a reasonable question, the student must first comprehend the text. The approach also has appeal because of the inherent role reversal—it is the student, not the teacher, who is doing the questioning. Reciprocal Questioning was introduced nearly half a century ago by Manzo (1969), who developed the technique while tutoring individual students. At certain points in a text, Manzo would pause and ask comprehension questions. After a while, it was the student's turn to pose questions. The impact on comprehension was so dramatic that Reciprocal Questioning (a title later shortened to ReQuest) was implemented with many variations and in a variety of contexts. Because tutorial situations (one student and one teacher) are limiting, the better-known variations have involved whole classes or small groups. The following are examples of two ReQuest variations that have proved effective:

- The teacher asks a number of postreading comprehension questions and then calls on volunteers. In true reciprocal fashion, however, they do not raise their hands to answer questions but to ask them. (Teachers who have used this variation know the importance of becoming familiar with the text beforehand!)
- The teacher begins by asking a question of one student, who must try to answer it. This student then becomes the questioner but asks another student rather than the teacher. After answering, the second student poses a question to the third, and so on, in popcorn fashion, until all students have had a turn.

Unless expectations are set, ReQuest can become a rapid-fire exercise in literal recall. By specifying in advance that only certain types of questions are acceptable, the teacher can elevate ReQuest to a level involving inferential thinking. For example, a few question starters might be placed on the board for students to choose from:

"Why did . . . ?"
"What would happen if . . . ?"
"What do you think will happen when . . . ?"
"How did . . . ?"

Like so many effective instructional approaches, ReQuest is not one that can be implemented without preparation on the part of teacher and students.

Students must understand what is expected of them. They must also come to recognize what makes a good comprehension question. To bring about this awareness, the teacher must model how to formulate questions. Such modeling gets at the "active ingredient" in ReQuest, which is the habit that all good readers have of posing questions to themselves as they read. Not all students develop this habit naturally. Teachers must help them. "By modeling strategic questioning for their students, teachers are instructing students about the kinds of questions they should be asking themselves while reading" (National Institute for Literacy, 2007, p. 29).

We have found the following suggestions helpful in implementing ReQuest. In using the technique with a whole class, let them know before they read and specify the kinds of questions they should be prepared to ask. In this way, they will focus on question generation as they read, and they will jot down a few questions for use afterward. When ReQuest is used in a small-group format, text-based questions can be addressed to individual group members or to the group as a whole. Our coaching template, presented in Figure 7.7, acknowledges this. It was, in fact, the possibility of small-group implementation that led to one of the best-known instructional approaches, Reciprocal Teaching, in which generating student-to-student questions plays a major part.

Reciprocal Teaching

Since you have already read about RT in Chapter 6, it probably will not surprise you that it was built on the demonstrated success of ReQuest. Palincsar and Brown (1984) used the idea of exchanging roles to develop a more ambitious approach. Remember that RT is used by students working in a small group as they make their way through an assigned text. After each text segment is read silently, the group leader asks questions and then engages in the additional procedures of clarifying and summarizing. Then a new sequence is initiated with a prediction. The leader asks questions about the segment, though others may ask questions as well.

We reprise RT here because it is a student-led, text-based discussion format with much to offer. By applying effective comprehension strategies to text after text, students begin to apply the strategies as a natural part of their independent reading. Not only does RT lead to better comprehension of assigned reading, it also leads students to become better comprehenders. But a few cautions must be kept in mind by any teacher considering RT. Successful participation does not happen overnight; the quality of an RT discussion is a reflection of the quality of student thinking.

Remember that you can read more about reciprocal teaching and view examples of it in practice in our open-access professional learning module at *www. comprehensivereadingsolutions.com/reciprocal-teaching*.

Coaching for Reciprocal Questioning
The strategy requires that students read with the purpose of formulating good text-based questions. I noticed
The strategy requires that you begin by asking a question. I noticed
The strategy requires that you engage students in asking and answering questions of their own. I noticed
The strategy allows you to use whole-class or small-group formats. I noticed

FIGURE 7.7. Coaching template for Reciprocal Questioning (ReQuest).

Questioning the Author

QtA offers another engaging, strategy-based approach to comprehending nonfiction. It is characterized by close reading of a text and a discussion that is guided by the teacher. Like RT, QtA is based on the idea that questioning should occur during reading rather than afterward. When questions are posed at the precise points where they are relevant, students can better understand their textual basis. Beck et al. (1997) summarized the approach this way:

> As text is read in class, the teacher intervenes at selected points and poses questions to prompt students to consider information in the text. Students respond by contributing ideas, which may be built upon, refined, or challenged by other students or by the teacher. Finally, students and the teacher work collaboratively, interacting to grapple with ideas and build understanding. (p. 8)

Here is an example of challenging nonfiction, excerpted from *The Longitude Prize*, a book by Joan Dash detailing how navigators solved the problem of determining their east–west position. This excerpt appears in Appendix A of the CCSS as an illustration of the kind of texts that 9th and 10th graders should be able to comprehend:

> Phoenicians, Greeks, and Romans tended to sail along the coasts and were rarely out of sight of land. As later navigators left the safety of the Mediterranean to plunge into the vast Atlantic—far from shore, and from the shorebirds that led them to it—they still had the sun and the North Star. And these enabled them to follow imagined parallel lines of latitude that circle the globe. Following a line of latitude— "sailing the parallel"—kept a ship on a steady east-west course. Christopher Columbus, who sailed the parallel in 1492, held his ships on such a safe course, west and west again, straight on toward Asia. When they came across an island off the coast of what would later be called America, Columbus compelled his crew to sign an affidavit stating that this island was no island but mainland Asia.

Now consider three comprehension questions based on this passage:

"How did sailors use shorebirds?"
"What does the author mean when she mentions the 'safety of the Mediterranean'"?
"Why does she tell the story of how Columbus forced his men to sign the paper swearing that they had reached Asia?"

The first question has a straightforward factual answer. It could easily be part of an IRE exchange. But Beck and her colleagues argue that students can often answer questions like this without understanding the deeper significance of the texts they read. On the other hand, the second and third questions are unlike the first. They cause students to think about why the author chose to include certain facts and wordings. That is, they go beyond extracting information and compel students to think about the author's craft. They may even call into question the author's traditional role as authority. For this reason, Beck and her coauthors refer to such questions as "queries," and they are the centerpiece of QtA.

Planning a QtA lesson involves three basic steps. First, the teacher carefully reads the text to identify major ideas that the students will need to construct along with probable trouble spots. In the excerpt from *The Longitude Prize*, a history teacher might well decide, for example, that a map of the Mediterranean would be a useful prop. Next, the teacher chooses where to divide the text into segments. The divisions will correspond to key ideas and may be as short as a paragraph or considerably longer. Finally, the teacher writes queries, which are of two kinds. Initiating queries are aimed at prompting meaningful thought about the content of the segment. The example above about the safety of the Mediterranean is an example of an initiating query. Follow-up queries require students to link facts within the text, or between the text and their prior knowledge. Of course, the further into a text the class goes, the more opportunities there are to make connections with earlier content.

A QtA discussion moves from segment to segment and queries are addressed when the relevant content is fresh in mind. Frequent references to the text are the norm. The teacher's role is to facilitate the thinking of the students as they address the queries. Beck and her colleagues recommend six tactics that the teacher can use. These are called "discussion moves."

1. *Marking* a student's comment involves stressing its importance. Here is an example based on *The Longitude Prize*:

   PETER: I don't think she means that the Mediterranean is all that safe. Just that it's safer than the Atlantic.

   TEACHER: I agree. Peter has made an important point. Safety is relative. Some places may be safer than others, but that doesn't mean there's no danger.

2. *Turning back* is a discussion move that can take one of two forms. A teacher can turn the discussion back to the students, placing the responsibility on them for clarifying their thoughts.

   PAIGE: (*responding to the query about Columbus*) I think he was afraid.

   TEACHER: Afraid of what?

   (The teacher can also turn the students' attention back to the text in cases where a student has clearly misread it.)

   PATRICK: I didn't think the Greeks ever crossed the Atlantic.

   TEACHER: Are you sure it says they did? Take another look.

3. *Revoicing* is a tactic for rescuing a student who is having a hard time expressing a response. "Revoicing is a kind of 'in other words' mechanism that
   helps students to express their own ideas" (Beck & McKeown, 2006, p. 96).

   JIMMY: I think Columbus thought his men might, well, not say what . . .

   TEACHER: You think he thought his men might say they never reached
   Asia?

   JIMMY: Yeah.

4. *Recapping* is a move used to quickly summarize the idea before moving
   on. Whether or not recapping is called for depends on the teacher's judgment about the students' understanding. It is a discussion move "that is
   useful when students have come to a place in their construction of ideas
   that seems to suggest they get it" (p. 97).

   TEACHER: So I think we can say that these sailors could navigate from
   east to west but that they never knew exactly how far north or south
   they were.

5. *Modeling* is a means of adding commentary to the text, through which
   the teacher demonstrates how a proficient reader makes connections and
   forms personal judgments.

   TEACHER: Wow, this really makes me appreciate how easy it is to tell where
   we are at any time with GPS. I can only imagine how scary it must have
   been to sail on a wooden ship and not know where you were.

6. *Annotating* is a discussion move through which the teacher adds information that is not in the text and that will probably aid the students' comprehension. Think of it as an oral footnote. The key is to judge in advance
   what the students are likely to know and not know.

   TEACHER: Now the Phoenicians lived right about here (*pointing to the
   map of the Mediterranean*) up until about 300 B.C. The Greeks were
   here, and Romans here. The Romans were last, but their empire was
   gone about 1,000 years before Columbus. So you can see how long
   sailors had to do without good navigation.

Before choosing to implement QtA, it's important to recognize a few of its
characteristics. Because the teacher must be on the scene to direct the discussion from one segment to the next, QtA is essentially a whole-class approach.
Although Beck and McKeown have maintained that it can also be used with
small groups, it is difficult to see how a teacher can use it effectively with multiple
groups functioning at the same time. In addition, because the teacher decides
which ideas are important for the students to explore through queries, QtA is
a teacher-directed approach. Although it encourages higher-order thinking, the
focus is determined in advance by the teacher. Note that we are not listing these
conditions as drawbacks, but they must be taken into account in planning. Figure
7.8 offers a coaching template for QtA.

Coaching for Questioning the Author
The strategy requires that you chunk text to initiate discussion during reading. I noticed
The strategy requires that you begin with an initiating query. I noticed
The strategy requires that you then use follow-up queries. I noticed
The strategy requires flexible use of discussion moves. I noticed

FIGURE 7.8. Coaching template for Questioning the Author (QtA).

Collaborative Reasoning

Collaborative Reasoning (CR) is an easy-to-implement approach to discussion. The main requirement is that the text involves a controversial issue. This may sound like a major limitation, but it's actually hard to imagine a text that is truly controversy free. CR was originally intended for use with literature, and Stahl and Shanahan (2004) have observed that it does not require much in the way of disciplinary knowledge. But the texts students encounter in science and social studies are often rife with contentious issues, and it appears to us that CR is a good way to use those issues as a means of learning effective argumentation. Figure 7.9 presents the steps in planning and implementing CR.

Note that the aim of CR is not to achieve consensus or even to persuade other group members to adopt a particular position. This is not to say that minds will not change. After all, "the students are expected to weigh the reasons and evidence offered and to decide whether to maintain or change their original position" (Chinn, Anderson, & Waggoner, 2001, p. 383). However, the goal is not to persuade others but to support a position with text-based evidence. That is the reason CR is so well suited to the Common Core expectation that students be able to engage in argumentation that includes relevant and sufficient evidence drawn from texts.

It is easy to see what led Wilkinson and Son (2011) to conclude that control is shared in CR by the teacher and the students. The teacher sets up the

Planning
1. Choose a text that involves an issue with at least two positions.
2. Create an Argument Guide. (This is an outline of the positions and the evidence in the text that supports each. It is not for the students but is created as a reminder to the teacher.)

Implementing
1. The teacher meets with a small, mixed-ability group and poses a question that captures the controversy. In the case of *A Doll's House*, discussed in Chapter 4, a question might be: "Was Nora justified in leaving her children at the end of the play in order to find meaning in her life?" This question must be deliberately answered yes or no.
2. The teacher reminds the group of the ground rules for CR: • Stick to the topic. • Do not talk when others are talking. • Try to look at both sides of the issue. • Make sure everyone has a chance to participate. • Respond to the idea and not to the person. (Clark et al., 2003, pp. 184–185)
3. Students are then given time to decide their position. In addition to yes or no, a student might take a third position or remain uncertain.
4. Group members then argue for their positions, making references to the text.
5. After the discussion, the group votes.
6. When the teacher rejoins the group, they discuss the results and their reasoning.

FIGURE 7.9. Steps in planning and implementing Collaborative Reasoning.

discussion by framing the question, but the students are then left to reason without input from the teacher, who is actually required not to take sides but merely facilitate the discussion when necessary. It is also easy to see how CR, unlike QtA, can be readily implemented in a small-group format. This is because the presence of the teacher is not always needed, and monitoring several groups at once is possible. Finally, it is easy to follow up CR with a writing task that calls upon students to make their arguments in written form. That possibility gives CR something in common with a related technique, the Devil's Advocate, discussed later in the chapter. A coaching template for CR appears in Figure 7.10.

Discussion Web

Discussion Web (Alvermann, 1991) is another strategy that centers on controversy. Like CR, it involves a question that forces a yes/no choice and compels students to think in terms of argumentation for or against a position. There are five steps:

1. The teacher introduces the reading selection in the typical way by building or activating background knowledge. Even though the teacher has thought of the controversial question in advance, it is not shared with the students before they read.
2. After students read, the teacher poses the question and asks the students to work in pairs to list the pros and cons, using a template like the one we've modified in Figure 7.11. They take turns jotting down points, using key words and phrases rather than whole sentences, and striving for an equal number of points for and against the question.
3. They then join another pair of students and the group of four works to build consensus by considering all of the evidence listed by each pair. This is a point where Discussion Web differs from CR, which does not stress the need for consensus. Students in each group of four are reminded that consensus does not mean unanimity and that it is all right if they disagree as individuals. The teacher also reassures them that dissenting views will be heard.
4. Once each group of four arrives at a consensus view, a spokesperson (appointed or elected) is given 3 minutes to report the group's decision and the *best* reason supporting it. The spokesperson is also charged with stating dissenting positions, if any.
5. After all of the groups have reported, the students write about their own conclusion, which may differ from their group's, in a short argumentative piece that provides the evidence supporting their view and attempts to counter contrary evidence.

Coaching for Collaborative Reasoning
The strategy requires that you create an argument guide in advance. I noticed
The strategy requires that students work in small groups of mixed ability. I noticed
The strategy requires that you remind students of the ground rules. I noticed
The strategy requires that students base their arguments on the text. I noticed
The strategy requires that the teacher not take a position. I noticed
The strategy requires that each group take a vote at the end of their discussion. I noticed

FIGURE 7.10. Coaching template for Collaborative Reasoning (CR)

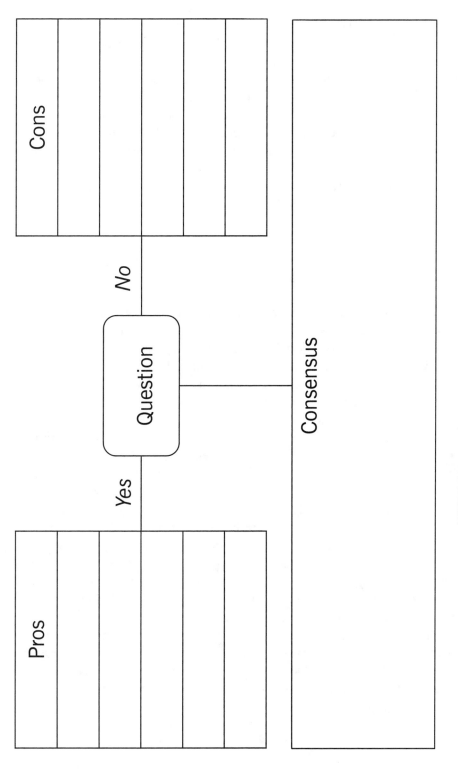

FIGURE 7.11. Student template for Discussion Web.

Discussion Web was developed for literature, and appropriate questions might take the form of "Was the main character justified in _____?" We see no reason, however, why it could not be applied to informational texts as long as an engaging issue can be identified. Stahl and Shanahan (2004) have also suggested that Discussion Web is a good way to encourage students to consider multiple texts: "Which of these two stories by Poe was the better written?" "Which of these two Saki stories had the better surprise ending?" What is important is not the outcome but the process. Like CR, Discussion Web "emphasizes the discourse leading to critical thinking" (Stahl & Shanahan, 2004, p. 107). We especially like the focus on argumentation, on the need to speak and to listen, and on the writing follow-up. All of these proficiencies are expectations of the Common Core. A coaching template for Discussion Web appears in Figure 7.12.

Devil's Advocate

Adolescents are seldom at a loss when it comes to taking positions on controversial issues. Submitting their positions to careful scrutiny is another matter, however, but that process is key to rational perspective taking, and it is at the heart of Common Core expectations regarding argument. Alvermann et al. (1984) have suggested that there is no better way to examine our own positions than by thinking through the evidence that supports a contrary view.

To prompt this kind of contrary thinking, they recommend an activity they appropriately call Devil's Advocate. It is a forerunner to Discussion Web, and it takes a very different turn by asking that students deliberately take a position they disagree with. The teacher poses an issue that involves two or more conflicting viewpoints. Students first work individually to prepare arguments for each position, even if they disagree with it. They base their arguments on the text (or text set) they have been reading. Each student writes a "position statement" for each view. The students are then paired and discuss with their partner the best arguments for each position. Together they decide whether a particular position can only be supported through faulty reasoning. The partners then discuss whether their original viewpoint has changed as a result of carefully considering the evidence supporting the other perspective. Each student then revises his or her position statement accordingly. The entire class then contributes to a discussion of the arguments in support of each position. As Manzo et al. (2009) observe, "One of three things may happen in a Devil's Advocate discussion: Positions may be strengthened, modified, or abandoned" (p. 216). A coaching template for Devil's Advocate appears in Figure 7.13.

Coaching for Discussion Web
The strategy requires that you pose a controversial question after students read. I noticed
The strategy requires that students work in pairs to complete the template. I noticed
The strategy requires that the partners join other partners and work in groups of four to reach consensus. I noticed
The strategy requires that a spokesperson from each group report the consensus view. I noticed
The strategy requires that spokespersons mention dissenting views. I noticed
The strategy requires that students follow up by writing about their own view and supporting it with evidence. I noticed

FIGURE 7.12. Coaching template for Discussion Web.

Coaching for Devil's Advocate
The strategy requires that students first work independently to prepare arguments for each position. I noticed
The strategy requires that students then work in pairs to discuss their arguments. I noticed
The strategy requires that the pairs decide whether an argument can only be supported through faulty reasoning. I noticed
The strategy requires that the students discuss whether their original viewpoint has changed. I noticed
The strategy requires that students be given a chance to revise their position statements after talking with a partner. I noticed
The strategy requires that the class discuss as a group the evidence for each position. I noticed

FIGURE 7.13. Coaching template for Devil's Advocate.

Final Thoughts

Postreading discussions are important for confirming and extending comprehension. They must, however, go well beyond the traditional recitation of facts
and focus instead on inference and interpretation. Teachers must strike a balance
between their need to transmit content and their students' need to think through
content collaboratively. Consequently, they must choose approaches to discussion
that encourage interaction among students both in small-group and whole-class
settings. This interaction must be focused on text and it must further comprehension. The most effective approaches to discussion possess these qualities. And,
perhaps surprisingly, they do not require teachers to cede too much control of
the discussion to their students, as long as they plan with care. Discussion also
presents excellent opportunities to meet the Common Core Standards regarding
speaking, listening, writing, and argumentation. Teachers tempted to skip discussion in order to get to the next unit, the next topic, or the next literary selection,
should think again. Discussion builds so many proficiencies at once that it is hard
to imagine a lesson component with more potential.

CHAPTER 8

Text-Based Writing
to Support Understanding

The aim of argument, or of discussion,
should not be victory, but progress.
—JOSEPH JOUBERT

To generalize is to be an idiot. To be
specific is the lone distinction of merit.
—WILLIAM BLAKE

Several years ago Bill Lewis thought it would be clever to feature the above two quotes prominently at the top of his AP syllabus. He did this because the quotes highlighted what he believed were the most important goals for his course:

1. Developing students' ability to read and discuss challenging literature.
2. Helping students successfully construct written analytic arguments about literary texts, which included choosing and connecting specific textual evidence to their arguments.

Bill eventually removed Blake's challenge from subsequent syllabi to prevent undue student stress on the first day of class. (Who wants to risk the possibility of feeling like an "idiot" at the very start of the school year?) The two quotes nevertheless represent the goals of the teacher's AP course, and they also fully reflect several pillars of the CCSS in reading and writing in *all* content areas. The CCSS focus on the ability of students to write a variety of text types, to evaluate authors' arguments in the texts they read, and to write arguments of their own using "valid reasoning and relevant and sufficient evidence" to support their claims. If we are to meet these CCSS demands, all content-area teachers will need to make text-based writing an integral part of their instruction, and will have to include a focused approach to argumentative writing in particular.

Our goals for this chapter are to provide you with a menu of text-based writing strategies that will help you prepare your students to use writing to improve their comprehension of content-area material, and then to share their understandings of that material with others. We begin the chapter with a discussion of why a shared responsibility for text-based writing across content areas is so important to the literacy development of our students. We then describe several text-based *summary* strategies that encourage students to synthesize important elements of their reading assignments, activities that will lead to better student comprehension. Last, we introduce several text-based writing strategies that will help you to extend your students' understanding of content-area texts through *written argument*, scaffolding their use of textual evidence to support their argumentative claims and engaging them in the mature ways of thinking that are demanded of them in college and the workplace.

Barriers to Text-Based Writing

After reading the first several chapters of this book, you might be saying to yourself that you fully understand the importance of supporting your students' literacy development through the strategic *reading* of content-area texts. However, you might be less excited about utilizing *writing* consistently in your instruction. We understand this reluctance. Because of our work in schools we know that it is sometimes difficult to "sell" writing across content areas, and there are many reasons for this. First, writing instruction is often thought to be the purview of the ELA or elementary teacher, not the responsibility of all middle school and high school content teachers. Second, some states, like Delaware, have removed writing from their state assessment regimen because of the expense of grading tests and concerns about the reliability of the scores. When writing falls off the state assessment radar (or if it is *pushed* off the radar because of other initiatives), administrators and classroom teachers can easily forget how important writing is to their students' learning in the content areas. Third, teachers are often concerned about the time it takes to grade written responses. Last, we understand that many high school teachers are concerned about the coverage of content and the very real time constraints that force them to make a choice between covering content and engaging students in extended reading or writing. In these battles, content coverage often wins.

While we think that all of these issues contribute to the relative lack of writing in schools, an overarching reason might be simply that teachers feel unprepared to do this work. Recent research demonstrates that many high school teachers (including ELA teachers!) do not feel that their education programs effectively prepared them to teach writing (Kiuhara et al., 2009). This might explain why content-area teachers rarely ask their students to engage in writing activities that require interpretation or analysis (Applebee & Langer, 2006) or to write texts that go beyond just a few sentences (Kiuhara et al., 2009). However, what research also shows is that if teachers feel more prepared to use and teach writing—because of their teacher preparation programs or professional development opportunities in their schools—they are more likely to use evidence-based writing practices in their classrooms and make adaptations for students who struggle with their writing (Kiuhara et al., 2009). We hope that this chapter will serve to prepare you to teach strategies that will help your students produce a variety of texts and make you more confident about using writing consistently in your classroom instruction.

Why Text-Based Writing—*and Why Me?*

So, why do you need to use writing in your content-area classroom? So far in this book we have focused on the text choices, reading processes, and instructional strategies that are important for improving student reading comprehension and meeting the robust demands of the CCSS. However, it is crucial that we don't forget the link between writing activities and reading comprehension. Although these are separate processes, research shows that having students write about the texts they read has a significant impact on the students' *reading* comprehension of these texts. As the National Commission on Writing puts it:

> If students are to make knowledge their own, they must struggle with details, wrestle with the facts, and rework raw information and dimly understood concepts into language they can communicate to someone else. In short, if students are to learn, they must write. (2003, p. 9)

The Carnegie Corporation has invested in explorations of this relationship between reading and writing. In their *Writing to Read* report, writing researchers Steve Graham and Michael Hebert (2010) demonstrate that some writing activities actually have a greater impact on reading comprehension than some well-accepted *reading comprehension* strategies! Although we will be highlighting features of this report later in the chapter, if you are interested in the impact of writing on comprehension you may download a free copy of the report at *www. carnegie.org/literacy* or *www.all4ed.org*.

This Carnegie report explores the impact of writing activities on reading comprehension, and the authors of the study identify three general categories of writing practices that strengthen student comprehension. Although at first glance the categories might seem too general to be helpful, they provide a solid reminder of what we need to think about in order to include more writing in our curriculum. These activities are represented in Figure 8.1.

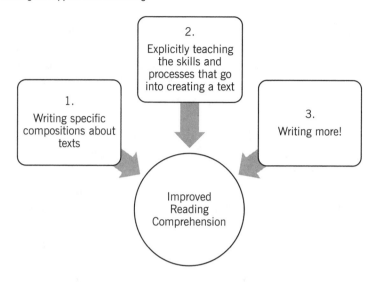

FIGURE 8.1. Writing activities that improve reading comprehension.

Although we represent the general recommendations as three separate types of activities in Figure 8.1, we believe the three must actually be implemented as a whole. For instance, the report recommends that students write specific compositions about the texts they read (Category 1). These compositions might include summaries, notes, personal responses, or written analyses. However, we claim that if students are going to write a summary of a text selection on cell division, or an analysis of a character in a chapter of *The Hunger Games* (Collins, 2010), or test questions that can encourage their peers to make inferences and think critically about the causes of the Revolutionary War, or notes on an article about genetically modified foods, then we also need to teach them the structure of these text types and the processes by which they can best produce them (Category 2). Furthermore, we know that if students are to become proficient writers, they are going to have to do a lot of writing (Category 3). Because students rarely engage in extended writing assignments, we need to think both about how we *assign* writing in our content-area classes and how we *teach* students to write the specific types of texts we assign. In order to do this, we need to plan strategically for connected reading and writing activities.

This truth is especially important for teachers of adolescents since every teacher must embrace writing in his or her discipline. Content areas demand discipline-specific ways of thinking, reading, and writing. When students move through the K–12 curriculum, their academic progress depends upon the acquisition of increasingly specialized skills and knowledge needed for success in content-specific coursework (Ferretti & De La Paz, 2011). As Heller and Greenleaf (2007) note, the "same old skills" are not enough if secondary students are to become competent with the very different content-area discourses they will be exposed to in college and the workplace. For example, a student writing an analysis of a poem by Robert Frost is going to use different reading and writing processes and different textual evidence than a student in social studies writing an analysis of population growth based on state maps and data tables. A student summarizing results of an experiment in a chemistry lab report will have a completely different set of expectations than a student documenting her problem-solving method in an advanced math course. If we are to help our students understand what it means to read, write, and think like historians, mathematicians, scientists, health professionals, literary critics, electricians, or auto body specialists, then we have to be explicit about how these experts make sense of texts and how they communicate their understanding to others. The best people to make this happen are the content-area teachers who have that expertise.

Now that we know about the positive effects of writing on content-area learning, and the shared responsibility for teaching and assigning writing that all content teachers must embrace, Graham and Hebert's "Write More" category makes a lot of sense! However, understanding when to use writing and how to help students produce texts can be difficult for teachers with already-full plates. The focus of the rest of this chapter, therefore, is to provide you with several specific writing strategies to help you see where and when writing can be used in your classroom.

Writing Activities That Work

In the previous section we highlighted the general writing activities that improve reading comprehension. However, we would like to spend some time unpacking the specific strategies that Graham and Hebert (2010) found improve student comprehension. Figure 8.2 identifies these strategies.

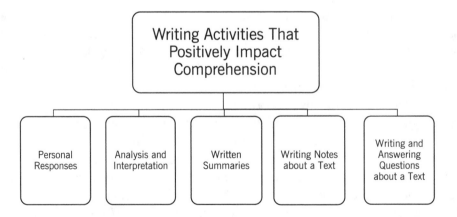

FIGURE 8.2. Writing activities that improve student comprehension.

Although there are a number of activities listed here that have a positive effect on student comprehension, we are going to focus on the two specific categories that we believe all content-area teachers need to embrace: summary writing and text-based argumentative writing. These activities pack a double punch: they improve reading comprehension (Graham & Hebert, 2010) and, when paired with explicit strategies that teach students *how* to write, they also improve writing quality (Graham & Perin, 2007). For busy teachers who are looking to maximize their instructional impact, this kind of "two-fer" (two for the price of one) represents an important avenue for effectively using classroom time.

You will notice that we chose strategies with less impressive research pedigrees than those we have recommended for supporting reading comprehension and building background knowledge; the available empirical literature is much smaller in the area of writing, especially across content areas. However, the strategies we present here have been recommended by well-respected teacher-educators, and used extensively in classrooms, and also form the basis of our own professional development work in middle schools and high schools embracing the challenges of the CCSS. You will also notice that the strategies that we chose for this chapter are focused on the production of short compositions, some no longer than a single sentence in length. We have made this choice because we favor short writing integrated into daily life rather than ponderous assignments that take a long time for students to complete and a long time for teachers to grade. Because connected reading and writing experiences are demanded in the CCSS, we want to present strategies that can easily be integrated into your content-area classroom.

Summary Writing

One of our literacy colleagues recently said, "If you had to commit to one type of content-area writing, you could do a lot worse than to choose summarizing as your focus." Although this is not the highest praise we have ever heard for summarizing, we agree with the essence of our colleague's thinking. Writing summaries of what is read is one of the most important activities for acquiring content-area knowledge (Graham & Hebert, 2010). However, although summarizing has been around for as long as there have been schools, writing summaries can be complex for students who struggle. It requires the reader/writer to identify main and supporting ideas and synthesize these ideas into a meaningful whole. The difficulty of this process was crystallized by the comments of a friend of ours who confessed about his own summarizing "strategy" in middle school: "Well, I plagiarized the first sentence of a passage, plagiarized a sentence from the middle of the passage, and then plagiarized the last sentence. I then misspelled a few words so the teacher would believe that I wrote it."

This might sound familiar to you if it approximates the process by which your own students go about producing summaries. Doug Buehl (2009), a literacy consultant and former teacher, argues that it is typical for students to attempt to write summaries by stringing together disconnected pieces of text while overlooking the main ideas and themes that animate them. Although stringing together ideas is certainly a summarizing "strategy," it is clearly not effective for helping students attain deep understanding of the content-area texts used in high school, and it certainly won't work in college. It is important, then, that we don't just *assign* students to summarize their content-area readings, but that we also explicitly *teach* the strategies through which they can learn to produce summaries.

The Magnet Summary Strategy

One of the most effective strategies that we have found in our work with schools is the Magnet Summary strategy (Buehl, 1993).

The Magnet Summary teaches students the two key skills needed to write effective summaries:

1. *Selecting* only the most important ideas and supporting details from a reading passage.
2. *Synthesizing* those details and main ideas into a coherent written text that captures the gist of the passage.

As with all reading and writing strategies, it is important to talk with your students about the importance of this one, to explicitly teach its steps, to model its use yourself with sample reading passages, and to provide the opportunity for collaborative classroom practice.

To teach Magnet Summaries, we agree with Buehl (2009) that you should begin by introducing the idea of "magnet words" to students, explaining that magnet words are the "main idea" words from a passage that "attract" other supporting ideas to them (Buehl, 2009). Then you can provide students practice in identifying magnet words in sample passages. This is a great time to talk to your students about the text features that often contain magnet terms (titles, headings, and subheadings) and to help them look for main ideas in opening or closing paragraphs. However, it is also important to let students know that magnet terms are not always found in these text features (Buehl, 2009).

Let's say that we are teaching a unit on the Great Depression and direct our students to read a short passage about Herbert Hoover from the excellent YA nonfiction book *FDR's Alphabet Soup: New Deal America 1932–1939* (Bolden, 2010). One passage of this book introduces students to Herbert Hoover and his failed attempts to control the downward financial spiral of the Great Depression. You could begin by having students quickly read the passage, looking for a "magnet term" that represents its content. In this case, the first paragraph of the selection mentions Hoover three times. Therefore, looking at the introductory paragraph can provide us with the magnet term: "Herbert Hoover," "the Hoover Presidency," or possibly, "Hoover and the Depression." When you introduce the idea of magnet words, we believe it is helpful to write the magnet word or phrase on the board to focus student attention on the central idea of the passage, while students write the word in the center of a page of notes or on a 3″ × 5″ card.

We would then direct our students to reread the passage, and when they finish to select the most important four or five words or short phrases from the passage that are "attracted" to that key magnet term. We suggest that when first teaching this strategy you direct students to choose fewer rather than more attractor terms. It is also important to help students at this point in the instruction to discuss the most important "attractor" words or phrases. For example, in the passage we have been describing, students could choose "Great Do-Nothing," "Ignored," "Rugged Individualists," "RFC," or "The Great Depression." These terms should be written on the board around the magnet term, and students can write their words on their 3″ × 5″ card. See Figure 8.3 for an example of what this card might look like.

After the magnet word and attractor terms are written down, real summarizing can begin. Here teachers should guide students in writing a summary that synthesizes the terms into a single sentence *and* (most importantly) demonstrates the relationship between the attractor and magnet terms. We suggest that you write your sentence on the board, while the students write their sentences on the back of their 3″ × 5″ cards. This part of the instruction is probably the most difficult because high school students often want to get away with just listing the terms, instead of combining them in ways that demonstrate their relationship. However, because you have already helped students determine the main idea (magnet word) and supporting ideas (attractor terms) the synthesis task will be

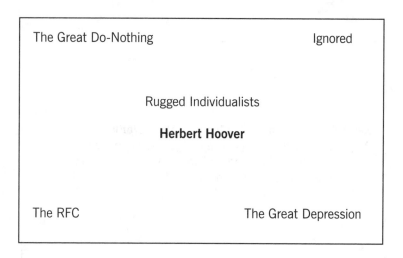

FIGURE 8.3. Sample Magnet Summary card.

much easier for them. Still, it is important to note that because of the difficulty of this task you should "think aloud" while you demonstrate this synthesizing process, explaining how you are connecting the words in your sentence. The think-aloud might go something like this:

"Since **Herbert Hoover** is the magnet term, I think I might start my sentence with that. Now I will look for a term that I can connect with it. '**Great Do-Nothing**' was his nickname, so I think that I will put that in the sentence and connect it with his name. It is a way to describe Herbert Hoover. I can write *Herbert Hoover was called the 'Great Do-Nothing.'*

"The Great Depression is the time period that this selection addresses, so I will use that next and add it to what I have. 'Herbert Hoover was called the "Great Do-Nothing" *during the Great Depression.'*

"OK. I know that a sentence has to have a verb so that it expresses a full idea. **Ignored** is a verb so I will use that. But who did Herbert Hoover ignore? Well, the passage seems to say that he ignored the people in the country during the Depression and he did that because he thought people should be '**Rugged Individualists**' and take care of themselves. I will write that idea down and connect it to what I have. 'Herbert Hoover was called the "Great Do-Nothing" during the Great Depression, *because he ignored people who he thought should be "rugged individualists."'*

"Good. I am almost done. I have only one term left . . . **RFC**. This is a big agency that Hoover created to bail out big businesses. How does this go with the idea of ignoring people? Well, he ignored people and instead tried to end the Depression by bailing out big businesses with the RFC. I will add that to the rest of my sentence. . . . "

Herbert Hoover was called the **"Great Do-Nothing"** during **the Great Depression** because he **ignored** people who he thought should be **"rugged individualists,"** and instead bailed out big businesses by creating the **RFC**.

FIGURE 8.4. Magnet Summary sentence.

After you model the process with this think-aloud, we suggest that you have students practice summarizing shorter passages in pairs or small groups. You can then gradually release responsibility to them, having them construct Magnet Summaries of their own. In the case of *this* Magnet Summary, the sentence that this process produces is represented in Figure 8.4.

As we mentioned, it is quite possible that during this phase of the instruction students might produce a sentence that is just a listing of the words with no real attempt at a meaningful synthesis. It is also quite possible that the magnet sentences they write will not be accurate. For instance, a student might write that the RFC was designed to help individual citizens, something that contradicts the textual information in the passage. During this part of the instruction it is important that you examine the magnet sentences that students produce in order to guide them in a discussion of what sentences best capture the gist of the passage. In this way, you are both teaching content about Hoover's role during the Great Depression and teaching your students to summarize.

Now that you understand the strategy, let's look at an actual passage that might be used in a biology lesson on evolution and animal behavior. Figure 8.5 contains a passage from a government publication on the evolutionary benefits of bird migration.

This could be a difficult passage for students to summarize without a procedure to follow. However, after they learn the Magnet Summary strategy, the task should become simpler. Students in groups, pairs, or working alone would first scan the text for text features or main ideas that could become the magnet term. It is very likely that they might choose "Evolution of Migration" because of its position as the heading of the passage. They would then write this term in the middle of their 3″ × 5″ card. While reading the passage, the students would then

---

EVOLUTION OF MIGRATION

The rigors of the annual migratory journey are balanced by benefits derived from species being able to inhabit two different areas during seasons when each region provides favorable conditions. Upland Sandpipers breeding in the grasslands of North America and wintering on the pampas of Argentina never experience winter. If it were not advantageous to make the trip twice a year, the behavior would not have evolved. . . . By departing in the spring from their wintering ranges to breeding areas, migrant species are probably assured of reduced interspecific competition for adequate space and resources such as ample food for themselves and their offspring.

Migration of Birds (USGS Publication)

FIGURE 8.5. Sample biology fact sheet.

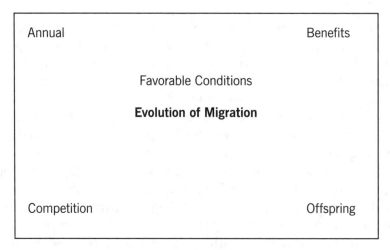

FIGURE 8.6. Magnet Summary card for migration passage.

look for the terms that are attracted to that magnet idea. In this case students might choose "annual," "benefits," "favorable conditions," "competition," and "offspring." All of these terms have a connection to either the concept of migration or evolution. Figure 8.6 demonstrates what a student's 3″ × 5″ card might look like after completing this step of the strategy.

It is now time for students to synthesize these words into a meaningful whole—one that shows the relationships among the words *and* represents the gist of the passage. Students might write something like the sentence in Figure 8.7.

It is clear that some students might pick different words than the ones we chose in our example. This is fine; it is consistent with the construction–integration theory of comprehension that defines comprehension for us. As long

The **evolution of migration** occurred because the **annual** movement of birds toward places with more **favorable conditions** had many **benefits**, including less **competition** for resources and healthier **offspring**.

FIGURE 8.7. Magnet Summary sentence for science passage.

as students can synthesize the terms they choose into a meaningful whole that represents the gist of the passage, we should allow them this freedom. However, it is still important for teachers to talk with students about their choices, and how some attractors might work better in their summaries than others. In our own experience, we found that if students have a difficult time synthesizing one of the attractor terms into their summary sentence, the attractor term might not be as important to the main idea as other terms. The act of trying to include a term by force-fitting it into the summary can highlight its relative unimportance and strengthen a student's focus on the main idea.

We believe that the Magnet Summary offers high school teachers a lot of flexibility. First, it is an excellent "pass out of class" strategy and a quick-check assessment of student comprehension of the reading done in class. However, it can also be used to summarize class discussions or synthesize course lecture notes. Additionally, this strategy can be expanded to accommodate summarizing longer pieces of text. For instance, if your students are reading a textbook chapter that includes several distinct subsections, they can be asked to write a one-sentence Magnet Summary for each of these sections. After they have written their sentences, they can then arrange them into a meaningful paragraph that summarizes the whole chapter. Similarly, we have seen the Magnet Summary strategy used as an end-of-unit review. At the start of the review, you could guide students in a discussion of what they believe are the four to six key "magnet" ideas from the unit. After deciding on these terms, students can generate the key words or phrases that are attracted to each word and construct sentences for these important unit topics. In the same way they made summaries of chapters, students can then arrange each of their Magnet Summary sentences into meaningful paragraphs that summarize their learning of a unit and focus them while they prepare for a quiz, test, or other assessment. The steps of the Magnet Summary Strategy plus a coaching template are provided in Figure 8.8.

The RAFT Strategy

The RAFT acronym has sometimes been utilized as an advanced organizer for reading, particularly reading primary source documents in history. However, as a summary strategy for reading, it encourages the synthesis of key ideas and provides students with a creative means for expressing these ideas in a variety of forms (Santa, 1988; Santa, Havens, & Valdes, 2004). For teachers who are concerned about meeting the CCSS demand that students "write routinely . . . for a range of tasks, purposes and audiences," the RAFT summary strategy is an excellent instructional routine. Additionally, in the *Writing Next* report, Graham and Perin (2007) identify the development of flexible writing as one of the primary goals of all writing instruction in schools. The RAFT strategy, which is directed at different audiences with different forms and topics, helps encourage this type of flexibility.

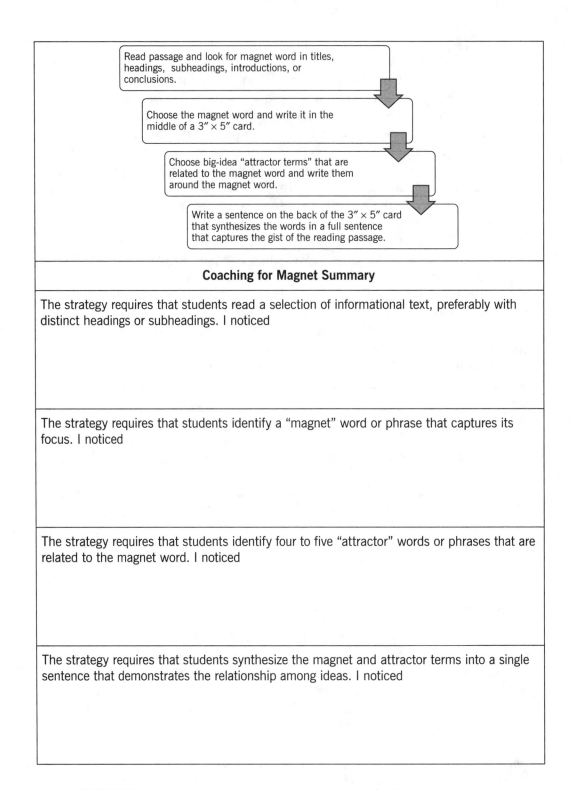

Coaching for Magnet Summary

The strategy requires that students read a selection of informational text, preferably with distinct headings or subheadings. I noticed

The strategy requires that students identify a "magnet" word or phrase that captures its focus. I noticed

The strategy requires that students identify four to five "attractor" words or phrases that are related to the magnet word. I noticed

The strategy requires that students synthesize the magnet and attractor terms into a single sentence that demonstrates the relationship among ideas. I noticed

FIGURE 8.8. Strategy summary and coaching template for Magnet Summaries.

The RAFT strategy is based on an easily remembered mnemonic. After students read, we encourage them to summarize their understandings by taking on a very specific *role* (R), writing to a particular *audience* (A), utilizing a specific *form* of writing (F), and addressing a specific *topic* in that form (T). In essence, we ask students to "transform" the main ideas of the text that they read into another form they are familiar with. Kyleen Beers calls this type of activity a "text reformulation" (Beers, 2002). The importance of reformulation is that it encourages deeper understanding of the relationships between main and subordinate ideas, because students are being forced to take what is most important from one type of text and then synthesize their understandings in creative ways. Figure 8.9 contains a few examples of RAFTs that teachers in science, math, history, and ELA might use to encourage students to synthesize textual material after their reading. The figure also provides a coaching template. These RAFTs were designed for an article on natural selection and Darwin's voyage, a textbook chapter in geometry, the short story "The Monkey's Paw," and a primary source account of the surrender at Appomattox Courthouse. Once students have the directions for their RAFTs, their brief compositions reflect both audience awareness and content knowledge. Their writing products can range in length, depending on both your teaching goals and the available time.

Although students will be familiar with the RAFT topics after completing their reading assignments, when introducing this summary strategy it may be helpful to begin the activity by sharing a specific example of the form of writing you are asking them to produce. Although students may have experience writing a speech or watching an infomercial, we would bet that many might need reminders about the elements of a haiku or a personal ad. Providing students examples of these text forms and talking about their salient features can make it much easier for them to summarize using this strategy. Additionally, students sometimes have difficulty understanding their roles when attempting RAFTs. One could imagine the difficulty some students might have understanding the complicated emotions of General Lee after losing the Civil War, or the strategic machinations of the ShamWow guy. However, it might be even more difficult for them to understand the point of view of a finch, or the completely inanimate viewpoint of a lonely triangle! Therefore, when using the RAFT strategy, Doug Buehl (2009) suggests that teachers provide students with the opportunity to brainstorm their roles with other students, identifying the key aspects of their role's *personality* that should be communicated, the important beliefs and feelings that make up their *attitude*, and the most crucial *information* they must share in that role.

Recently in one of our content-area literacy classes, we provided our students—who were all student teaching at the time—a short reading on violent weather and the formation of tornadoes from a ninth-grade earth and space science text. We asked them to summarize this reading in the RAFT format in Figure 8.10, and an example of what one student produced is represented in

Science	Math
R: Galapagos cactus finch	R: Single triangle
A: Galapagos vampire finch	A: Another lonely triangle
F: Tweet (Twitter feed)	F: Personal ad
T: I like my beak adaptation	T: Looking for "triangle congruence" and corresponding angles

ELA	History
R: ShamWow guy (or other infomercial persona)	R: General Lee
A: Late-night TV viewer	A: General Grant
F: Infomercial	F: Haiku
T: A monkey paw from Jacobs's short story "The Monkey's Paw"	T: My surrender

Coaching for RAFT

The strategy requires that you select a passage of informational or narrative text. I noticed

The strategy requires that you provide a clear role for students to write from. I noticed

The strategy requires that you provide an audience for students to write to. I noticed

The strategy requires that you provide a form to write in and discuss the salient features of that form. I noticed

This strategy requires that you provide a topic drawn from the readings for students to write about. I noticed

FIGURE 8.9. Sample RAFTs from content area texts and coaching template.

Role:	Frustrated teacher
Audience:	Assistant principal
Format:	Discipline referral statement
Topic:	Student Tornado's behavior

FIGURE 8.10. RAFT "example."

Figure 8.11. Our students had no trouble taking on the role of frustrated teacher, nor were they unfamiliar with the disciplinary statement format! However, as they found out, reformulating an informational science text into a new genre can take some thinking. They had to determine the main ideas of the passage and then transform those main ideas in a way that met the demands of the disciplinary writing that teachers are sometimes, unfortunately, required to do. However, in Figure 8.11 you can see that our student writer was able to creatively combine important textual information in way that demonstrated a sophisticated understanding of the passage and provided a few laughs for some tired student teachers. The creativity and synthesis required for this type of writing are important benefits of this strategy.

The SWBS Strategy

Like the RAFT strategy, the SWBS (Somebody Wanted But So) strategy (Macon, Bewell, & Vogt, 1991) is a focused summarizing strategy that provides students with a clear mnemonic scaffold to summarize texts. It encourages students to identify the main actors in a content-area reading, to look at the motivation and desires of these actors, to identify conflicts that get in the way of the actors achieving their goals, and to determine how these conflicts are resolved. Although this summary strategy works well in the ELA content area for summarization of

Mr. Stormchaser: There was an incident in my class today involving one of my students, Tornado. Tornado was destructive to school property, littered, and was disruptive/uncooperative. It seems that a rapid upward movement of warm, moist air touched off the incident. He got very upset and destroyed lots of school property as he spun through the room. He picked up dirt, which gave him a dark complexion, and then dropped it, littering school grounds. I previously had a conference with Tornado telling him to stay away from cooler winds blowing in a different direction when he has warm, moist air moving upward, but he did not listen. Although the destruction lasted only a minute or two, this matter should be referred to scientists who should look into radar and other detection methods so we can be prepared for Tornado the next time around.

FIGURE 8.11. Sample RAFT summary for violent weather passage.

Content Area	Somebody	Wanted	But	So
Biology	Jean-Baptiste Lamark	To explore why organisms change and develop over time	His idea about how they change was incorrect (for example, he thought that giraffes got long necks from parent giraffes stretching to eat leaves).	Darwin had to come along to explain how organisms really change over time.
History	Christopher Columbus	To find a better way to sail to India to make trade easier for Spain	He ran into what is now Cuba.	He claimed it for Spain and became one of the first explorers to begin trade with the New World.
American literature	Peyton Farquhar	Wanted to escape his hanging at Owl Creek Bridge	The rules of reality say that those who are hanged do not escape death.	He dreamed about escaping only to be pulled back to reality when the rope breaks his neck at the end of the story.
Applied mathematics	A carpenter	To find if the deck he built was perfectly square	He only had a long tape measure and his knowledge of the Pythagorean theorem.	He used the theorem and measured the diagonals. When he saw that the diagonals were equal, he knew the deck was square.

FIGURE 8.12. SWBS summary strategy.

short stories, novels, and narrative poems, this framework also works well for informational texts that feature individuals or groups of people who overcome conflict to achieve specific goals. Additionally, we have found that math teachers find this strategy very helpful for getting students to summarize problem-solving procedures from their math textbooks. Figure 8.12 offers a few simple examples that use the SWBS strategy to scaffold student understanding of the actors, conflicts, and resolutions. They are drawn from a variety of high school content-area texts—including math! You will also find a coaching template in Figure 8.13 to guide your reflection.

Argumentative Writing

Because the first of the CCSS Writing Anchors states that students must "write arguments to support claims in an analysis of substantive topics or texts, using valid reasoning and relevant and sufficient evidence," it is quite clear that we cannot rest upon our laurels when our students are able to effectively summarize texts in writing. Students must not only be able read and write to acquire the

Coaching for SWBS
The strategy requires that you select a passage of informational or narrative text. I noticed
The strategy requires that students identify the main actor in the reading. I noticed
The strategy requires that students identify a goal for that actor. I noticed
The strategy requires that students identify a barrier to achieving that goal. I noticed
This strategy requires that students identify how the main actor overcame the barrier or reconciled himself to the situation. I noticed

FIGURE 8.13. SWBS coaching template.

gist of a text, but must also do something (often analytical and argumentative) with that understanding. This is for a very good reason. In *Clueless in Academe*, Gerald Graff (2003) maintains that argument and persuasion are at the core of academic studies beyond high school, the "hidden curriculum" that undergirds all academic discourse, and the unifying factor of what has increasingly become "a vast disconnected clutter of subjects, disciplines and courses" (p. 3). Additionally, Graff argues that argument and persuasion are the key elements of becoming a fully engaged member of a literate and democratic society, where people must engage in argument about important ideas. This claim is supported by Deborah Meier (2002), who writes that disagreement and argument fuel intellectual growth and understanding, and that children must be initiated into these mature ways of thinking if our civic life is to survive.

It is not surprising, then, that the authors of the CCSS identify argumentative writing as the "cornerstone" of the writing standards and suggest that simple opinion writing should be an instructional focus in even the earliest of grades (NGA and CCSSO, 2010). Children can begin to develop argumentative skills through the construction of basic opinion essays that seek to convince an audience through emotional appeals and by using only the evidence that is favorable to their points of view. However, middle school and high school students must, instead, engage in reasoning and written communication practices that depend on logical appeals that contain clear claims, evidence from content-area texts, and warrants (connections between evidence and claims) (Hillocks, 2011). This is the difference between what is called *persuasive writing* and the more mature *argumentative writing* that is the focus of the CCSS.

To illustrate, let's look at a few sample CCSS performance tasks from Appendix B of the Standards document. Four of these tasks are included in Figure 8.14.

Students compare George Washington's Farewell Address to other foreign policy statements, such as the Monroe Doctrine, and *analyze* how both texts *address similar themes and concepts* regarding "entangling alliances."

Students *analyze how* Abraham Lincoln in his Second Inaugural Address *unfolds* his examination of the *ideas* that led to the Civil War, paying particular attention to *the order in which the points are made, how* Lincoln *introduces and develops* his points, *and the connections that are drawn between them.*

Students *evaluate* the *argument and specific claims* about the "spirit of liberty" in Learned Hand's "I Am an American Day Address," *assessing the relevance and sufficiency of the evidence and the validity of his reasoning.*

Students *determine the purpose* and *point of view* in Martin Luther King Jr.'s "I Have a Dream" speech and *analyze* how King *uses rhetoric to advance* his position.

FIGURE 8.14. CCSS performance tasks for informational text.

Not only are all of these tasks highly demanding, but many of them require students to carefully analyze the arguments of others before constructing an argument of their own. Whether it be building an argument about the similarities between documents, arguing for or against the sufficiency and validity of a historical argument, or arguing for their view of the purpose of a speech, students must understand how arguments are constructed by others and be able to use logical appeals and textual evidence to build robust arguments of their own.

We trust that looking at these demanding reading and writing tasks will encourage you to commit to using text-based argument in your classroom. Understanding argument will help students comprehend complex text, and it will ultimately prepare them to engage in the great debates that are a part of the study of literature, history, sciences, and our democratic institutions. However, although you probably understand the importance of encouraging students to use textual information to form an argument in your classroom, you might not know how to teach them to do so effectively. Below we provide an instructional strategy you can use to get started with text-based argument.

CSQT

Bill Lewis developed and we all used a specific text-based writing strategy that aligns well with the CCSS demands for text-based argument. This strategy was originally designed to help students in an ELA classroom use quotes and other textual evidence to back their arguments about literature. We found that although many students could generate claims about literature ("I think the character does not grow emotionally," "The ending of Huck Finn is stupid!" "I think that Gatsby is a tragic figure"), students had a much more difficult time finding textual evidence to support their claims and often could not explain the relationship between their evidence and claims. We knew that explicit instruction would be needed to overcome this difficulty, so we developed a strategy that could be used to explicitly teach students the elements of the writing that they needed to produce. Based on the mnemonic CSQT (see Figure 8.15), students are prompted (1) to state a clear claim (C) about their reading, (2) to find a quote in the text that backs their claim and provides contextual information that "sets up" the quote for the reader (S), (3) to embed the quote in their written text (Q), and, most important, (4) to "tie in" (T) the quote to their claim by explaining how the quote supports that claim. Although originally designed as a strategy for arguments about literature in ELA, CSQT has been used across disciplines to help students use textual evidence to support their claims.

We have found that it is often the "tie-in," or what argumentation specialists call the "warrant," that is the most difficult for students to produce. Students will often just restate their quotes instead of developing a true tie-in sentence that connects their quoted evidence to their claims. Therefore, it is important to spend instructional time with this element of the mnemonic until students can produce

C=Claim
• State your opinion.

S=Setup
• Introduce your quote.
• Tell how it fits in the text.

Q=Quote
• Share a quote that illustrates your opinion.

T=Tie-in
• Tell your reader how your quote shows your opinion is right.

FIGURE 8.15. The CSQT strategy mnemonic.

tie-ins on their own. As Hillocks (2011) states, warrants are commonsense rules, scientific principles, or laws that are generally accepted as true. Therefore, the teacher's role at this stage of instruction is to make sure that students can generate these rules.

Let's make this more concrete. Here are some prompts well suited to the CSQT frame:

"What is the narrator's mood and how does the poet use language to develop that mood?"

"Is Martin Luther King Jr.'s 'I Have a Dream' speech practical or inspirational?"

"Is the main character in 'The Most Dangerous Game' a dynamic individual?" Explain whether you believe that Rainsford has changed in the story.

The prompts must encourage students to choose a side, or commit to a point of view. The answer to the prompt cannot be found explicitly in the reading itself. Students must make inferences to craft their argumentative responses.

These writing prompts reflect the arguments that students are required to make in dynamic ELA and history classrooms. Additionally, they are very similar to CCSS performance tasks that require close reading of texts and an analysis of how authorial choices impact the reader. However, an additional benefit to this type of open-ended question is that multiple answers can be supported with the text. For example, a group of high-achieving 11th graders were asked to make and defend a claim about the mood of the narrator of a humorous poem about the approach of winter. It was a challenging assignment because the evidence was conflicting. Parts of the poem suggested that the speaker is happy. Different portions indicated that the speaker is sad or even afraid about the coming of winter. The students resolved the conflict by claiming that the narrator is confused, perhaps even unstable. This claim, they found, accounted best for the evidence and their citations supported it well. The students worked together to produce the CSQT that appears in Figure 8.16.

There are very few groups of students who will produce something this sophisticated in their first efforts at CSQT. However, this example shows us what can be achieved when we are explicit about the elements of an effective argument. Let's break down what the students do here. They begin their argument with a clear *claim* that seeks to reconcile the conflicting signals the narrator provides the reader. The students then *set up* two short quotes by explaining their places in the poem (at the beginning and end). Then they provide those *quotes*, which demonstrate the conflicting moods, and finally craft a *tie-in*, in which they warrant their evidence by generating a rule about how quick shifts in emotion are often symptomatic of confusion. In this way, they link their quotes to their claim.

However, in this paragraph the group of students go even further, using evidence about the structure of the poem and then developing a tie-in about how a break in the rhyme scheme in the last couplet reinforces the broken and confused mood. Not only is the ability to link the structure of a piece of writing to its meaning and effect part of the CCSS, this is also one of the content-specific expectations that we mentioned above. In the ELA content-area, experts often look for breaks in rhyme or meter because those breaks may signal that the poet is bringing attention to something important.

Besides being a solid argument, this example also provides us with insight into the flexibility of the strategy. CSQT can be expanded to prompt students to provide multiple quotes and tie-ins (as the student group did in Figure 8.16), to use one long quote and one short quote, or two quotes and a single tie-in that would explain both quotes. There are many effective combinations of quotes and

---

The narrator's mood is confused, and as the poem progresses she seems to become more emotionally unbalanced. The reason this is so is because in the beginning of the work she is very happy, "clap[ping] with glee" at the sudden snowfall. However, at the end of the poem, the mood switches to a threatening one, the poet warning "not to go to that shopping mall." A quick switch in emotion like this shows that the narrator may be emotionally unbalanced and confused about the beginning of winter. In addition, the poet ends with the haunting lines: "when you get at home in bed, / Thoughts of frost they fill your little mind!" The poem up to that point is filled with perfect rhymes. However, in this case the expected rhyming word, *head*, does not appear. This jars the reader's expectations and could demonstrate that the writer, herself, feels confused and jarred by the coming winter.

FIGURE 8.16. Sample CSQT response.

tie-ins that teachers can talk with students about as they learn to craft text-based arguments. However, having a common language to talk about these writing choices makes students much more likely to be able to use them effectively.

With careful attention to the development of prompts, CSQT can be used in *all* content areas to help make claims and inferences and use relevant and sufficient evidence to defend them. For instance, a science teacher we know recently gave his students a CSQT performance task for an informational text that described the different types of damage that can occur during an earthquake. These included damage from tsunamis, fires, ground liquefaction, and landslides. The prompt, with a sample CSQT paragraph, is shown in Figure 8.17.

This is a solid argument, and one of the reasons is that the teacher's prompt required students to make an argument based on inferences from a content-area text. In no part of the reading assignment was there a section that explicitly told students where people should build houses in earthquake zones. The students had to make those inferences and apply the textual information to create their argument. Then, following the CSQT strategy, the student stated a clear claim, set up and used quotes drawn from the text, and explained the relevance of this evidence to her claim. What is also interesting about this example is that this student used both quotes and paraphrased information about tsunamis to back her opinion. At this stage of the instruction, we think this use of paraphrased information can be helpful and would suggest that you systematically introduce students to other types of evidence besides quotations. In addition to paraphrased text, this could include facts gleaned from maps, charts, or graphs, or evidence based on mathematical calculations. In fact, several schools we work with have changed the Q of the CSQT to an E to introduce students to a broader understanding of what is relevant and sufficient *evidence*. We are in favor of this change. However,

---

Based on the information in this article, construct an argument for where and how you would build a house in an earthquake-prone area to avoid suffering damage from a quake.

The safest place to live would be someplace built on a bedrock mountaintop, away from the sea and designed to withstand motion. When earthquakes strike, they can cause great changes to the surrounding land and widespread damage to buildings that are on it. The textbook states that ground motion could "completely destroy buildings, especially buildings on unlithified sediment which can liquefy and then slide down hills" (p. 257). Building my house on bedrock would eliminate the problems with this kind of damage, particularly if the bedrock is at the top of a mountain; this would avoid landslides. Also, if the house is properly designed, it could withstand the movements during the earthquake. The third reason building on a bedrock mountaintop is a good idea is because it avoids an indirect effect of earthquakes: tsunamis. These "seismic sea waves" can cause greets amounts of damage near the coastal areas with waves as high as 10 meters (p. 261). Even though these waves are very big, if I am on a mountaintop away from the sea my house will not be in danger no matter how big the waves get.

FIGURE 8.17. CSQT prompt and sample argument for earthquake text.

even though we agree that moving students toward a CSET mnemonic is help-ful, especially to content-area teachers outside of ELA, we suggest starting with quotes since it is very easy for students to combine setups, evidence, and tie-ins into an indistinguishable blob in early stages of instruction.

The ability to formulate clear, concise arguments with text-based evidence is an advanced literacy skill. Therefore, students will need lots of support, many opportunities to practice with a variety of texts in all content-area classrooms, and feedback on the quality of their efforts. Once mastered, though, the basic struc-ture of CSQT (or CSET) can be used to complete extended writing assignments and research papers. Students constructing an argumentative essay—on the pri-mary cause of the Revolutionary War, the theme of Robert Frost's "After Apple Picking," or whether a manned flight to Mars is reasonable and responsible—can use individual CSQTs or CSETs as their supporting paragraphs, constructing as many as they need to support their broader overall argument.

There are clearly many variations of CSQT and CSET that can lead to the same outcomes. We present a coaching template in Figure 8.18. Keep in mind there is a natural interface between CSQT and some of the discussion techniques we presented in the previous chapter. Discussion Web and Devil's Advocate, in particular, both involve making notes in support of arguments, and they could lead seamlessly into an approach like CSQT.

The Save the Last Word for Me Strategy

It may be the case that your students have difficulty with the CSQT/CSET strat-egy and need more support in connecting evidence to claims. It might also be the case that you want a quick "exit ticket" strategy that can serve as a check on stu-dent comprehension while also encouraging students to choose and explain their textual evidence. The Save the Last Word for Me strategy could be a good choice for you. Although there are a number of variations of this strategy (see Buehl, 2009; Vaughan & Estes, 1986), it can be quite simple and supports the claim/evidence/tie-in connection that is sometimes difficult for students to develop.

To begin using this strategy we suggest that you start by giving your students a clear purpose for reading a particular passage (a practice we have encouraged throughout this book!). For instance, an ELA teacher might ask students to read a short story and specifically focus on the foreshadowing in it. A health teacher might ask students to read a passage on smoking and concentrate on the ill effects smoking has on the body. A history teacher might ask students to read a primary source document concerning the framing of the Constitution and to determine whether the writer is from a northern or southern state. After the students read the passage, the teacher hands each a 3″ × 5″ card and asks them to find a quote related to a critical question. The ELA teacher might ask students to find a quote that is the best example of foreshadowing in the short story. The health teacher might ask students to find a quote that represents what the student believes to be

Coaching for CSQT
The strategy requires that you select a passage of informational or narrative text. I noticed
The strategy requires that you develop a prompt that is argumentative and requires students to make inferences. I noticed
The strategy requires that students develop a claim for their argument. I noticed
The strategy requires that students identify quotes that support their claim and provide contextual information that helps the reader to understand the quote. I noticed
This strategy requires that students develop a tie-in sentence that explains the relevance of the quote to the student's claim. I noticed

FIGURE 8.18. CSQT coaching template.

the most dangerous hazard of smoking. The history teacher might ask students to find a quote that provides important evidence of whether the writer has northern or southern sympathies.

After writing their quote on the front of the card, students should then be asked to write a "tie-in"-type sentence on the back that ties the quote to the focus question. For example, let's say our ELA teacher wants her students to read the highly anthologized short story "The Gift of the Magi" by O. Henry because of its use of foreshadowing. As you may recall, this story tells of the struggles of a poor couple who do not have enough money to buy each other Christmas presents. Each decides to sell something precious in order to get the money needed to buy a present: the husband his watch, and the wife her beautiful hair. Much to their surprise when they open their presents, the wife finds that her husband has bought her combs for her now-missing hair, and her husband finds a beautiful chain for his now-missing watch. Figure 8.19 (on p. 162) represents a Save the Last Word for Me card that a student might construct for this text, together with a coaching template.

In this example, the student chooses a quote that repeatedly refers to money. She then provides an explanation of how the repetition of monetary need foreshadows the desperate action that the character will eventually take. Although a very concise form of writing for students—and an easy-to-evaluate assessment for teachers—the Save the Last Word for Me strategy provides students with valuable practice in identifying, explaining, and connecting relevant and specific evidence to important questions, as well as an efficient means of assessing student understanding of content-area concepts.

Final Thoughts

In order to develop into skilled readers, writers, and thinkers, our students need explicit instruction concerning the processes and genre expectations for producing a variety of written texts (Graham & Perin, 2007). They also need to practice the summarizing and argumentation activities that positively impact their comprehension (Graham & Hebert, 2010). However, these writing strategies cannot be limited to the ELA content-area classroom. If we are to help our students develop the skills necessary to meet the demands of college and the workplace, we need to make connected reading and writing activities a part of *every* content-area classroom. Hopefully this chapter has given you a number of ideas about how to use summaries and argumentative writing to enhance content-area learning in your classroom.

Quote:	Explanation:
"One dollar and eighty-seven cents. That was all. And sixty cents of it was in pennies. Pennies saved one and two at a time by bulldozing the grocer and the vegetable man and the butcher. . . . Three times Della counted it. One dollar and eighty-seven cents. And the next day would be Christmas."	This is the best example of foreshadowing because the author reinforces how poor the character is by repeating how much she has: "One dollar and eighty-seven cents." Because it is clear that the holidays are approaching and she has no money, we can expect her to do something desperate to get that money, which she eventually does by cutting her hair!

Coaching for Save the Last Word for Me
The strategy requires that you select a passage of informational or narrative text and provide a focus for reading. I noticed
The strategy requires that you provide students with a focus question. I noticed
The strategy requires that you help students identify a quote that serves as evidence for the focus question. I noticed
The strategy requires that you help students explain the connection between the quote and the focus question. I noticed
This strategy requires that you help students identify how the main actor overcame the barrier or reconciled himself or herself to the situation. I noticed

FIGURE 8.19. Save the Last Word for Me strategy card and coaching template.

CHAPTER 9

Research in the Content Areas

It is nothing short of a miracle that modern methods of instruction
have not yet entirely strangled the holy curiosity of inquiry.
—ALBERT EINSTEIN

In our last chapter we addressed how important connected writing activities
are to our students' comprehension of challenging content-area texts, and we
provided a number of summary and text-based argumentative strategies that
can help students to synthesize and extend their understanding of content-area
material. We also addressed how these strategies provide teachers with a "two-
for-the-price-of-one" instructional benefit: increasing comprehension while also
improving our students' writing quality. However, text-based and summary writing is not sufficient. In order to meet the demands of the CCSS and build the
skills needed for college and beyond, we have to guide our students in sustained
research and inquiry. These opportunities will require that our students connect
personally with content, extend their understanding of the disciplines, and share
their enhanced understanding with others. In short, we need to utilize classroom
practices that nurture Einstein's belief in the centrality of inquiry to our students'
literacy development and motivation to learn.

The CCSS Anchor Standards for Writing highlight this need. In the standards document the authors stress that students must be able to use "research
to build and present knowledge," and they have provided three specific Anchor
Standards that are related to that goal. Anchor Standards 7–9 appear in Figure
9.1.

It is clear from these Common Core writing anchors that content-area teachers must think hard about how to include both short-term and extended research
and inquiry activities into *all* content-area curricula. This makes good sense to us.
The students we teach in college must be able to engage in research and inquiry,
and some cannot. That may be because many schools relegate research activities
to ELA classrooms alone. To be college and career ready, students must learn

Anchor 7	Anchor 8	Anchor 9
Conduct short as well as more sustained research projects based on focused questions, demonstrating understanding of the subject under investigation.	Gather relevant information from multiple print and digital sources, assess the credibility and accuracy of each source, and integrate the information while avoiding plagiarism.	Draw evidence from literary or informational texts to support analysis, reflection, and research.

FIGURE 9.1. CCSS Anchor Standards related to research.

to explore interesting questions in all content areas by finding credible information and synthesizing it accurately and creatively. To equip them to do this,
we have to engage our students with the tools of inquiry that discipline-specific
experts actually use. As Ferretti and Lewis (2013) argue, success in content-area
learning means acquiring discipline-specific ways of reading, thinking, and writing. Teachers who can design instruction that provides insight into disciplinary
knowledge and skills are a must. Research is one such skill.

This might seem to be a daunting challenge! Those teachers who are questioning their ability to integrate more writing might also be concerned about
how to squeeze extended research and inquiry activities into their schedule. Others might struggle with understanding what "research" and "inquiry" actually
mean in their content areas, especially if the standard "research paper" is their
only model. Still others, although currently including research or inquiry activities in their instruction, might be dissatisfied with the results, and/or feel over-
burdened by their demands.

These concerns and questions are understandable, and we have faced these
same questions in our own work with students. The goal of this chapter, therefore, is to provide you with an understanding of what research and inquiry mean
within content-area classes, and to provide you with a number of tools and strategies for helping students use inquiry to enhance and extend their understanding
of content-area material. We begin the chapter by briefly exploring the history of
the research, or "library," paper and contrasting that with the goals of inquiry
and research in the CCSS. We then identify a number of important inquiry tools
that students must become familiar with to be successful researchers in our digi-
tally sophisticated society. Because the relevance and credibility of evidence is an
important part of the CCSS, we offer a framework for helping students evaluate
the evidence they find. We end with a discussion of methods by which students
can share the fruits of their inquiry, including digital formats.

We hope that by the end of the chapter you have a solid understanding of
how to incorporate research into your content area. We hope you will see that real
tools of inquiry are important to student success in college and the workplace.
However, we also hope that by thinking hard about how to use research and
inquiry in content-area classes you can both fire students' "holy curiosity" and

engage them with the 21st-century literacies that will be critical to their future success.

A Short History of Research in the Content Areas

When we think of "research," what may come to mind for most of us is the standard research paper. Many of us will remember the research papers we wrote in our high school and college courses, the packs of 3″ × 5″ note cards that we used, the construction of outlines, the formatting and citation issues we faced, and—for those of us who are old enough—the tedious typing of pages and use of messy correction fluid on "onion skin" paper. Although many of these images seem dated (particularly typewriters and correction fluid!), the research paper as it is assigned in current secondary classrooms has not significantly changed since its introduction in the 1920s (Davis & Shadle, 2000). However ubiquitous, the formal research paper may be, we believe that it is not always helpful to students, limits teachers' understanding of the forms that research and inquiry can take in the classroom, and is often ineffective for achieving content-area goals. It is certainly insufficient to meet the research and inquiry demands of the CCSS.

The debate about the usefulness of the research paper is not new. As early as 1958, the Shop Talk feature of the *English Journal* contained a robust discussion about the uses and usefulness of this traditional form. Teachers and academics debated when it should be introduced, how many words the papers should be, the number of footnotes it should contain, and, most important, whether it should be used in high schools at all (Burton, 1958). However, a note about a 1957 conference discussion on what to call the research paper is one of the most illuminating elements of this old *English Journal* debate. Burton (1958) writes that during this conference, college and high school teachers agreed that the term "library paper" is a more accurate description than "research paper" because "teachers should not lead students to suppose that they are doing real research when they are in reality doing rather simple reports" (Burton, 1958, p. 291).

Although written over half a century ago, this admission that the research paper is not a legitimate form of inquiry is as relevant today as it was in 1958. Instead of engaging students in research and inquiry activities that build and extend content-area knowledge, much of what we call research is really about producing simple reports on the work that others have already done (Davis & Shadle, 2000). To quote Samuel Johnson yet again, a writer may "turn over half a library to make one book." Fast-forward two centuries and the traditional research report is much the same. It simply repackages what is already known. These reports are often tedious for students—what one author has called an "exquisite torture" (Dellinger, 1989, p. 31)—and unhelpful for teachers, who have a difficult time using the form to extend their students' understanding of important content-area concepts.

A 1967 article on teaching the research paper process inadvertently summed up the problem. Attempting to calm teachers' fears that the research paper is too challenging for high school students, Neman (1967) remarked, "Such a paper, although difficult, is, after all, achieved through the performance of almost *mechanical techniques*" (p. 263). For those of us who are hoping to meet the CCSS demands of deep understanding, analysis, and reflection, the mechanistic and procedural conception of the research paper can be unhelpful at best, and a waste of time at worst. Therefore, as we move forward to incorporate the CCSS research and inquiry demands into our own instruction, we have to answer the question that Dellinger (1989) asked over 20 years ago: "Can we teach our students how to do *real* research instead of tediously 'clipping and stitching' together meaningless reports of others' research?" (p. 32).

"Real Research"

You might be asking yourself what the term "real research" actually means. This is an important question because it can begin productive conversations about how we can change instruction in order to include real research in course design. Real research involves teaching students to use the tools of inquiry that are *actually used* by those in the real world of content-area disciplines. If literacy is the capacity to use the most powerful tools for accessing and conveying important information (Wilhelm, 2010), then our job as content-area teachers is to identify those powerful tools, share them with students, and give them the practice they need to master them.

For instance, in Chapter 8 we highlighted a number of text-based summarizing strategies, including Magnet Summaries, that can help students synthesize multiple resources in their academic research (Shanahan, 2013). Additionally, we explained the CSQT/CSET strategy and how it could be a useful tool for writing extended argumentative compositions that could include research papers, and as a framework for sharing the results of our students' research and inquiry activities with others. These ideas followed naturally from the practices we outlined in Chapter 7 for encouraging text-based discussion. However, even though we believe these text-based discussion and writing strategies are helpful for synthesizing textual information and writing a text-based argument, they are only two tools—among many—that students need in order to collect and convey meaningful information. In addition to using summarizing and text-based writing frameworks such as CSQT/CSET, students need to be given practice using many other tools of inquiry that can help them move from reporting on the research of others to creating and sharing knowledge of their own.

Figure 9.2 represents what we believe are the four categories of inquiry tools that are critical for conducting effective research in content-area classrooms. First, we believe that students must be given practice with the real-life tools of data

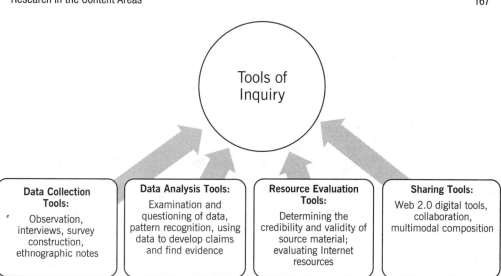

FIGURE 9.2. Tools of inquiry.

collection. We all have used the library and Internet to research information that is important to us, and many of us have had our students do the same. However, we must also help students to think outside the "library paper" framework to include other means of collecting important data, including the use of interviews and surveys, as well as the practices of making field observations, taking notes on what is observed, and collecting relevant artifacts. These ethnographic skills not only help students develop a more comprehensive understanding of real research and inquiry but can also provide them with a deeper understanding of society (Beach & Finders, 1999) and their place within it.

Second, we believe that students must be provided with the skills needed to analyze and question the data they collect and to let their questions and claims emerge from that data. Although we will address this point later in the chapter, we agree that too often students are asked to develop their research questions and claims without first immersing themselves in the data that can best inform their inquiry (Hillocks, 2010, 2011). That is, they make a thesis statement and selectively search for evidence to support it. Inquiry activities are characterized by setting clear research goals, collecting and analyzing data, and then applying what was learned (Graham & Perin, 2007). If students are trying to apply learning before being thoroughly grounded in the data, we believe that they are losing out on the opportunity to understand what research and inquiry mean, as well as the opportunity to utilize the analytic and interpretive skills needed to be successful in college and the workplace.

In conjunction with data analysis skills, students should also be provided with strategies and frameworks for evaluating the relevance and credibility of source material they collect, particularly information they find on the Internet.

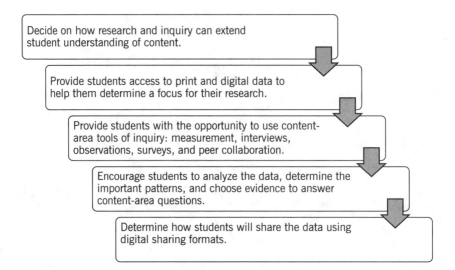

FIGURE 9.3. Research project steps.

Last, they must be provided with a variety of forms for sharing the fruits of their research and inquiry and given practice using digital technology to create multimodal texts—those that creatively combine traditional print with graphics and sound (Karchmer-Klein, 2013). Each of these tools is explained in the sections that follow. However, Figure 9.3 provides a visual depiction of the steps teachers can take to develop content-area research projects that utilize these inquiry tools.

Data Collection Tools

For those of us who have been brought up with the "library paper" as the primary mode of research in high school, it is understandable that we haven't thought much about other modes of inquiry we might use in our content-area classrooms. However, if we are going to meet the demands of the CCSS, engage students in research that creates knowledge (instead of rehashing it), and teaches students to analyze and interpret data, then we are going to have to think more broadly about the tools students use to collect that data. Fieldwork and ethnographic skills (Beach & Finders, 1999) must be part of the mix.

What is fieldwork and what does it look like as a means to collect data in the content areas? In her work on best practices for teaching adolescent writing, writing researcher Dolores Perin (2013) described an instructional study related to the writing of lab reports by secondary science students that serves as a model (Keys, 2000). After studying the concept of soil erosion in the classroom, students made observations and created careful notes about an area surrounding the school that was undergoing significant soil erosion. The students collected data about soil, made careful measurements of the erosion they saw, represented their data in charts, and developed questions and claims by interpreting the data with their peers. Students were then guided in writing a scientific report in which they had to state opinions about what they saw and reinforce them with actual data. In this science classroom, students practiced with the actual tools of scientific inquiry, including scientific measurement practices, as well as the methods by which data are meaningfully represented and shared with others: tables, charts, and graphs, and, eventually, the construction of a scientific report based on these data.

There is more to data than measurement. High school ELA teacher Karen Moynihan (2007) designed a project related to the nonfiction book *The Orchid Thief*. The book explores the subculture of orchid fanatics and the lengths to which some collectors go in acquiring exotic specimens. Wanting students to extend their understanding of this type of subculture and gain facility with legitimate tools of inquiry, Moynihan designed a research project in which students explored one type of "collectible" (i.e., Barbie dolls, comic books, figurines, Pez dispensers, political buttons) and the subculture of people who collect it. In addition to library research, students were encouraged to gather information from collector websites and blogs, as well as from the official websites of the companies that produced the collectible objects that students were interested in.

Moynihan did not stop there. Besides collecting print and digital data, students were encouraged to go to flea markets and events where these objects were traded in order to observe and take notes on the interactions they saw there. Moynihan guided her students in designing short interview protocols, encouraged them to post the questions on collector blogs and websites, and recommended that they conduct personal interviews with knowledgeable collectors. Students in this project were not only meeting the CCSS demands to "gather relevant information from multiple print and digital sources," they were also collecting data with the real-life tools of inquiry that writers and novelists actually use. They were conducting interviews and developing the "people-watching" ethnographic skills of making field observations and notes.

This type of research and inquiry project could also be used in a history classroom. After completing a unit on the Cold War, the Red Scare, and the Cuban Missile Crisis, students could explore multiple print and digital resources about the time period in order to understand the psychological impact of these threats on the American people. They might access old issues of *Life* magazine from the 1950s and 1960s and examine the advertisements in these articles in order to understand what people cared about and what they bought. They might also look for online data related to nuclear bomb testing to track the proliferation of those tests during the Cold War era. Accessing these print and digital texts will provide important information from which students can begin to make sense of this time period. However, to extend their understanding of these threats and their impact on real people, students could design interview questions for adults who lived through those troubling times, questions related to their attitudes toward the former Soviet Union, their fear of nuclear catastrophe, and their experiences related to the Korean or Vietnam War. Once collected and added to the other information that students find, these interviews could round out a rich data set from which important content-specific questions about the Cold War and its impact could then be explored.

Although the ability to interview people is primarily limited to contemporary historical topics, we stress that data collection, analysis, and the public display of evidence in order to back claims are the discipline-specific tools that historians actually use (Monte-Sano & De La Paz, 2012). Furthermore, teaching students interviewing skills can help them understand that historical documents are essentially social interactions, grounded in specific social and historical contexts (Wineburg, 1991). The dialogic interactions required to plan and carry out a successful interview reinforce the skills that historians use to make sense of texts, which include looking at the biases of those being studied and the context in which they are embedded, and comparing what interviewees say with other data that students find. These are the "sourcing," "contextualization," and "corroboration" skills that Wineburg (1991) identifies as being essential to disciplinary thinking in history.

Data Analysis Tools

One of the most important research and inquiry tools is the ability of students to engage in analyzing and interpreting multiple sources of data to make and support argumentative claims. Because of the increased availability of information, researchers believe that students must be taught to "work across" resources in order to synthesize and create meaning (Goldman, 2009). However, writing researcher George Hillocks (2010, 2011) argues that few students are taught this critical skill in high school. This can be a significant problem since this type of thinking is clearly part of the CCSS Anchor Standards related to research. Instead of developing claims and important questions by immersing themselves in data first, Hillocks claims that most students are asked to form their ideas about content-area questions in a data-less vacuum. For instance, in a biology classroom students might be asked to take a side on the question of whether genetically modified plants are helpful or harmful *before* they are asked to explore data related to the question. Such data include yield levels of modified versus unmodified plants, data related to environmental impacts of genetically modified crops, costs of modified versus unmodified seeds, and interview data from the farmers whose livelihoods depend on these products.

In an ELA classroom, a teacher may ask her students to commit to whether they believe that the ending of *Huckleberry Finn* is flawed *before* they are asked to immerse themselves in the critical conversations about the book that are occurring in literary journals, academic and personal blogs, and other digital and print sources of literary analysis. In a history classroom, students might be asked to develop an opinion on whether the financial difficulties our country is currently undergoing are similar to those of the Great Depression *before* looking at unemployment numbers, stock market averages, or interview data from individuals who were impacted by the events of either era. Unfortunately, these data-less prompts are often a part of state assessments of writing because critical content knowledge is often purposely left out so as not to give an advantage to those students with more background knowledge (Hillocks, 2002). However, when these data-less approaches are adopted by content-area teachers, they can reinforce bad habits in students, and they are not representative of the discipline-specific inquiry activities they will be required to complete in college.

Instead of conditioning our students to form opinions first, without looking at data, Hillocks (2010, 2011) believes that teachers must first engage them in the interpretation and analysis of sets of data from which important questions and claims can then emerge. He lays out a framework for inquiry that we find quite helpful. The process he describes is represented graphically in Figure 9.4.

In Hillocks's model, students should be provided the opportunity to examine data related to important content-area concepts. They should be encouraged by their teachers to look for patterns in the data, ask questions related to what they see, and reexamine the data set in order to form answers to these questions or develop an argumentative claim. Students should then be encouraged to go back into the data to choose relevant examples that support their answer and claims.

What might classroom inquiry look like given this framework? Here is an example drawn from one of our YA literature classes at the University of Delaware. Bill Lewis wanted to engage his students—all preservice ELA teacher

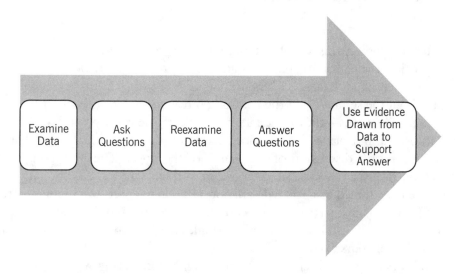

FIGURE 9.4. Hillocks's process for using data.

candidates—in an inquiry activity related to the importance of the science fiction and fantasy genres to adolescent readers, and wanted to have them apply what they found to an evaluation of the award-winning YA fantasy/sci-fi novel *Going Bovine* by Libba Bray (2009). Understanding how to meet the needs of young adults through strategic literature choices is a key focus of this course, and therefore providing preservice ELA teachers practice in the evaluation of YA literature is a primary course goal.

Instead of asking students to engage in an uninformed discussion about whether *Going Bovine* meets the needs of YA readers without researching data relevant to the question, Bill had his students *examine the data*. Groups of class members examined a number of sources: the 2012 Teens' Top Ten Nominations book list (Young Adult Library Services), several YA fantasy and sci-fi literature blogs written by teens, and a few written by knowledgeable adults (teachers, media specialists, and YA literature fans). From these data, Bill encouraged his students to *ask questions* about what they saw in collaborative groups, specifically focusing on what adolescents and YA literature enthusiasts believe makes an effective fantasy or sci-fi novel.

Students then *reexamined the data* to begin developing evaluative criteria in their small groups based on their research. Then as a full class they decided on the following criteria from the data they collected:

1. The novels of this genre must involve an important quest.
2. The use of magic or technology in the novels must be engaging but believable.
3. The choices of the main characters must have global significance (choices that can save or end the world, instead of saving or ending a relationship).
4. The main characters should be flawed but must grow and change across the course of the novel.

After developing this set of criteria, students were now better prepared to make a critical evaluation of the novel and *answer the question* about whether it meets the needs of adolescent readers. Instead of inventing a thesis statement in a vacuum about the suitability of the text for YA readers—a practice against which Hillocks (2011) warns—these students were able to use research and inquiry to make informed and principled decisions based on data, and they were able to engage in a robust discussion of the merits of the novel. Their opinions were founded on relevant criteria that emerged from their data set. Additionally, for those time-constrained teachers who are not sure that research and inquiry activities can fit into their instructional schedules, this inquiry and discussion activity took only 1 hour of instructional time—a single class session—while accomplishing a number of course goals.

Besides being an efficient use of time, highly motivating to students, and clearly related to content-area goals, this example also meets the demands of the

CCSS surrounding research and inquiry. The activities are related to focused content-specific questions (Writing Anchor Standard 7) and require students to gather, analyze, and evaluate relevant information from a variety of sources (Writing Anchor Standard 8) and to draw evidence from literary or informational texts to support analysis, reflection, and research (Writing Anchor Standard 9). Unlike the "clip and stitch" approaches critiqued by Dellinger (1989) that were described at the beginning of this chapter—through which students merely repackage information from others' work—here students are able to create their own knowledge through research and inquiry activities.

Data Evaluation Tools

Although the data collection and analysis tools are important, it is also clear that we need to teach students the skills to evaluate the resources they find, particularly those found on the Internet. Content-area teachers at the high school level certainly know that the Internet is both a boon and a curse when it comes to student research and inquiry—a boon because of the quick and easy access to information, but a curse because of the vast differences in the quality and credibility of information found there. Although the ubiquity of electronic information provides students with an increased opportunity to draw on multiple information sources, researchers agree that the need to evaluate those sources has also increased (Goldman, 2009). Therefore, providing students with practice evaluating data *before* they begin the inquiry process is crucial to their development as researchers.

Although it may seem counterintuitive, one excellent resource for teaching students these evaluation skills is the use of purposely fictitious websites that can be found on the web itself. Whenever we talk about evaluating source material with teacher education students, we always make sure to show them a number of questionable Internet resources on which to practice their evaluative skills. One of our favorite fake websites is an alternative site about the city of Mankato, Minnesota (*http://city-mankato.us*). Not only does this site provide inaccurate (and humorous) information about the balmy 70-degree average winter temperatures of the town, its extensive underwater city in the middle of the Minnesota River, and its circa 1300 B.C. pyramid that now serves as the state university campus, it also provides teachers the opportunity to help their own students evaluate the information on the Internet for its accuracy and its validity. A similar site that we recommend is the Save the Pacific Northwest Tree Octopus site (*http://zapatopi. net/treeoctopus*), which contains similarly false but entertaining information about tree-climbing octopi and the means by which concerned citizens can get involved in the preservation of this rare species. What is chilling about this site is the fact that many proficient adolescent readers, prompted to examine its contents, accepted them at face value (Leu & Castek, 2006).

However, besides having exemplars of obviously inaccurate websites on which to practice their skills, it is also important for students to be provided with a framework for making these evaluations on their own. One of the better heuristics that we have found is from Frank Cioffi's text on argumentation (2005), in which he provides a helpful guideline for making decisions about the credibility of Internet resources. In order to help teachers understand this evaluation process we have turned these guidelines into a step-by-step flow chart, with the first two steps represented in Figure 9.5. Using the flow chart, we can evaluate one of the fake Internet sources that we just mentioned, the site for the Pacific Northwest tree octopus. Asking ourselves whether the site has an author, we see that it does (Lyle Zapato). However, following Cioffi's suggestion, we then Googled the author's name, which elicited a number of hits, with many of the results containing words such as "fake," "myth," and "fictitious." After our first question, therefore, we are already quite suspicious about the credibility of this site and the accuracy of the information it contains. Moving on to our second question, we see that Zapato is not associated with a government agency or university. Instead, the site mentions that he is associated with the highly suspect Wild Haggis Conservation Society, another mark against the credibility of this resource. (Haggis is a Scottish dish that sometimes contains calf offal—in other words, B.S.!)

Our third and fourth questions are represented in Figure 9.6. This set of questions encourages us to evaluate the spelling and language usage of the site

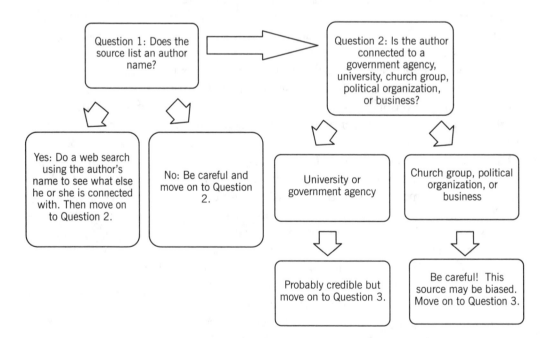

FIGURE 9.5. Analyzing Internet sources: Questions 1 and 2.

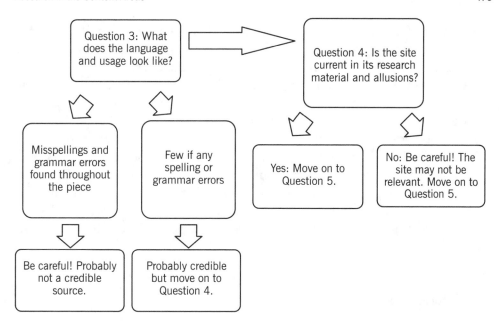

FIGURE 9.6. Analyzing Internet sources: Questions 3 and 4.

and to look for obvious misspellings or grammar errors. Although the site's text is impeccably worded and spelled, a quick check on the Links tab brings us links to the "yeti crab," the "flying squid," and "fur-bearing trout," descriptions of which reinforce the absurdity of the information contained within the site as a whole. The site does contain updated information, which is the focus of question 4, including recent blog postings.

However, question 5 (see Figure 9.7) raises yet another red flag, since the site contains a banner ad for the book *Aluminum Foil Deflector Beanie: Practical*

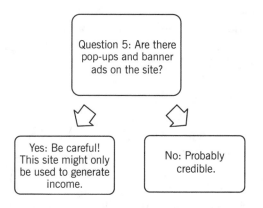

FIGURE 9.7. Analyzing Internet sources: Question 5.

Mind Control Protection for Paranoids (Zapato, 2003). The inclusion of this advertisement makes this more likely to be a site focused on making money instead of offering legitimate information about an endangered species.

Because the site fails a number of the credibility control tests, it is most likely that the information on this site is not accurate and is instead created solely for the reader's entertainment (as well as to make a little money for the site designer). However, as Cioffi (2005) states, even though a site fails a number of these tests, it does not necessarily mean that the site and its information are worthless. It is just that we have to approach it with a more critical and discerning eye. For those of us who are concerned about helping our students assess the credibility and accuracy of researched sources, which is a focus of Writing Anchor Standard 8, Cioffi's evaluation framework can give students practice in developing these critical analysis skills.

Data Sharing Tools

After being provided access to the tools that allow them to collect and analyze data and evaluate the credibility of their source material, students must be allowed to develop facility with the modern tools of sharing their data with others. Although our 1967 term-paper-writing guide assures teachers that once data are collected, the "hardest work is already behind" and that the paper can "tend to almost write itself" (Nemen, 1967, p. 268), teachers who desire to meet the demands of the CCSS must provide their students much more experience with the modern tools that allow them to share knowledge. These go well beyond the standard research paper. Not only must students be able to share what they find by writing in a variety of genres—argumentative, expository, and narrative—they must also be able to use digital technology to interact, collaborate on projects, and share (Dalton, 2012). As Ranker (2007) points out, in an increasingly digital world literacy practices are more likely to take place on a screen instead of on a page. Our colleague Rachel Karchmer-Klein highlights the importance of teaching students how to compose using multimodal digital texts (those using pictures, text, graphics, sound, and hyperlinks) if they are going to develop the 21st-century skills they need to be successful in this digital environment. And as Dalton (2012) maintains, students must come to think of themselves as *designers* of multimedia texts and to develop the critical knowledge of how different "modes carry meaning" when communicating with others. Many standard research projects do not encourage students to take on this new and important designer's role.

We believe it is essential to consider the literacy skills that students use to share their research because too often there is a divide between school-like literacies and those that are used in real life. We also believe that this divide can significantly undermine the importance of what happens in school in the minds of our adolescent students, reducing their motivation for the research and inquiry tasks that are important to their development. For example, several years ago one of our children was given a research assignment in a math class that involved creating a poster about a famous mathematician. Students in his class were asked to research their mathematician, highlight four important aspects of that person's life using text and pictures, and connect what they found to some of the concepts they had covered in that year's class. However, although the posters were "multimodal," in that they combined text and pictures, there were no digital elements to the project, and students in the course were required to *handwrite* the informational blurbs on their posters in order to prevent blatant plagiarism from Internet sources. Plagiarism is a significant problem for adolescent writers (Perin, 2013); however, by cutting off the digital production and design methods that are so important to adolescents and to content-area experts—including the very basic use of word processing—projects such as these have the effect of widening the divide between school literacies and real-world literacies. As biologist E. O. Wilson has stated, projects such as these are more about the "doing of school" instead of doing what happens in the real world of the disciplines (cited in Wilhelm, 2010, p. 13).

We would suggest that a better method for sharing student information might be for teachers to encourage their students to use Web 2.0 tools. Web 2.0 is a general term for technologies, like blogs and wikis, that allow authors to create and share their work with audiences but also allow those audiences to collaborate with the author and respond to what has been created (Karchmer-Klein, 2013). Because of how rapidly technology changes, a detailed discussion of current technology would quickly date this chapter. However, we provide some examples of how we might use technology as a general framework for sharing student research so that you can integrate the most current technology into your own instruction.

For instance, instead of individually creating a handwritten *paper* poster on famous mathematicians, groups of students might instead work collaboratively on a Glogster *digital* poster about that mathematician. The Glogster tool (found at *http://edu.glogster.com*) is an online platform for students and teachers to share information through creative multimodal mixes of text, photos, music, graphics, videos, and other attached data files. Once they are created, students and teachers can embed these digital interactive posters in class websites or blogs, Facebook pages or tweets, or in a teacher's digital library. Projects such as these meet the CCSS demands for research and writing much more effectively than our paper mathematician project. They help students to integrate multiple print and digital resources (Writing Anchor 7) to convey complex ideas and information through the selection and organization of content (Writing Anchor 2) and to use technology to "produce and publish writing and to interact and collaborate with others" (Writing Anchor 6). Also, for those of us who have had to throw away countless yellowing and peeling student-created posters at the end of a school year, the ability to collect and share student inquiry through digital means can be an efficient and effective means to manage student work—not to mention saving it to inform the work of future students.

Similarly, data about the lives of mathematicians might be presented in a digital narrative format. Karchmer-Klein (2013) identifies two such applications for iPads. These are the *Toontastic* and *iBook Author* apps, which allow students to create multimodal digital stories that include the ability to add video and sound and, in the case of *Toontastic*, to animate their stories by adding music, dialogue, and movement. Through use of these digital storytelling tools, students can select the most important elements of their mathematician's life and illustrate them in a way that conveys the individual's significance to the overall development of mathematics. Additionally, the ability of students to transform the informational texts that were the focus of this inquiry project into narrative ones—a process that reading expert Kylene Beers calls "text reformulation" (Beers, 2002, p. 160)— provides students practice in making inferences, and in identifying main ideas, themes, and causal relationships (Beers, 2002). Although Karchmer-Klein (2013) warns that teachers must help students avoid the pitfalls of focusing only on the "bells and whistles" of these digital tools instead of on selecting modes that lead to a unified message, we believe that Web 2.0 applications offer our students a means to share the fruits of their research and inquiry activities in ways that bridge the gap between real-life literacies and those that students use in school. And as technology continues to develop, the possibilities for real-world sharing will continue to grow.

A Word about Collaboration as a Tool of Inquiry

One of the common threads in many of the research and inquiry activities in this chapter is that they involve substantive collaboration and sharing among students. Whether it be researching and debating in groups to develop evaluative criteria for a YA sci-fi text; collecting, discussing, and writing about erosion data as a science class; or designing, sharing, and commenting on electronic posters that represent the lives and accomplishments of famous mathematicians on a math classroom blog; effective research and inquiry involves the co-construction of understanding with other people. Unfortunately, research and writing in secondary classrooms is often carried out as a solitary pursuit limited to interactions between teacher and student (Boscolo & Gelati, 2013), with students reminded to do their own work and to think for themselves (Dellinger, 1989).

This conception does little to foster the interactive communication needed to motivate students, or to build literate communities of practice that (1) use research and writing as a means of extending student understanding of content-area concepts and (2) serve as a means of self-expression and relationship building inside and outside the classroom (Newell, Beach, Smith, & VanDerHeide, 2011; Nolen, 2007). In our work as academics and in our professional development work, most, if not all, of the important research and professional projects that we are involved in happen collaboratively. Your reading of this book is certainly proof of that, and its quality would be significantly diminished without the collective expertise of all of us working together. However, collaborative projects are not limited to the work done in schools or in academic pursuits. Most workplace writing takes place in collaboration with others (Hart-Landsberg & Reder, 1995; Perin, 2013), and much of that collaboration happens at a distance via the use of technology (Schriver, 2012). Furthermore, research demonstrates that when collaborative arrangements are used in writing instruction, and students can help other students with critical components of the writing process, writing quality improves (Graham & Perin, 2007). Because of its links with the real world of the disciplines and the workplace, and because of the overall improvement of individual writing skills, it is no wonder that the CCSS identify collaboration—and the use of technology as a vehicle for that collaboration—as one of the writing anchors that are critical for student success.

Final Thoughts

Unlike the formulaic and mechanistic "library paper" described at the beginning of this chapter, real research and inquiry means applying discipline-specific knowledge and tools to questions that are important to students. It means providing students with the real-life tools of inquiry needed to gather and collect data related to those questions and practice in analyzing and representing them. It also means establishing a collaborative framework for students to work together and then share their findings in creative ways. These are the skills that the CCSS specifically target, and content-area teachers will be responsible for incorporating research and inquiry into regular instruction to build the 21st-century skill set that students need to be successful.

CHAPTER 10

Leading for Change

Leaders are best when people barely know they exist.
When their work is done, their aim fulfilled, people
will say, "We did it ourselves!"

—LAO TZU

We work in schools that want to change instruction in order to change student achievement. We work side by side with administrators and teachers, and sometimes we are able to help schools make changes. Sometimes we are not. The fact that we are not always successful has led us to reflect together and to study research on teacher change. In this chapter, we are going to provide a brief primer on the research on teacher learning and change, and then invite you to engage the CCSS as a school-based team, establishing a very specific implementation vision, gathering the resources your plan demands, mapping your plan onto your instructional calendar, creating a comprehensive teacher support system, and eventually linking evaluation to implementation. That's a lot. But that is what it will take.

Changing or Tweaking

Often we get a call from an administrator or coach who says that a group of teachers (sometimes an entire school) has used one of our books in a book study and then launched a change initiative. At other times, a group of teacher leaders who have attended large-scale professional development (PD) with us over time and redelivered to their peers for implementation will invite us to come and observe and then provide an after-school session. All too frequently, what we observe is business-as-usual (BAU) instruction, or BAU with one or two twists and tweaks. Those after-school sessions are typically very awkward; the school is expecting us to celebrate and endorse its model, but we are cornered into comparing what we saw with what we said or wrote. We have had this same experience so many times that we have learned not to accept these invitations without an extensive conversation about exactly what leaders think has actually changed.

We are not the only PD team to experience failure. (And believe us when we say that we try to learn from it!) Actually, the quality of the PD that teachers typically endure is usually so poor that they are accustomed to looking for a tiny tweak, some morsel that they can take away. PD is usually planned and provided locally by individuals whose content knowledge is similar to that of the teachers (Hill, 2009). They may not be able to envision instruction that is different from BAU in their district because they have neither read about, planned, or seen it.

We do not fault school and district leaders for this. We see their numbers dwindling due to budget cuts while their responsibilities increase. They simply lack the time and opportunity to read and study in order to plan or administer high-quality, coherent PD. Unfortunately, however, they tend to adopt multiple innovations at the same time (Guskey, 2009; see also Guskey & Yoon, 2009). This approach can result in either surface-level goals, monitored in quick walk-throughs, with relatively little reflection on whether teachers are learning or instruction is changing (Webster-Wright, 2009).

Make no mistake about our message here. The CCSS are totally new. They are aggressive. Implementation will require wholesale change in how we think about instruction across content areas. It will not be accomplished with a few tweaks.

Barriers

If you have endured much low-quality PD and engaged in selective, incremental changes to your instructional routines, it makes sense to consider what such PD has done to your belief system. Guskey (1986) argues that PD is typically designed without attention to what motivates teachers to actively engage. The Cognitive–Affective Model of Conceptual Change (Ebert & Crippen, 2010; Gregoire, 2003) posits that the main reasons teachers do not change their instruction are

1. From the outset they do not think the PD applies to them personally.
2. Even if they concede its relevance, they lack the skills or motivation to carry out the instruction.

In order for CCSS to be realized in a school, *all* teachers must be convinced that the standards require them to make changes *and* that they will be supported as they do.

An individual might view this combination as a carrot and a stick: The CCSS require that I change my instruction (a stick) but people in my school will help me (a carrot). Though teaching may feel at times like a lonely business, change cannot be. Teacher learning is heavily influenced by social interactions with peers and with PD providers (Marrero, Woodruff, Schuster, & Riccio, 2010). As you build these social interactions, you can create a culture in which participation in PD and experimentation in the classroom co-evolve (Kazemi & Hubbard, 2008).

The CCSS will require something that researchers call collective teacher efficacy (CTE). CTE is the result of long-term, coherent efforts to develop knowledge and practices, allow teachers to collaborate and share their skills, examine the relationship between practice and achievement, and involve teachers in decision making (Brinson & Steiner, 2007). CTE demands both *knowledge* from outside the school (like the contents of this book) and *process* inside the school.

Creating a Specific Vision

We are going to provide you with a road map for building CTE, using our vision of CCSS implementation as a case study. If you engage with us here, you will be able to see whether you're ready to embrace this model. If you are not, please keep searching. Achieving high-level, meaningful, flexible knowledge and skills for students requires a substantially new vision. Figure 10.1 provides our vision for transforming middle school and high school experiences for students.

You will see that the core of our vision is not reading or writing, but knowledge. Literacy is a tool to build knowledge, not an end in itself. That's why we became literacy researchers. Bill Lewis was a high school English teacher; Sharon Walpole was a high school history teacher; Mike McKenna was (believe it or not) a middle school math *and* English teacher. We each had very strong content-area training. However, we all realized that to achieve our content-area goals, we had to understand the development of reading and writing better. That's what led us from schools to universities.

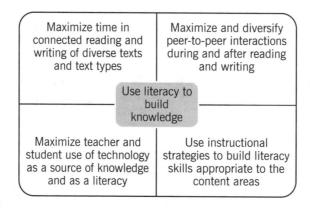

FIGURE 10.1. A new vision for middle school and high school.

In Figure 10.1, you will also see four separate contributors to this mission: time, interaction, technology, and instructional strategies. We thought carefully about interaction and technology as we chose, tested, and recommended instructional strategies, and we have created a short list of strategies that we presented in the first nine chapters of this book. In Figure 10.2 we reprise them for you both as a conceptual review and to show that we mean business when we say that a vision is something specific.

If your school were using this book to establish a schoolwide CCSS initiative, we would expect to see *only* these strategies if we were to visit. Or, before we

How Will You Build Background Knowledge?
• Visual Text? • Concept of Definition? • Semantic Feature Analysis? • Preview? • PreP? • Graphic Organizer? • Concept Map? • Student-Generated Questions?
How Will You Group?
• Whole Class? • Individual? • Pairs? • Homogeneous Small Group? • Heterogeneous Small Group?
How Will Students Read and Collaborate?
• Reading Guide? • Reading Road Map? • PALS? • Reciprocal Teaching? • Jigsaw?
How Will You Plan and Manage Discussion?
• ReQuest? • Questioning the Author? • Collaborative Reasoning? • Discussion Web? • Devil's Advocate?
How Will Students Write to Deepen Understanding?
• Magnet Summary? • RAFT? • SWBS? • CSQT? • Save the Last Word for Me? • "Real" Research?

FIGURE 10.2. Schoolwide instructional strategies.

came, you would have sent us a schoolwide chart like this one, showing exactly which of these instructional strategies you have embraced, along with those additional ones you have selected. A schoolwide instructional vision must be very specific to be enacted.

Gathering the Resources Your Vision Demands

Once you have a vision, the nuts and bolts really matter. We know many effective administrators who spend time creating a vision but realize that they need a partner with a very different skill set to identify the resources that will be required. When you think about resources, think of people, time, texts, and data. Figure 10.3 represents these resources.

People

If you are a leader reading this book, or a teacher working in a school without strong instructional leadership, you may be thinking that this kind of specific vision could never be realized in your school. You might be right. In that case, your school will have to add people to your team, at least temporarily. In our long-term collaborations with schools, we have partnered with administrators and teacher leaders to inform the schoolwide instructional vision; it is that work in middle and high schools that informed the creation of this book. Investment in the people you need is required for change. Since the CCSS is a national movement, you will have choices as you seek out consultants.

All schools spend some of their scant resources on PD for teachers. Some districts sponsor very large conferences on teacher release days, with hundreds of sessions from which teachers may choose. Others send just a few teachers and

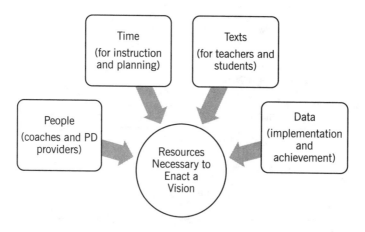

FIGURE 10.3. Resources typically needed for instructional change.

leaders to conferences that require extensive time and travel. It might be more cost-effective for districts to hire full-time PD specialists with very high levels of content expertise to serve many schools. Unfortunately, this may mean that central office instructional supervisor positions go to individuals outside the organization, rather than to those who have worked their way up. We know many, many central office staff members who will readily admit that they were promoted to take a PD position in a content area in which they have no relevant expertise. That practice simply has to stop.

Regardless of whether the school looks outside to consultants or within the district office for a PD designer, teachers are also going to need classroom-level support. The best administrators we know figure out how to reserve one of their teaching positions for a coach. A coach, to us, is an individual whose job is to provide service to teachers, rather than students, by facilitating collaborations outside the classroom and by providing modeling and feedback for work inside the classroom (Walpole & McKenna, 2012). In a schoolwide PD initiative with a vision, the coach's job is to relentlessly support teachers as they attempt to understand and implement the vision.

Time

While no one ever seems to have enough time, leaders can vastly change the time for teaching and learning in schools—if they truly want things to change. Let's think first about time from the perspective of students. Administrators who work with us often ask this question: "How often do you actually expect all teachers to assign reading and writing. Once a week? Once in each unit?" They generally gasp when we say, "Every single day." We work in schools with 90-minute instructional blocks; 90 minutes without meaningful reading and writing is 90 minutes wasted. For 45- to 50-minute blocks, we can envision days linked together. For example, Monday might be used for building background knowledge, but then Tuesday, Wednesday, and Thursday could be devoted to peer-oriented reading, writing, and researching. That would leave Friday for sharing or discussion. Either of these plans would be a radical shift in the use of time for nearly every teacher.

This also means a radical shift in the way a teacher plans instruction. Essentially, the real work of teaching will happen during planning, with the actual instructional day being much less teacher focused. That means we need more time for teacher planning and that time has to be used differently. Planning can no longer be the time when teachers make copies or phone calls; they actually have to be engaging collaboratively in the design of CCSS lessons. In Delaware, all schools have had to reserve 90 minutes each week for teacher planning during contract hours. While it may have been a painful planning process, schools accomplished it. Therefore, we know that it is possible. And 90 minutes each week is the very least amount of time that teachers will require—assisted, if possible, by a coach. It will also have to be augmented by chunks of paid time in the summer. Given the fiscal realities most school systems currently face, this will be a very hard pill to swallow. But if we don't change what we are doing, we are not going to get different results. And the CCSS require different results.

Texts

We have yet to visit a middle school or a high school with adequate text resources for students. Again, the fiscal burden is real here; there is little money for updating textbooks or supplementing with the kind of rich resources students will need *on a daily basis* to meet the cross-textual demands of the CCSS. To get a sense of how important multiple texts are, visit the website of the two organizations designing CCSS outcome tests: the Partnership for Assessment of Readiness for Colleges and Careers (PARCC; *www.parcconline.org*) and the Smarter Balanced Assessment Consortium (SBAC; *www.smarterbalanced.org*). You will see that performance assessments will demand that students synthesize and think across content-area texts *during the exam*; that means this sort of access must become the normal business of school.

Remember that we define *text* broadly. We include traditional print textbooks and trade books, surely, but also visual texts of all kinds as well as texts accessed only electronically. Embracing technology as the source of a wide variety of texts will be essential; that means schools must be wired for access, classrooms must be equipped with Internet-ready devices, and firewalls must allow students to access information outside of the school. Obviously, individual schools will be in different places in their access to technology; they will have to evaluate the costs and benefits of buying print resources and accessing digital ones.

Teachers need texts, too. Those texts must provide access to new knowledge if your vision calls on new knowledge. Though we don't yet see a time when we will have no bookshelves, we can say that nearly all of the information we needed to write this book was accessed electronically through our university libraries. Teachers don't usually have to go to these archival sources, though, and there is more knowledge available to them for free now than ever before. Like students doing "real" research, however, they have to be savvy consumers of web-based knowledge. Figure 10.4 provides a list of our go-to sites.

Data

As CCSS changes are implemented, they will have to be evaluated for their impact. Evaluation demands data. We will suggest a relatively simplistic heuristic for leaders here, represented in Figure 10.5. Clearly, it doesn't make sense to spend time considering data absent a vision and the resources to realize it. Clearly, our idea of schoolwide implementation requires an instructional strategies document like the one in Figure 10.2. And it also clearly requires that teachers have support

The websites listed here contain a variety of resources for professional learning (PL). Most offer materials free for download.

Comprehensive Reading Solutions. Our own open-access site comprising PL modules on a variety of topics. Note in particular the modules on Teaching Technical Vocabulary, Reading Guides, Introduction to Argument, Building Background Knowledge, Reciprocal Teaching, and Peer-Assisted Learning Strategies.

www.comprehensivereadingsolutions.com

Common Core State Standards Initiative. The official site of the CCSS, where you may download the standards, the not-to-be-overlooked appendices, and background reports.

www.corestandards.org

AdLit. This site, developed by WETA in Washington, offers an abundance of information about adolescent literacy. Especially useful are how-to summaries of a variety of research-based instructional techniques.

www.adlit.org

ReadWriteThink. Organized by grade ranges, the IRA's site for professional learning offers lesson plans, strategy guides, webinars, and more.

www.readwritethink.org

Center on Instruction. Sponsored by RMC Research Corporation, a nonprofit with interests in STEM, ELL, and Special Education as well as literacy. The site provides reports, instructional strategy descriptions, and many other resources.

www.centeroninstruction.org

Lexile Framework. Explains how Lexiles work and provides a searchable database of thousands of books and many primary source documents. An analyzer tool allows you to upload any sample of text and obtain the Lexile instantly. Operated by MetaMetrics.

www.lexile.com

FIGURE 10.4. A selection of trustworthy knowledge sources for teachers.

somehow, in the form of coaching. Once these components are all in place, data analysis makes sense. Figure 10.5 requires that student achievement data not be analyzed absent meaningful data on teachers' implementation. We can't go from a vision of instruction to changes in achievement. We have to go from a vision to a nuts-and-bolts plan for realizing it, to sustained implementation. Then and only then can we know whether sustained implementation is associated with desirable outcomes. And we will also know whether specific teachers or teams of teachers are realizing better outcomes by enacting variations on the vision; those variations can then be incorporated by all. Since the CCSS are a very new set of goals for teaching and learning, we recommend that leaders focus on changing instruction to align with the standards first, and analyzing student achievement data later.

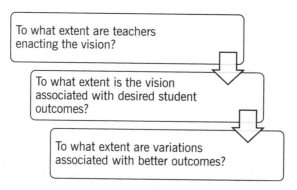

FIGURE 10.5. Rethinking data.

Gathering data on the extent to which teachers are enacting a vision must go beyond simple walk-through checklists. We believe that making a thoughtful match between an instructional goal, a text, and an instructional strategy—on a daily basis across content areas—is the key to realizing our vision for the CCSS. That will mean that some data can be collected in teacher planning time; the products teachers produce together to guide their work will be concrete representations of their understanding of the vision. Additional data can come only from observation. Walk-throughs can help a leader know *whether* teachers are using time and instructional strategies in line with the vision; only longer observations can tell *how well* they are doing so.

Final Thoughts: Making It All Make Sense

We know that this is a lot. You are going to have to pace yourself. In the broad scheme of things, you typically have summer work time to collaborate on your vision and gather the resources you need. During the school year, though, things happen fast. When you have set time for teachers to work together, you can create a blueprint of sorts for that time. Remember to build in cycles; teachers will have to wrestle with the standards, read and discuss new ideas, connect them to their goals for building knowledge, write lesson plans, teach from those plans, and reflect on the extent to which their plans helped them meet their goals. If they do this together, with the help of a coach, their efforts are more likely to yield schoolwide changes in instruction.

We can tell you about one such group, to whom this book is dedicated. They are inspirational to us. They work at William Penn High School in New Castle, Delaware. They include Jake Nagy (an experienced English-teacher-turned-coach), Tim Hein (a young history teacher), Megan Bone (a midcareer science teacher), Katie Sabol and Christine View (young math teachers), and their principal, Jeff Menzer.

In year 1, Jeff allowed the teacher team to attend monthly trainings with Bill Lewis and Sharon Walpole. In those trainings, they spent 3 hours in large-group PD sessions and 3 hours in professional learning community collaborations. Each month we taught one of the broad themes in this book: the structure of the standards, understanding text difficulty, building background knowledge, during-reading strategies, discussion, and text-based writing. In between, they went back and tried these things.

In year 2, Jeff assigned them to one team, with a core group of students to share. They agreed to use a small set of instructional strategies fairly exclusively. They met as a professional learning community (PLC) and problem-solved. They worked through issues with other state and local mandates. They figured out how to make it work. And they met with Sharon periodically for support.

In year 3, Jeff moved Jake from the classroom to a coaching position. The team was disbursed, but they were tasked as PLC leaders for the rest of the 9th- and 10th-grade teachers. Jake worked with Sharon and with Mike McKenna to reshape web-based PD modules to make sure that there was a consistent source of knowledge for teachers. He also decided how to order them. PLC time was reserved for learning. Mike came and did walk-throughs with Jake.

Year 3 also involved intense focus on unit design. Jake decided that content-area teams needed to see what full units looked like. They could use these units to start their instruction in year 4 and also as templates to work together on additional ones. Their goal, in year 4, is to have a schoolwide instructional brand consistent with the demands of the CCSS and the realities of their resources. And we will be right there with them, mostly because our conversations nearly always start with "You'll never believe what happened today." We'll see what happens tomorrow.

Text Set Examples from English Language Arts

After we determine our instructional objective, we pick a set of texts that, taken together, build knowledge through reading and connected writing activities. In ELA instruction there is often a target text, so the other texts in the set are designed to build the background knowledge this text requires. Then we select the instructional strategies and procedures to use for each text, maximizing student responsibility. In the examples that follow, we will show you the choices we made to make the target texts, *A Doll's House* by Henrik Ibsen and *Animal Farm* by George Orwell, accessible to high school ELA students, and map each unit onto a calendar.

Example 1: Male and Female Roles in *A Doll's House* by Henrik Ibsen

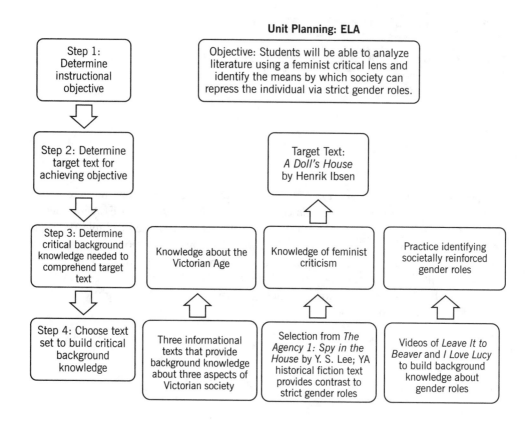

Our Objective

Students will analyze *A Doll's House* using a feminist critical lens and identify the ways that society can repress individuals through strict gender expectations.

First Texts (Video with T-Chart Graphic Organizer)

We begin to build student understanding of societally determined gender roles by showing two short video clips, one from *Leave It to Beaver* and one from *I Love Lucy* (CCRA R.7). While viewing these clips the students will use a T-Chart graphic organizer as a viewing guide. On the left side of the organizer, they will write descriptions of how men are depicted and what activities they engage in. On the right side, students will write descriptions of how women are depicted and the activities they engage in. At the end of the videos, students will share their observations with the teacher, who will compile responses on the board while clarifying and leading a short discussion of the gender roles of the 1950s.

Second Texts (Differentiated Informational Text Set, with Magnet Summaries)

We build more specific knowledge of the Victorian Age and gender expectations through the use of differentiated informational texts. The teacher assigns students to homogeneous reading groups based on reading ability. For those reading below grade level, students will be reading a two-page Internet text on Victorian manners. On-grade-level readers will be reading a three-page magazine article on Victorian entertainment. Above-grade-level readers will be reading a longer section of an academic discussion of Victorian corsets and their relationship to the oppression of women (CCRA R.10). After students read their articles in groups, each group will write a Magnet Summary of their informational text. They will then jigsaw to form heterogeneous groups to combine the sentences from all groups into a magnet paragraph (CCRA W.2). Groups will share magnet paragraphs with the whole class and discuss the main qualities of the Victorian era. The teacher will make connections between the Victorian Age and the 1950s era depicted in the video texts.

Third Text (Canonical Target Text, RAFT Strategy)

Now that students have enough background information about societally determined gender roles and the Victorian Age, they are now ready to begin reading *A Doll's House*. Before reading Act I, the teacher will preview the reading with the Listen–Read–Discuss strategy and a focus question that encourages students to see how each character takes on a specific gender role. They will start reading Act I of the text in pairs, each member of the pair taking either the male or female lead and determining the gender roles that each character plays (CCRA R.1, R.2). After reading the act, students will complete a RAFT (CCRA W.2, W.4) for their roles:

Role: Nora Helmer (female lead character)
Audience: Herself
Format: Diary entry
Topic: My marriage to Torvald

Role: Torvald Helmer (male lead character)
Audience: Himself
Format: Journal entry
Topic: My marriage to Nora

Fourth Text (Contemporary YA Text, CSQT Argumentative Writing)

After reading the first act of *A Doll's House*, the teacher has students read several selections from *The Agency 1: Spy in the House* by Y. S. Lee in Reciprocal Teaching (RT) groups. As we stated in Chapter 4, this text features a main female character who works outside the strict gender boundaries of the Victorian era. The teacher will provide students with the following purpose before reading: Do you believe this Victorian woman plays a gender role that is similar to or different from Nora's in *A Doll's House* (CCRA R.2, R.9)? Using the CSQT strategy, students will construct a short argument using textual evidence drawn from both books (CCRA W.1).

Fifth Texts (Two Video Versions of *A Doll's House*, Venn Diagram, Informational Writing)

To provide students with experience comparing interpretations of a source text (CCRA R.7, R.9), students will view two versions of Act II of *A Doll's House*. For the first half of the act students will view the 1973 version starring Jane Fonda, and for the second half they will view the 1992 BBC version. Students will be asked to focus on the interpretations of the characters in each version, with female students focusing on the depiction of Nora and male students focusing on the depiction of Torvald. Students will complete a Venn diagram to organize the differences and similarities in the two video interpretations of the source material and write a short informational paragraph explaining the similarities and differences.

Instructional Calendar for *A Doll's House* by Henrik Ibsen

Day 1
As a large group, students will view video clips of *Leave It to Beaver* and *I Love Lucy*, complete a T-Chart, and discuss men's and women's societally determined roles in the video texts.

Day 2
In small homogeneous groups, students will read one of three informational texts on the Victorian era and complete magnet sentences and magnet paragraphs for each of the three texts.

Day 3
In pairs, students will read Act I of *A Doll's House*, completing RAFTs for Nora and Torvald that summarize the characters' feelings about their marriage and focusing on the Victorian standard of what marriage should be.

Day 4
In RT groups, students will read selections from *The Agency 1: Spy in the House*. Groups will complete CSQT argumentative writing on whether main character is similar to or different than Nora from *A Doll's House*.

Day 5
Students will view two video versions of Act II. Students will complete a Venn diagram comparing and contrasting how the video texts depict Nora and Torvald as characters, and the way that each character interprets his or her gender role.

Day 6
Based on their Venn diagrams, students will cowrite an informational text comparing and contrasting the two video depictions of these characters and engage in a discussion of the characters and their roles based on their paragraphs.

Day 7
Students will read the first half of Act III in groups of five, each student taking one of the five roles. After reading, students will complete a Save the Last Word for Me card for their character. Each card will contain a quote from the character that best represents the character's understanding of his or her gender role and an explanation of that quote.
Day 8
Students will read the second half of Act III in pairs. After students complete the play, they will write a short argument about whether they believe that Nora's decision to leave Torvald and her children at the end of the play was the correct decision. Based on their arguments, students and teacher will discuss Nora's concluding decision and whether it was correct, and why Ibsen ended the play this way.
Day 9
For homework, students will be asked to conduct a short interview with a family member and ask how that member fought against a societally reinforced gender role. In small groups, students will share their interview information and begin constructing a Glogster poster that depicts what they found and compares the interview information to *A Doll's House*.
Day 10
Student groups will finish the Glogster poster and present it to the full class, discussing what they found about gender expectations in *A Doll's House* and the lives of their family members.

Example 2: Totalitarianism and the Human Spirit in *Animal Farm* by George Orwell

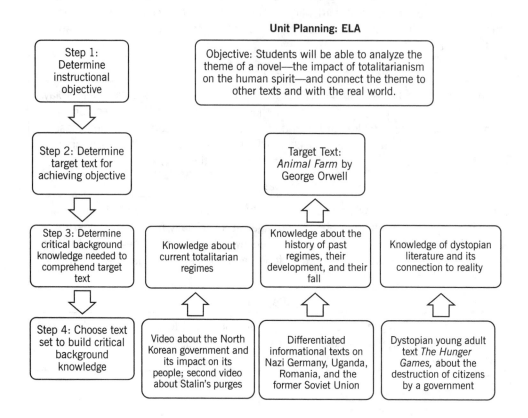

Unit Planning: ELA

Step 1: Determine instructional objective

Objective: Students will be able to analyze the theme of a novel—the impact of totalitarianism on the human spirit—and connect the theme to other texts and with the real world.

Step 2: Determine target text for achieving objective

Target Text: *Animal Farm* by George Orwell

Step 3: Determine critical background knowledge needed to comprehend target text

Knowledge about current totalitarian regimes

Knowledge about the history of past regimes, their development, and their fall

Knowledge of dystopian literature and its connection to reality

Step 4: Choose text set to build critical background knowledge

Video about the North Korean government and its impact on its people; second video about Stalin's purges

Differentiated informational texts on Nazi Germany, Uganda, Romania, and the former Soviet Union

Dystopian young adult text *The Hunger Games,* about the destruction of citizens by a government

Our Objective

Students will analyze the theme of *Animal Farm* by George Orwell: the impact of totalitarianism on the human spirit.

First Text (Video with Informational Writing Activity)

We begin to build student understanding of the impact of totalitarianism on the human spirit by showing excerpts from the National Geographic documentary video *Welcome to North Korea* (CCRA R.7). While viewing these clips, students will use a viewing guide to note examples of the impact of oppression of the North Korean regime on the human spirit. After discussing these examples, students will write a paragraph (CCRA W.2) making a conjecture about how North Korea became such a dysfunctional society and share their conjectures as part of a concluding classroom discussion.

Second Texts (Differentiated Informational Texts on Totalitarianism with Summary Writing)

To build background knowledge about totalitarian regimes, we chose four short informational texts that describe the history of several of these regimes (CCRA R.1, R.10). These texts are differentiated by Lexile and students will be organized into homogeneous "expert" groups based on reading level. Weaker readers will be reading a short article on the rise and fall of the former Soviet Union. Average readers will be reading either a three-page article on the rise of Nazi Germany or an Internet text on the repressive Ugandan government of Idi Amin. Stronger readers will be reading a four-page article on the early years of the Socialist Republic of Romania. After students read their articles in groups, students will be assigned to a "jigsaw" group, each group containing at least one member from each of the "expert" groups. Groups will discuss the similarities between these totalitarian regimes and their impact on the people living there. They will then construct a summary paragraph (CCRA W.2) on the key similarities of these regimes and share it with the class.

Third Text (Canonical Target Text, Informational Writing)

Now that students have enough background information about different forms of totalitarianism and its impact on the individuals living in these societies, they are ready to start reading *Animal Farm*. They will be reading this text in pairs and small groups throughout the unit, and will start reading the opening chapters in small groups with a number of during-reading scaffolding strategies and connected writing activities. Students will begin reading the first chapter of the novel in cooperative groups with a reading guide. This guide encourages students to make connections between the oppression of the animals, the developing philosophy of the character Old Major, the propaganda that supports this new animal government, and the real totalitarian regimes that students read about in their informational texts (CCRA R.9).

Fourth Text (Contemporary YA Text, CSQT Argumentative Writing)

After reading the first six chapters of *Animal Farm* students will read several selections from the popular YA text *The Hunger Games* by Suzanne Collins. This dystopian novel depicts a future totalitarian regime that forces the society to sacrifice some of their children in an annual fight-to-the-death competition. Students will read the selections from the novel in RT groups and be asked whether they believe that the societies in *The Hunger Games* and *Animal Farm* are similar. Using the CSQT strategy, students will construct a short argument using textual evidence drawn from both books to support their opinions (CCRA W.1, R.1).

Fifth Text (Video Text, Viewing Guide Comparison with *Animal Farm*)

Before reading Chapter 7 of *Animal Farm*, which deals with the purging of individual characters from the increasingly oppressive animal society, students will view a short video text on Stalin's purges in the former Soviet Union, and complete a viewing guide to list important facts about Stalin's purges (CCRA R.7). Students will then individually read Chapter 7 of the novel to look for aspects of the purges in *Animal Farm* that are like Stalin's purges (CCRA R.9, R.10).

Instructional Calendar for *Animal Farm* by George Orwell

Day 1
As a large group, students will view documentary video clips from *Welcome to North Korea* and write a short paragraph while they make a conjecture about how the society became this dysfunctional.
Day 2
In homogeneous "expert" groups, students will read informational texts on the former Soviet Union, the Third Reich, Romania, and Uganda under Idi Amin. Then in "jigsaw" groups, students will write a short informational paragraph that summarizes the similarities between these regimes.
Day 3
Students will read the first chapter of *Animal Farm* in homogeneous groups with a reading guide.
Day 4
Students will read Chapters 2 and 3 of *Animal Farm* in heterogeneous groups with a reading guide. Students will construct a summary writing activity that connects these chapters with the history of the totalitarian nations.
Day 5
Students will read Chapter 4, "Battle of the Cowshed," in heterogeneous groups in an RT framework. After reading the chapter, students will make text-to-self/world connections between the ceremonies developed by the animals and ceremonies in our own society.
Day 6
Students will read Chapters 5 and 6 in a PALS reading framework.
Day 7
Students will read selections from *The Hunger Games* in RT groups. After reading, students will construct a CSQT argument on whether they believe the society of *The Hunger Games* is similar to that which is being created in *Animal Farm*.
Day 8
Students will view the short video text on Stalin's purges and complete the left side of their T-Chart. Students will then read Chapter 7 on the farm purges and complete the right side of the chart, comparing both purges and the use of propaganda.

Day 9
Students will read Chapters 8 and 9 in heterogeneous RT groups. After reading, students will summarize the chapters in a Reader's Theater framework that converts the two chapters into a 1-minute dramatic summary and prediction about how the novel will end.
Day 10
Students will read the final chapter with the PALS reading framework and compare their predictions to what happens at the end of the novel. As a summary of the novel, students will be asked to construct a "soundtrack" for the novel, identifying one song per chapter and an explanation of the songs' connections to each chapter of the book.

APPENDIX 2

Text Set Examples from History/Social Studies

After we determine our instructional objective, we pick a set of texts that, taken together, build knowledge through reading and connected writing activities. In history and social studies instruction, the CCSS encourage teachers to use a variety of difficult primary and secondary source texts as the target of instruction. The texts in these sets are designed to build the background knowledge needed for comprehending complicated texts. Then we select the instructional strategies and procedures to use for each text, maximizing student responsibility. In the examples that follow, we will show you the choices we made to make *The Declaration of Independence* and W. E. B. Du Bois's *Niagara Movement Speech* accessible to high school history students, and map each unit onto a calendar.

Example 1: *The Declaration of Independence* and Its Connection to Current Political Debate

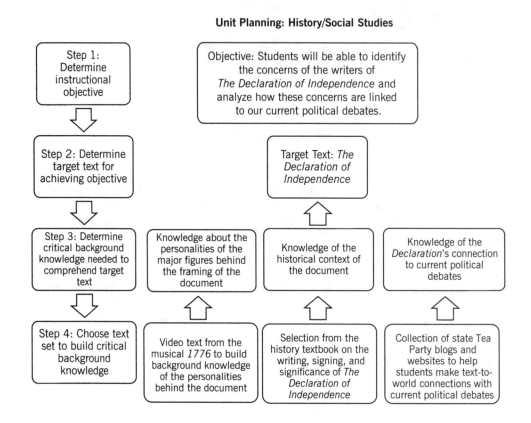

Unit Planning: History/Social Studies

Step 1: Determine instructional objective

Objective: Students will be able to identify the concerns of the writers of *The Declaration of Independence* and analyze how these concerns are linked to our current political debates.

Step 2: Determine target text for achieving objective

Target Text: *The Declaration of Independence*

Step 3: Determine critical background knowledge needed to comprehend target text

Knowledge about the personalities of the major figures behind the framing of the document

Knowledge of the historical context of the document

Knowledge of the *Declaration*'s connection to current political debates

Step 4: Choose text set to build critical background knowledge

Video text from the musical *1776* to build background knowledge of the personalities behind the document

Selection from the history textbook on the writing, signing, and significance of *The Declaration of Independence*

Collection of state Tea Party blogs and websites to help students make text-to-world connections with current political debates

Our Objective

Students will identify the concerns of the writers of *The Declaration of Independence* (CCRA R.1, R.5, R.10) and the impact of the Age of Reason on the framing of the document and its structure. Students will extend their understanding by linking the concerns expressed in the document with the concerns of current political debates.

First Texts (Video with Character Map)

We begin to build student understanding of the political context of the revolutionary time period and the concerns of the primary political players in the writing of the declaration. We show our whole-group students several short video clips from the musical *1776* (CCRA R.7), and while viewing these clips the students will use a viewing guide to describe the main characters: Thomas Jefferson, Benjamin Franklin, and John Adams. Students will share their observations with the class, with the teacher clarifying responses and discussing the personalities and concerns of the characters.

Second Texts (Informational Text with RT Groups and Graphic Organizer)

We build more specific knowledge of the context of *The Declaration of Independence* through the use of the course textbook. The textbook selection addresses the ideas of the Age of Reason and the contextual factors behind the meeting of the Continental Congress, the writing of the *Declaration*, and the document's structure (CCRA R.1, R.2). The teacher assigns students to small heterogeneous RT groups and assigns them a final product for their group work: a graphic organizer on large newsprint that synthesizes the background of the Continental Congress, the *Declaration*, and key vocabulary. Groups will share their graphics for the textbook selection and post them in the classroom to guide the reading of *The Declaration of Independence*.

Third Text (Canonical Target Text and Reading Guide)

Now that students have enough background information on the context, structure, and key vocabulary related to *The Declaration of Independence*, they are now prepared to read the document. In small heterogeneous groups, students will read the declaration with a reading guide that strategically chunks the document into its parts: introduction, conclusion, and the lists of colonist complaints organized by category (CCRA R.1, R.2, R.5). After reading the document, students will share their summaries of each of the *Declaration*'s sections and discuss the colonist concerns, the rhetorical effect of the document's structure, and its link to broader Age of Reason ideas (CCRA R.1, R.2, R.5).

Fourth Text (Internet Texts with Save the Last Word for Me and Informational Writing)

After reading and discussing *The Declaration of Independence*, students in pairs will access the websites of state Tea Party groups that have been identified by the teacher. Using their reading guide from *The Declaration of Independence*, students will identify key quotes from the websites that are linked to the specific colonist complaints and write those quotes on one side of a 3″ × 5″ card (CCRA R.7, R.9). Then, students will explain the link between these quotes and the specific complaints of the colonists during the American Revolution. Student pairs will then use the information on these cards to write a short informational composition that compares the concerns of the revolutionary time period with the concerns of these political groups (CCRA W.2, W.9)

Instructional Calendar for _The Declaration of Independence_

Day 1
As a large group, students will view video clips of the movie musical _1776_ and complete character map graphic organizers for Thomas Jefferson, John Adams, and Benjamin Franklin.

Day 2
In small heterogeneous RT groups, students will read a textbook selection on the background and structure of _The Declaration of Independence_ and create a graphic organizer that synthesizes the information.

Day 3
In heterogeneous groups, students will read the entire text of _The Declaration of Independence_ with a reading guide.

Day 4
In pairs, students will access state Tea Party websites and complete Save the Last Word cards for concerns that are shared between these groups and those of the time of the American Revolution. Students will write a composition that compares these concerns.

Day 5
Full-class discussion of _The Declaration of Independence_ and its impact on current political debates.

Example 2: The Progressive Era, Injustice, and Inequality

Unit Planning: History/Social Studies

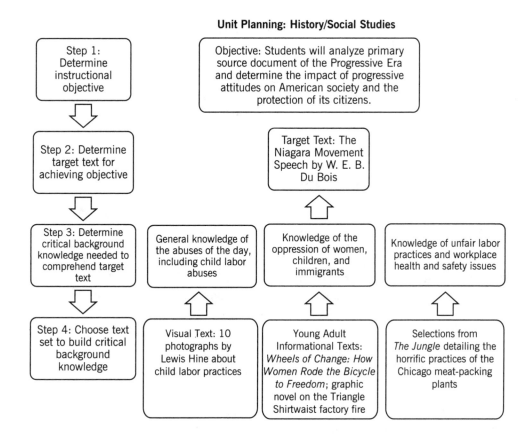

Our Objective

Students will analyze primary and secondary source documents of the Progressive Era and determine the impact of progressive attitudes on American society, and the rights of citizens, including the right to racial equality.

First Texts (Primary Source Photographs with Graphic Organizer)

We begin to build student understanding of the abuses of the time period with 10 photographs from Lewis Hine that are focused on child labor (CCRA R.7). We show our whole group of students the 10 photographs while students complete a viewing guide where they identify the subject of the photograph, the most important detail of the photograph, and a theme or message that the photograph is trying to convey. After students are finished viewing the photographs, they will write a short summary paragraph based on individual themes they identified in the set of photographs that tell them something about the era these children lived in (CCRA W.2). Students will share their themes with the full class.

Second Texts (YA Nonfiction Texts and Reading Guides on Women's Rights)

In homogeneous RT groups, students will read three nonfiction selections from the YA nonfiction texts. The strongest readers will read selections from *Wheels of Change: How Women Rode the Bicycle to Freedom* by Sue Macy. The middle group of readers will read selections from *Kids at Work: Lewis Hine and the Crusade Against Child Labor* by Russell Freedman. Weaker readers will read selections from the graphic nonfiction text *The Triangle Shirtwaist Factory Fire (A Graphic History)* by Jessica Gunderson, Charles Barnett III, and Phil Miller (CCRA R.1, R.2). After students read their selections, they will develop a poster to share with the class that depicts the dangers and abuses of the age regarding women, children, and immigrants, and how these abuses began to change during the Progressive Era.

Third Text (Canonical Literature Selections with Reading Guide)

Individually, students will read three selections from *The Jungle*, by Upton Sinclair (CCRA R.10). This canonical text graphically depicts the unfair labor practices of Chicago meatpacking plants and the dangers those practices posed to workers and consumers. The three sections that detail the horrific conditions in the plants are accompanied by a reading guide that helps students focus on the most important elements of the reading and summarize and synthesize the information about the industry abuses that is highlighted in the three sections. Students and teacher will engage in a discussion of the abuses (CCRA R.1, R.2, W.2).

Fourth Text (Target Primary Source Document and Informational Writing)

In PALS reading pairs, students will read the Niagara Movement Speech by W. E. B. Du Bois (CCRA R.10). This speech highlights the oppression of African Americans during this era and demands that they are provided the same rights as other Americans. A reading guide will help students compare and contrast the fight for racial equality during this era with the fight for women's, children's, and immigrant rights that is detailed in the other texts (CCRA R.9).

Fifth Text (Student-Created Multimedia Text)

Using their reading guide from the W. E. B. Du Bois speech, students will work in small groups to construct a multimedia presentation that compares and contrasts the fight for racial equality with the fight for children's, women's, and immigrants' rights. The presentations can include digital pictures from the Internet, Progressive Era songs, and other sounds and/or images that convey the similarities and differences (CCRA W.7-W.9).

Instructional Calendar for the Progressive Era

Day 1
As a large group, students will view 10 photographs from Lewis Hine depicting the abuses of child labor. Students will complete a graphic organizer that helps them analyze the messages of the photos. In homogeneous reading groups students will then read one of three informational texts that provide information on child labor, women's rights, and immigrants' rights.
Day 2
In their small homogeneous groups, students will construct posters that summarize and synthesize the information from their nonfiction readings and share with the class.
Day 3
Individually, students will read three selections from *The Jungle* by Upton Sinclair with a reading guide and engage in a full-class discussion of the labor abuses and safety issues of the age.
Day 4
In PALS reading pairs, students will read the Niagara Movement Speech by W. E. B. Du Bois and begin to identify the similarities and differences between the fight for racial equality in this speech and the fight for the rights of children, women, and immigrants.
Days 5 and 6
In small research groups, students will use their graphic organizers from day 4 to construct a digital presentation that compares and contrasts the fight for racial equality with that of other groups. It should include photos, songs, and other types of digital media that illustrate the similarities and differences.

Text Set Examples from Science

After we determine our instructional objective, we pick a set of texts that, taken together, build knowledge through reading and connected writing activities. Then we decide on the instructional strategies and procedures to use for each text, maximizing student responsibility. In the examples that follow, we will show you the choices we made to make our units on cell division and earthquakes accessible to high school science students, and map each unit onto a calendar.

Example 1: Cell Division and the Impact of Environmental Factors on the Process

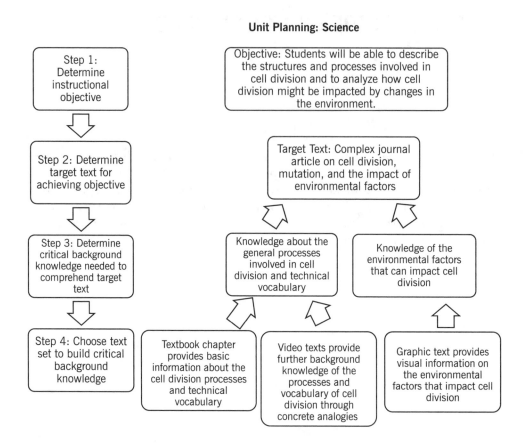

Unit Planning: Science

Step 1: Determine instructional objective

Objective: Students will be able to describe the structures and processes involved in cell division and to analyze how cell division might be impacted by changes in the environment.

Step 2: Determine target text for achieving objective

Target Text: Complex journal article on cell division, mutation, and the impact of environmental factors

Step 3: Determine critical background knowledge needed to comprehend target text

Knowledge about the general processes involved in cell division and technical vocabulary

Knowledge of the environmental factors that can impact cell division

Step 4: Choose text set to build critical background knowledge

Textbook chapter provides basic information about the cell division processes and technical vocabulary

Video texts provide further background knowledge of the processes and vocabulary of cell division through concrete analogies

Graphic text provides visual information on the environmental factors that impact cell division

Our Objective

Students will be able to describe the structures and processes involved in cell division and analyze how cell division might be impacted by changes in environment.

First Text (Classroom Textbook with Six-Step Graphic Organizer)

We begin to build the appropriate background knowledge by using the classroom textbook to get an overview of the process of mitosis and the "gist" of the steps in the asexual reproduction of cells (CCRA R.2). Students are divided into heterogeneous reading groups, each group provided with graphic organizers that represent the six phases of cell division covered in the reading selection. Students will complete their graphic organizers in these reading groups and discuss the phases of mitosis as a whole group.

Second Texts (Video Texts with Argument)

We now build more specific knowledge of mitosis with video texts. We found four different student-created analogies that we captured from YouTube. All of the videos compare the process of mitosis to something easier for students to understand: a soccer team tryout, a house, a 1970s-style athletic tube sock, and a synchronized swimming contest. As a whole group, students will utilize a six-section reading guide similar to the one they used for the textbook reading (CCRA R.4, R.7). Each student will be responsible for identifying the elements of the analogies that are related to the six steps in the process of mitosis. Then in groups, students discuss the analogies and decide which of the four videos they believe is the most comprehensive depiction of the process given their reading of the biology text. Students will write an argument that supports their opinion on which video is the best and share it with the whole group (CCRA W.1).

Third Text (Data Table and Summary Writing)

Now that students have enough background information about the process of mitosis, and the content vocabulary to talk about it (CCRA R.4), we give students a complex data table in heterogeneous groups (CCRA R.7). The data table presents information about the impact of environmental factors on mitosis. We ask students to evaluate the chart and write a short summary composition on the environmental factors that would most likely lead to mutation and cancer.

Fourth Text (Journal Article and Extended Metaphor)

Students are now ready to read the journal article on the impacts of the environment on mitosis. In PALS reading pairs, students will read the six-page article and summarize the impact of environment on the process of cell division (CCRA R.2, W.2). To extend their understanding of mitosis, students will create an original metaphor for these cell division processes, which include the possibility of mutation, and present their metaphors to the class using a digital format (CCRA W.6).

Instructional Calendar for Cell Division

Day 1
In small heterogeneous reading groups, students will read the textbook section on mitosis and highlight the six steps on a graphic organizer. After reading, students and teacher will discuss the steps of the process.
Day 2
As a full group, students will view four different student-created videos that compare mitosis to another object or concept. Using their knowledge of the process from day 1, students will create a short argument that supports one of the videos as being the best depiction of the process.

Day 3
In heterogeneous reading groups, students will analyze a chart on the impacts of environment on mitosis and write a short summary on the factors most likely to impact mitosis.

Day 4
In PALS reading pairs, students will read a complex journal article on the impact of environmental factors on mitosis, including the possibility of mutations that cause cancer. Students will produce their own metaphor of the process, which includes the possibility of mutation.

Day 5
Students will work on metaphors and present their metaphors for discussion to the whole class.

Example 2: The Impact of Earthquakes

Unit Planning: Science

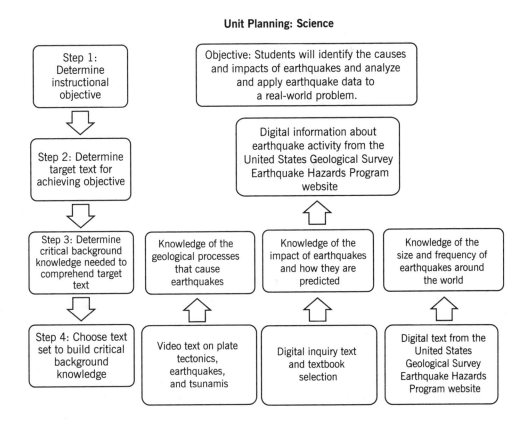

Our Objective

Students will be able to identify the causes and impact of earthquakes and analyze and apply seismologic information to real-world problem solving.

First Texts (Inquiry Project with Digital Texts)

We begin to build appropriate background knowledge for this unit on earthquakes through a short inquiry activity. In heterogeneous groups, students will use the Internet to research one of five severe earthquakes that struck in heavily populated areas across the globe (CCRA R.7). Using a graphic organizer, students will note the area of the globe where each earthquake struck, the specific types of damage that it caused, its impact on human life, and any preventive or safety measures that followed the quake. Each group will present its findings to the other groups in a short PowerPoint presentation. After a discussion of the commonalities among the earthquakes, students will write a summary of all the earthquake information that the groups found.

Second Text (Video Text with Vocabulary Organizer)

We continue building the appropriate background knowledge for this unit on earth-quakes by providing students with a video text that describes the causes of earthquakes, the geological processes related to plate tectonics, and the relationship between earth-quakes and tsunamis. While viewing the video, students will complete a vocabulary guide in which they will write summarized definitions and examples of key vocabulary terms for the unit. The terms will then be discussed and added to a classroom "word wall" for the duration of the unit (CCRA R.4, R.7).

Third Text (Class Textbook and Timeline)

We now build more specific knowledge of the causes of earthquakes through reading a textbook selection. In pairs, students will read about how scientists attempt to predict earthquakes and the geological processes behind them. Students will complete a timeline of the geological processes that cause earthquakes (CCRA R.2-3).

Fourth Text (Digital and Print Informational Texts and Argumentative Writing)

In small groups, students will be directed to the United States Geological Survey Earth-quake Hazards Program website. There they can explore digital representations of earth-quake activity around the world, as well as the magnitude, depth, and intensity of earth-quakes (CCRA R.7). Using this information, students will summarize the data that they find by highlighting the most and least likely regions to experience an earthquake (CCRA W. 2). Students will then read a recent newspaper account of Italian seismolo-gists who were imprisoned for manslaughter when they incorrectly predicted the risk of an earthquake in their own country. Finally, based on the earthquake information that they have read and researched, students will write an argument in support of or against the Italian seismologists (CCRA W.1, W.9).

Instructional Calendar for Earthquake Unit

Day 1
In heterogeneous groups, students will participate in a short inquiry activity during which they will research 1 of 5 earthquake events and present a PowerPoint summary of key information about their quake and its impact to the full class.
Day 2
As a full class, students will view a video on plate tectonics, earthquakes, and tsunamis. Students will complete a vocabulary graphic organizer based on the definitions and examples of those definitions in the videos. Discussion of key vocabulary will follow.

Day 3
In pairs, students will read a textbook selection on the how seismologists predict earthquakes and the geological processes that cause them. Students will complete a timeline reading guide on which they will summarize these processes in chronological order.
Day 4
In heterogeneous groups, students will read and analyze digital data on earthquake activity around the world and write an informational composition on the most and least likely regions to experience an earthquake. Students will then read a recent newspaper account of Italian seismologists who were imprisoned for manslaughter when they incorrectly predicted the risk of an earthquake in their own country. Using the information gleaned from their reading, students will discuss whether the imprisonment of these scientists was just.
Day 5
Students will write an argument against or in support of the imprisonment of the Italian scientists based on the earthquake information from the unit and their discussion on day 4.

References

ACT. (2006). *Reading between the lines: What the ACT reveals about college readiness in reading*. Iowa City, IA: Author.

Alexander, P. A., & Fox, E. (2011). Adolescents as readers. In M. L. Kamil, P. D. Pearson, E. B. Moje, & P. P. Afflerbach (Eds.), *Handbook of reading research* (Vol. 4, pp. 157–176). New York: Routledge.

Alexander, P. A., Kulikowich, J. M., & Jetton, T. L. (1994). The role of subject-matter knowledge and interest in the processing of linear and nonlinear texts. *Review of Educational Research, 64*, 201–252.

Alozie, N. M., Moje, E. B., & Krajcik, J. S. (2010). An analysis of the supports and constraints for scientific discussion in high school project-based science. *Science Education, 94*, 395–427.

Alvermann, D. E. (1991). The Discussion Web: A graphic aid for learning across the curriculum. *Reading Teacher, 45*, 92–99.

Alvermann, D. E., Dillon, D. R., & O'Brien, D. G. (1987). *Using discussion to promote reading comprehension*. Newark, DE: International Reading Association.

Applebee, A., & Langer, J. (2006). *The state of writing instruction: What existing data tell us*. Albany, NY: Center on English Learning and Achievement.

Barthes, R. (1985). Day by day with Roland Barthes. In M. Blonsky (Ed.), *On signs* (pp. 98–117). Baltimore, MD: Johns Hopkins University Press.

Beach, R., & Finders, M. G. (1999). Students as ethnographers: Alternative research projects. *English Journal, 89*(1), 82–90.

Bean, T. W., & Harper, H. (2009). The "adolescent" in adolescent literacy: A preliminary review. In K. D. Wood & W. E. Blanton (Eds.), *Literacy instruction for adolescents: Research-based practice* (pp. 37–53). New York: Guilford Press.

Beck, I. L., & McKeown, M. G. (2006). *Improving comprehension with Questioning the Author: A fresh and expanded view of a powerful approach*. New York: Scholastic.

Beck, I. L., McKeown, M. G., Hamilton, R. L., & Kucan, L. (1997). *Questioning the Author: An approach for enhancing student engagement with text*. Newark, DE: International Reading Association.

Beck, I. L., McKeown, M. G., & Omanson, R. C. (1987). The effects and uses of diverse vocabulary instructional techniques. In M. McKeown & M. E. Curtis (Eds.), *The nature of vocabulary acquisition* (pp. 147–163). Hillsdale, NJ: Erlbaum.

Beers, K. (2002). *When kids can't read: What teachers can do*. Portsmouth, NH: Heinemann.

Benjamin, R. (2012). Reconstructing readability: Recent developments and recommendations in the analysis of text difficulty. *Educational Psychology Review, 24*, 63–88.

Bentley, F., Kennedy, S., & Semsar, K. (2011). How not to lose your students with concept maps. *Journal of College Science Teaching, 41*, 61–68.

Berliner, D. C., & Biddle, B. J. (1995). *The manufactured crisis: Myths, fraud, and the attack on America's public schools*. Reading, MA: Addison-Wesley.

Bloome, D., & Egan-Robertson, A. (1993). The social construction of intertextuality in classroom reading and writing lessons. *Reading Research Quarterly, 28*, 304–333.

Bolden, T. (2010). *FDR's alphabet soup: New Deal America 1932–1939*. New York: Knopf Books for Young Readers.

Boscolo, P., & Gelati, C. (2013). Best practices in promoting motivation for writing. In S. Graham, C. A. MacArthur, & J. Fitzgerald (Eds.), *Best practices in writing instruction* (2nd ed., pp. 284–308). New York: Guilford Press.

Brenner, D., & Hiebert, E. H. (2010). If I follow the teachers' editions, isn't that enough? Analyzing reading volume in six core reading programs. *Elementary School Journal, 110*, 347–363.

Bright, A. (2011). Writing Homer, reading Riordan: Intertextual study in contemporary adolescent literature. *Journal of Children's Literature, 37*(1), 38–47.

Brinson, D., & Steiner, L. (2007, October). *Building collective efficacy: How leaders inspire teachers to achieve*. Washington, DC: Center for Comprehensive School Reform and Improvement.

Buehl, D. (1993). Magnetized: Students are drawn to technique that identifies key words. *WEAC News & Views, 29*(4), 13.

Buehl, D. (2009). *Classroom strategies for interactive learning*. Newark, DE: International Reading Association.

Burton, K. (1958). Some further thoughts on research papers. *English Journal, 47*(5), 291–292.

Carmichael, S. B., Wilson, W. S., Porter-Magee, K., & Martino, G. (2010). *The state of state standards—and the Common Core—in 2010*. Thomas B. Fordham Institute. Available at *www.edexcellence.net/publications/the-state-of-state-of-standards-and-the-common-core-in-2010.html*.

Carr, S. C., & Thompson, B. (1996). The effects of prior knowledge and schema activation strategies on the inferential reading comprehension of children with and without learning disabilities. *Learning Disability Quarterly, 19*, 48–61.

Carrell, P. L. (1983). Three components of background knowledge in reading comprehension. *Language Learning, 33*, 183–207.

Cazden, C. B. (1988). *Classroom discourse: The language of teaching and learning*. Portsmouth, NH: Heinemann.

Center on Education Policy. (2011). *States' progress and challenges in implementing Common Core State Standards*. Washington, DC: Author.

Chesky, J., & Hiebert, E. H. (1987). The effects of prior knowledge and audience on high school students' writing. *Journal of Educational Research, 80*, 304–313.

Chinn, C. A., Anderson, R. C., & Waggoner, M. A. (2001). Patterns of discourse in two kinds of literature discussion. *Reading Research Quarterly, 36*, 378–411.

Cioffi, F. L. (2005). *The imaginative argument: A practical manifesto for writers*. Princeton, NJ: Princeton University Press.

Clark, A., Anderson, R. C., Kuo, L., Kim, I., Archodidou, A., & Nguyen-Jahiel, K. (2003). Collaborative reasoning: Expanding ways for children to talk and think in school. *Educational Psychology Review, 15*, 181–198.

Coburn, C. E., Pearson, P. D., & Woulfin, S. (2011). Reading policy in the era of accountability. In M. L. Kamil, P. D. Pearson, E. B. Moje, & P. P. Afflerbach (Eds.), *Handbook of reading research* (Vol. 4, pp. 157–176). New York: Routledge.

College Board. (2012). *The SAT report on college and career readiness: 2012*. Princeton, NJ: Author.

Collins, S. (2010). *The hunger games*. New York: Scholastic.

Complete College America. (2012). *Remediation: Higher education's bridge to nowhere*. Washington, DC: Author.

Cronin, J., Dahlin, M., Adkins, D., & Kingsbury, G. G. (2007). *The proficiency illusion*. Washington, DC: Thomas B. Fordham Institute.

Crossley, S. A., Greenfield, J., & McNamara, D. S. (2008). Assessing text readability using cognitively based indices. *TESOL Quarterly, 42*, 475–493.

Dalton, B. (2012). Multimodal composition and the common core state standards. *Reading Teacher, 66*, 333–339.

Davis, R., & Shadle, M. (2000). "Building a mystery": Alternative research writing and the academic act of seeking. *College Composition and Communication, 51*, 417–446.

Dellinger, D. G. (1989). Alternatives to clip and stitch: Real research and writing in the classroom. *English Journal, 78*(5), 31–38.

Dexter, D. D., & Hughes, C. A. (2011). Graphic organizers and students with learning disabilities: A meta-analysis. *Learning Disability Quarterly, 34*, 51–72.

Dodson, S. (2011). *100 books for girls to grow on*. New York: HarperCollins.

Duke, N. K. (2000). 3.6 minutes per day: The scarcity of information texts in first grade. *Reading Research Quarterly, 35*, 202–224.

Dunston, P. J., & Gambrell, L. B. (2009). Motivating adolescent learners to read. In K. D. Wood & W. E. Blanton (Eds.), *Literacy instruction for adolescents: Research-based practice* (pp. 269–286). New York: Guilford Press.

Dweck, C. S. (2007). *Mindset: The new psychology of success*. New York: Random House.

Ebert, E. K., & Crippen, K. J. (2010). Applying a cognitive–affective model of conceptual change to professional development. *Journal of Science Teacher Education, 21*, 371–388.

Eco, U. (1979). *The role of the reader*. Bloomington: Indiana University Press.

Eeds, M., & Wells, D. (1989). Great conversations: An exploration of meaning construction in literature study groups. *Research in the Teaching of English, 23*(1), 4–29.

Ferretti, R. P., & De La Paz, S. (2011). On the comprehension and production of written texts: Instructional activities that support content-area literacy. In R. E. O'Connor & P. F. Vadasy (Eds.), *Handbook of reading interventions* (pp. 326–355). New York: Guilford Press.

Ferretti, R. P., & Lewis, W. E. (2013). Best practices in teaching argumentative writing. In S. Graham, C. A. MacArthur, & J. Fitzgerald (Eds.), *Best practices in writing instruction* (2nd ed., pp. 113–140). New York: Guilford Press.

Fry, E. (2002). Readability versus leveling. *Reading Teacher, 56*, 286–291.

Fulton, M. (2010). *State reports on the cost of remedial education: Getting Past Go Project*. Denver, CO: Education Commission of the States.

Gallavan, N. P., & Kottler, E. (2007). Eight types of graphic organizers for empowering social studies students and teachers. *Social Studies, 98*, 117–123.

Goldman, S. R. (2009). Literacy in the digital world: Comprehending and learning from multiple sources. In M. G. McKeown & L. Kucan (Eds.), *Bringing reading research to life* (pp. 257–284). New York: Guilford Press.

Graesser, A. C., Millis, K. K., & Zwann, R. A. (1997). Discourse comprehension. *Annual Review of Psychology, 48*, 163–189.

Graff, G. (2003). *Clueless in academe: How schooling obscures the life of the mind*. New Haven, CT: Yale University Press.

Graham, S., & Hebert, M. A. (2010). *Writing to read: Evidence for how writing can improve reading*. A Carnegie Corporation Time to Act Report. Washington, DC: Alliance for Excellent Education.

Graham, S., & Perin, D. (2007). *Writing next: Effective strategies to improve writing of adolescents in middle and high schools*. New York: Carnegie Corporation of New York.

Grant, M., Lapp, D., Fisher, D., Johnson, K., & Frey, N. (2012). Purposeful instruction: Mixing up the "I," "we," and "you." *Journal of Adolescent and Adult Literacy, 56*, 45–55.

Gregoire, M. (2003). Is it a challenge or a threat? A dual-process model of teachers' cognition and appraisal processes during conceptual change. *Educational Psychology Review, 15*, 147–179.

Guskey, T. R. (1986). Staff development and the process of teacher change. *Educational Researcher, 15*(5), 5–12.

Guskey, T. R. (2009). Closing the knowledge gap on effective professional development. *Educational Horizons, 87*, 224–233.

Guskey, T. R., & Yoon, K. (2009). What works in professional development? *Phi Delta Kappan, 90*, 495–500.

Guthrie, J. T., & McCann, A. D. (1996). Idea circles: Peer collaborations for conceptual learning. In L. B. Gambrell & J. F. Almasi (Eds.), *Lively discussions! Fostering engaged reading* (pp. 87–105). Newark, DE: International Reading Association.

Guzzetti, B. J. (2009). Lessons on literacy learning and teaching: Listening to adolescent girls. In L. Christenbury, R. Bomer, & P. Smagorinsky (Eds.), *Handbook of adolescent literacy research* (pp. 372–385). New York: Guilford Press.

Hacker, D. J., & Tenent, A. (2002). Implementing reciprocal teaching in the classroom: Overcoming obstacles and making modifications. *Journal of Educational Psychology, 94*, 699–718.

Hart, E. R., & Speece, D. L. (1998). Reciprocal teaching goes to college: Effects for postsecondary students at risk for academic failure. *Journal of Educational Psychology, 90*, 670–681.

Hart-Landsberg, S., & Reder, S. (1995). Teamwork and literacy: Teaching and learning and Hardy Industries. *Reading Research Quarterly, 30*, 1016–1052.

Hartman, D. K., & Allison, J. M. (1996). Promoting inquiry-oriented discussions using multiple texts. In L. B. Gambrell & J. F. Almasi (Eds.), *Lively discussions! Fostering engaged reading* (pp. 106–133). Newark, DE: International Reading Association.

Heller, R., & Greenleaf, C. (2007). *Literacy instruction in the content areas: Getting to the core of middle and high school improvement*. Washington, DC: Alliance for Excellent Education. Retrieved from *www.all4ed.org/files/LitCon.pdf*.

Helms, J. W., & Helms, K. (2010). Note Launchers: Promoting active reading of mathematics textbooks. *Journal of College Reading and Learning, 41*, 109–119.

Herber, H. L. (1970). *Teaching reading in content areas*. Englewood Cliffs, NJ: Prentice Hall.

Hiebert, E. (2012). The Common Core State Standards and text complexity. *Teacher Librarian, 39*(5), 13–19.

Hiebert, E., & Pearson, P. D. (2012). What happens to the basics? *Educational Leadership, 70*(4), 48–53.

Hill, H. (2009). Fixing teacher professional development. *Phi Delta Kappan, 90*, 470–476.

Hillocks, G. (2002). *The testing trap: How state writing assessments control learning*. New York: Teachers College Press.

Hillocks, G. (2010). Teaching argument for critical thinking and writing: An introduction. *English Journal, 99*(6), 24–32.

Hillocks, G. (2011). *Teaching argument writing, grades 6–12: Supporting claims with relevant evidence and clear reasoning*. Portsmouth, NH: Heinemann.

International Reading Association. (2012). *Adolescent literacy: A position statement of the International Reading Association*. Newark, DE: Author. Available at *www.reading.org/Resources/ResourcesByTopic/Adolescent/Overview.aspx*.

Ivy, G., & Broaddus, K. (2000). Tailoring the fit: Reading instruction and middle school readers. *Reading Teacher, 54*, 68–78.

Jetton, T. L., & Alexander, P. A. (2004). Domains, teaching, and literacy. In T. L. Jetton & J. A. Dole (Eds.), *Adolescent literacy research and practice* (pp. 15–39). New York: Guilford Press.

Johnson, D. D., & Pearson, P. D. (1984). *Teaching reading vocabulary*. New York: Holt, Rinehart and Winston.

Karchmer-Klein, R. (2013). Best practices in using technology to support writing. In S. Graham, C. A. MacArthur, & J. Fitzgerald (Eds.), *Best practices in writing instruction* (2nd ed., pp. 309–333). New York: Guilford Press.

Kazemi, E., & Hubbard, A. (2008). New directions for the design and study of professional development: Attending to the coevolution of teachers' participation across contexts. *Journal of Teacher Education, 59*, 428–441.

Keys, C. W. (2000). Investigating the thinking processes of eighth grade writers during the composition of a scientific laboratory report. *Journal of Research in Science Teaching, 37*, 676–690.

Kintsch, W. (1988). The role of knowledge in discourse comprehension: A construction-integration model. *Psychological Review, 95*, 163–182.

Kintsch, W. (1994). Text comprehension, memory, and learning. *American Psychologist, 49*, 294–303.

Kiuhara, S. A., Graham, S., & Hawken, L. S. (2009). Teaching writing to high school students: A national survey. *Journal of Educational Psychology, 101*, 136–160.

Langer, J. A. (1981). Pre-reading plan (PReP): Facilitating text comprehension. In J. Chapman (Ed.), *The reader and the text* (pp. 125–131). London, UK: Heinemann.

Langer, J. A. (1984). Examining background knowledge and text comprehension. *Reading Research Quarterly, 19*, 468–481.

Langer, J. A., & Nicolich, M. (1981). Prior knowledge and its effect on comprehension. *Journal of Reading Behavior, 13*, 373–381.

Lemke, J. (2011). The secret identity of science education: Masculine and politically conservative? *Cultural Studies of Science Education, 6*, 287–292.

Lenski, S. D. (1998). Intertextual intentions: Making connections across texts. *Clearing House, 72*(2), 74–80.

Lesko, N. (2001). *Act our age! A cultural construction of adolescence.* New York: Routledge.

Leu, D. J., & Castek, J. (2006, April). *What skills and strategies are characteristic of accomplished adolescent users of the Internet?* Paper presented at the meeting of the American Educational Research Association, San Francisco, CA.

Loveless, T. (2012). *How well are American students learning?* Washington, DC: Brown Center on Education Policy, Brookings Institution. Available at *www.brookings.edu*.

Mackey, M. (1997). Good-enough reading: Momentum and accuracy in the reading of complex fiction. *Research in the Teaching of English, 31*, 428–458.

Macon, J. M., Bewell, D., & Vogt, M. (1991). *Responses to literature: Grades K–8.* Newark, DE: International Reading Association.

Manzo, A. V. (1969). The ReQuest procedure. *Journal of Reading, 13*, 123–126.

Manzo, A. V., & Casale, U. P. (1985). Listen–Read–Discuss: A content reading heuristic. *Journal of Reading, 28*, 732–734.

Manzo, U. C., Manzo, A. V., & Thomas, M. M. (2009). *Content area literacy: A framework for reading-based instruction* (5th ed.). Hoboken, NJ: Wiley.

Marrero, M., Woodruff, K., Schuster, G., & Riccio, J. (2010). Live, online short-courses: A case study of innovative teacher professional development. *International Review of Research in Open and Distance Learning, 11*, 81–95.

Marzano, R. J. (2004). *Building background knowledge for academic achievement: Research on what works in schools.* Alexandria, VA: Association for Supervision and Curriculum Development.

McKenna, M. C. (2001). Development of reading attitudes. In L. Verhoeven & C. Snow (Eds.), *Literacy and motivation: Reading engagement in individuals and groups* (pp. 135–158). Mahwah, NJ: Erlbaum.

McKenna, M. C. (2011). Issues and trends in American literacy education: When irresistible forces meet an immovable object. *Korean Literature and Language Education, 8*, 23–43.

McKenna, M. C., Franks, S., & Lovette, G. (2011). Using reading guides with struggling readers in grades 3 and above. In R. L. McCormick & J. R. Paratore (Eds.), *After early intervention, then what? Teaching struggling readers in grades 3 and beyond* (2nd ed., pp. 207–220). Newark, DE: International Reading Association.

McKenna, M. C., & Robinson, R. D. (2013). *Teaching through text: Reading and writing in the content areas* (2nd ed.). Boston: Allyn & Bacon/Vango.

McKenna, M. C., & Walpole, S. (2007). Assistive technology in the reading clinic: Its emerging potential. *Reading Research Quarterly, 42*, 140–145.

McKeown, M. G., Beck, I. L., & Blake, R. G. K. (2009). Rethinking reading comprehension instruction: A comparison of instruction for strategies and content approaches. *Reading Research Quarterly, 44*, 218–253.

McKeown, M. G., Beck, I. L., Omanson, R. C., & Pople, M. C. (1985). Some effects of the nature and frequency of vocabulary instruction on the knowledge and use of words. *Reading Research Quarterly, 20*, 522–535.

McNamara, D. S., Kintsch, E., Butler-Songer, N., & Kintsch, W. (1996). Are good texts always better?: Interactions of text coherence, background knowledge, and levels of understanding in learning from text. *Cognition and Instruction, 14*, 1–43.

Mehan, H. (1979). *Learning lessons.* Cambridge, MA: Harvard University Press.

Meier, D. M. (2002). *In schools we trust.* Boston, MA: Beacon Press.

Mesmer, H., Cunningham, J., & Hiebert, E. (2012). Toward a theoretical model of text complexity for the early grades: Learning from the past, anticipating the future. *Reading Research Quarterly, 47*, 235–258.

Miller, S. D. (2003). How high- and low-challenge tasks affect motivation and learning: Implications for struggling learners. *Reading and Writing Quarterly, 19*, 39–57.

Monte-Sano, C., & De La Paz, S. (2012). Using writing tasks to elicit adolescents' historical reasoning. *Journal of Literacy Research, 44*, 273–299.

Moore, D. W., Bean, T. W., Birdyshaw, D., & Rycik, J. A. (1999). *Adolescent literacy: A position statement for the Commission on Adolescent Literacy of the International Reading Association.* Newark, DE: International Reading Association.

Moynihan, K. E. (2007). A collectibles project: Engaging students in multimodal research and writing. *English Journal, 97*(1), 69–76.

National Commission on Writing. (2003, April). *The neglected "R": The need for a writing revolution.* Available at *press.collegeboard.org/releases/2003/national-commission-writing-americas-schools-and-colleges-calls-writing-revolution.*

National Council of Teachers of English. (2012). *Resolution on teacher expertise and the Common Core State Standards.* Urbana, IL: Available at *www.ncte.org/positions/statements/teacherexpertise.*

National Governors Association Center for Best Practices & Council of Chief State School Officers. (2010). *Common Core State Standards.* Washington, DC: Author.

National Institute for Literacy. (2007). *What content-area teachers should know about adolescent literacy.* Washington, DC: National Institute of Child health and Human Development. Available at *www.adlit.org/researchbytopic/24446.*

National Institute of Child Health and Human Development. (2000). *Report of the National Reading Panel. Teaching children to read: An evidence-based assessment of the scientific research literature on reading and its implications for reading instruction* (NIH Publication No. 00-4769). Washington, DC: U.S. Government Printing Office.

Nelson, J., Perfetti, C., Liben, D., & Liben, M. (2012). *Measures of text difficulty: Testing their predictive value for grade levels and student performance.* New York: Student Achievement Partners.

Neman, B. S. (1967). A handbook for the teaching of the research paper. *English Journal, 56*, 262–268.

Newell, G. E., Beach, R., Smith, J., & VanDerHeide, J. (2011). Teaching and learning argumentative reading and writing: A review of research. *Reading Research Quarterly, 46*, 273–304.

Nolen, S. (2007). The role of literate communities in the development of children's interest in writing. In S. Hidi & P. Boscolo (Eds.), *Writing and motivation* (pp. 241–255). Oxford, UK: Elsevier.

O'Brien, D., Stewart, R., & Beach, R. (2009). Proficient reading in school: Traditional paradigms and new textual landscapes. In L. Christenbury, R. Bomer, & P. Smagorinsky (Eds.), *Handbook of adolescent literacy research* (pp. 80–97). New York: Guilford Press.

Organisation for Economic Co-operation and Development. (2010). *PISA 2009 results: Learning trends: Changes in student performance since 2000* (Vol. 5). Paris: OECD Publishing. Retrieved July 15, 2011, from *dx.doi.org/10.1787/9789264091580-en.*

Palincsar, A. S., & Brown, A. L. (1984). Reciprocal teaching of comprehension-fostering and comprehension-monitoring activities. *Cognition and Instruction, 1,* 117–175.

Perin, D. (2013). Best practices in teaching writing for college and career readiness. In S. Graham, C. A. MacArthur, & J. Fitzgerald (Eds.), *Best practices in writing instruction* (2nd ed., pp. 48–70). New York: Guilford Press.

Peterson, R., & Eeds, M. (2007). *Grand conversations: Literature groups in action* (Updated ed.). New York: Scholastic.

Pritchard, M. E., Wilson, G. S., & Yamnitz, B. (2007). What predicts adjustment among college students? A longitudinal panel study. *Journal of American College Health, 56*(1), 15–22.

RAND Reading Study Group. (2002). *Reading for understanding: Toward an R&D program in reading comprehension.* Santa Monica, CA: RAND. Available at *www.rand.org/pubs/monograph_reports/MR1465.*

Ranker, J. (2007). A new perspective on inquiry: A case study of digital video production. *English Journal, 97*(1), 77–82.

Raphael, T. E., & McMahon, S. I. (1994). Book Club: An alternative framework for reading instruction. *Reading Teacher, 48,* 102–116.

Ravitch, D. (2010). *The death and life of the great American school system: How testing and choice are undermining education.* New York: Basic Books.

Rosenblatt, L. (1978). *The reader, the text, and the poem: The transactional theory of the literature work.* Carbondale, IL: Southern Illinois University Press.

Rothman, R. (2011). *Something in common: The Common Core Standards and the next chapter in American education.* Cambridge, MA: Harvard Education Press.

Rothman, R. (2012). Laying a common foundation for success. *Phi Delta Kappan, 94*(3), 57–61.

Rupley, W. H., & Slough, S. (2010). Building prior knowledge and vocabulary in science in the intermediate grades: Creating hooks for learning. *Literacy Research and Instruction, 49,* 99–112.

Rybarczyk, B. (2011). Visual literacy in biology: A comparison of visual representations in textbooks and journal articles. *Journal of College Science Teaching, 41*(1), 106–114.

Santa, C. M. (1988). *Content reading including study systems.* Dubuque, IA: Kendall/Hunt.

Santa, C. M., Havens, L. T., & Valdes, B. J. (2004). *Project CRISS: Creating independence through student-owned strategies.* Dubuque, IA: Kendall/Hunt.

Schnick, T., & Knickelbine, M. (2000). *The Lexile framework: An introduction for educators.* Durham, NC: MetaMetrics.

Scholastic & MetaMetrics. (1999). *Scholastic Reading Inventory using the Lexile Framework: Technical manual, Forms A and B.* New York: Scholastic.

Schriver, K. (2012). What we know about expertise in professional communication. In V. W. Berninger (Ed.), *Past, present, and future contributions of cognitive writing research to cognitive psychology* (pp. 275–312). New York: Psychology Press.

Schwartz, R. M., & Raphael, T. E. (1985). Concept of definition: A key to improving students' vocabulary. *Reading Teacher, 39,* 198–205.

Shanahan, T. (2013). Best practices in writing about text. In S. Graham, C. A. MacArthur,

& J. Fitzgerald (Eds.), *Best practices in writing instruction* (2nd ed., pp. 309–333). New York: Guilford Press.

Smith, M. W., & Wilhelm, J. D. (2009). Boys and literacy: Complexity and multiplicity. In L. Christenbury, R. Bomer, & P. Smagorinsky (Eds.), *Handbook of adolescent literacy research* (pp. 360–371). New York: Guilford Press.

Southern Regional Education Board. (2006). *Getting students ready for college and careers.* Atlanta, GA: Author. Available at *www.sreb.org.*

Sprague, M. M., & Keeling, K. K. (2009). Paying attention to girls' literacy needs. In K. D. Wood & W. E. Blanton (Eds.), *Literacy instruction for adolescents: Research-based practice* (pp. 187–209). New York: Guilford Press.

Stahl, S. A., & Jacobson, M. G. (1986). Vocabulary difficulty, prior knowledge, and text comprehension. *Journal of Reading Behavior, 18*, 309–323.

Stahl, S. A., Jacobson, M. G., Davis, C. E., & Davis, R. L. (1989). Prior knowledge and difficult vocabulary in the comprehension of unfamiliar text. *Reading Research Quarterly, 24*, 27–43.

Stahl, S. A., & Shanahan, C. (2004). Learning to think like a historian: Disciplinary knowledge through critical analysis of multiple documents. In T. L. Jetton & J. A. Dole (Eds.), *Adolescent literacy research and practice* (pp. 94–115). New York: Guilford Press.

Stanovich, K. E. (1986). Matthew effects in reading: Some consequences of individual differences in the acquisition of literacy. *Reading Research Quarterly, 21*, 360–407.

Stevens, R., & Slavin, R. E. (1995). Effects of a cooperative learning approach in reading and writing on academically handicapped and nonhandicapped students. *Elementary School Journal, 95*, 241–262.

Surber, J. R., & Schroeder, M. (2007). Effect of prior domain knowledge and headings on processing of informative text. *Contemporary Educational Psychology, 32*, 485–498.

Taboada, A., & Guthrie, J. T. (2006). Contributions of student questioning and prior knowledge to construction of knowledge from reading information text. *Journal of Literacy Research, 38*, 1–35.

Tarchi, C. (2010). Reading comprehension of informative texts in secondary school: A focus on direct and indirect effects of reader's prior knowledge. *Learning and Individual Differences, 20*, 415–420.

Todd, M. L., & Higginson, T. W. (Eds.). (1890). *Poems of Emily Dickinson.* Boston, MA: Roberts Brothers.

Valencia, S., Stallman, A. C., Commeyras, M., Pearson, P. D., & Hartman, D. K. (1991). Four measures of topical knowledge: A study of construct validity. *Reading Research Quarterly, 26*, 204–233.

van Dijk, T. A., & Kintsch, W. (1983). *Strategies of discourse comprehension.* New York: Academic Press.

Vaughn, J. L., & Estes, T. H. (1986). *Reading and reasoning beyond the primary grades.* Boston, MA: Allyn & Bacon.

Vaughn, S., Klingner, J. K., Swanson, E. A., Boardman, A. G., Roberts, G., Mohammed, S. S., et al. (2011). Efficacy of collaborative strategic reading with middle school students. *American Educational Research Journal, 48*, 938–964.

Vaughn, S., Swanson, E., Roberts, G., Wanzek, J., Stillman-Spisak, S., Solis, M., et al. (2013). Improving reading comprehension and social studies knowledge in middle school. *Reading Research Quarterly, 48*, 77–93.

Waggoner, M., Chinn, C., Yi, H., & Anderson, R. C. (1995). Collaborative reasoning about stories. *Language Arts, 72*, 582–589.

Walpole, S., & McKenna, M. C. (2012). *The literacy coach's handbook: A guide to research-based practice* (2nd ed.). New York: Guilford Press.

Webster-Wright, A. (2009). Reframing professional development through understanding authentic professional learning. *Review of Educational Research, 79*, 702–739.

Wilhelm, J. (2010). Technology in our schools: A call for a cost/benefit analysis. *Voices from the Middle, 17*(3), 44–46.

Wilkinson, I. A. G., & Son, E. H. (2011). A dialogic turn in research on learning and teaching to comprehend. In M. L. Kamil, P. D. Pearson, E. B. Moje, & P. P. Afflerbach (Eds.), *Handbook of reading research* (Vol. 4, pp. 359–387). New York: Routledge.

Williamson, G., Fitzgerald, J., & Stenner, A. (2013). The Common Core State Standards' quantitative text complexity trajectory: Figuring out how much complexity is enough. *Educational Researcher, 42*(2), 59–69.

Willingham, D. T. (2009). *Why don't students like school?* San Francisco: Jossey-Bass.

Wineburg, S. (1991). Historical problem solving: A study of the cognitive processes used in the evaluation of documentary and pictorial evidence. *Journal of Educational Psychology, 83*, 73–87.

Wineburg, S. (2001). *Historical thinking and other unnatural acts: Charting the future of teaching the past.* Philadelphia: Temple University Press.

Wolsey, T. D., & Lapp, D. (2009). Discussion-based instruction in the middle and secondary school classroom. In K. D. Wood & W. E. Blanton (Eds.), *Literacy instruction for adolescents: Research-based practice* (pp. 368–391). New York: Guilford Press.

Wood, K. D. (2011). Bridging print literacies and digital literacies using strategy guides. *Journal of Adolescent and Adult Literacy, 55*, 248–252.

Zakaluk, B. L., & Samuels, S. J. (1988). Toward a new approach to predicting text comprehensibility. In B. L. Zakaluk & S. J. Samuels (Eds.), *Readability: Its past, present and future* (pp. 121–144). Newark, DE: International Reading Association.

Index

Page numbers in *italic* refer to figures or tables.

Accelerated Reader program, 32
Adolescent development
    fixed mindset versus growth mindset in, 26
    gender differences in, 19
    literacy instruction in context of, 17–18
Advanced Placement curriculum, 28
Agency 1, The: Spy in the House (Lee), 52
Alexander, P. A., 17–18, 21–22, 117–118
Alozie, N. M., 117
Alvermann, D. E., 117, 132
Anchor Standards
    CCSS structure, 8–9
    College and Career Readiness, *9*
    for Reading. *See* Reading, Anchor
        Standards for
    for Speaking and Listening, 9, 115, *115*
    for writing, 177
Anderson, R., 120
Animal Farm (Orwell), 191, 196–199
An Inconvenient Truth (Gore), 93, *94*
Annotating, 126
Argumentative thinking and writing
    CCSS objectives for, 10–11, 152–154
    rationale for teaching, 153
    strategies for enhancing, 152–161
Assistive technologies, 109
ATOS, 32–33, 35
Attractor words, 143
Authentic discussion, 117

Authorial intent, 12, 58, 74
Autobiography of My Dead Brother (Meyers),
    102

B

Background knowledge
    in anchor standards for reading, 10
    components of, *60,* 60–61, 62
    cycle of building, 64, *64*
    definition of, 58, 60
    importance of, 58–59, 61–62, 64
    movement toward domain knowledge with,
        62–64, *63*
    previewing for, 74–81
    in text representation theory, 45–47
    use of text sets to build, 48–50
    writing activities to build, 81–85
Barthes, R., 42
Bean, T. W., 17
Beck, I., 120, 124–125
Beers, K., 149, 178
Berliner, D. C., 2
Blogs, 177
Bone, M., 188
Book Club, 119–120
Book Thief, The (Zuzak), 102
Bray, L., 172

Brookings Institution, 5
Brown, A. L., 103, 122
Buehl, D., 141–142, 149
Burton, K., 165

C

Carnegie Corporation, 138
Categories of skills for reading, 10–13
Cato Institute, 5
Cazden, C. B., 116
CCSS. *See* Common Core State Standards
Cell division, 54–56, 210–212
Center for Best Practices, 5
Cioffi, F., 174, 176
Class discussion
    balance between transmission and
        participation in, 117–118, *118*
    CCSS requirements for, 114–116
    characteristics of effective, *116,* 116–119
    Collaborative Reasoning approach to, *128,*
        128–129, *130*
    controversial topics in, 128, 129, 132
    Devil's Advocate technique, 132, *134*
    Discussion Web technique, 129, *131,* 132,
        133
    effective questioning strategies for, 114,
        114
    goals for, 135
    initiate–respond–evaluate model, 116–117
    Questioning the Author technique,
        124–126, *127*
    Reciprocal Questioning technique, 121–
        122, *123*
    Reciprocal Teaching technique, 122
    recitation model, 116–117
    resistance to nontraditional forms of, 117
    in small groups, 118–119, *119*
    as teacher-controlled questioning, 112–114
    teacher stances for, 119–120, *120*
Click and clunk, 90
Clueless in Academe (Graff), 154
Cognitive–Affective Model of Conceptual
    Change, 181
Cognitive proficiencies for reading
    comprehension, 10–13
    apprenticeship models for learning, 91–92
    construction of meaning, 42, *42,* 45
    discipline-specific, 139–140

instructional stances for, 87–88
    text representation theory, 41–47
Cognitive psychology, 87
Collaborative learning. *See* Cooperative groups
Collaborative Reasoning, 120, *128,* 128–129,
    130
Collaborative Strategic Reading, 88–90, *89*
Collective teacher efficiency, 182
College and Career Readiness Anchors, 8, *9*
College and workplace readiness, 2, 7, 8, 28,
    29
Collins, S., 102
Common Core State Standards (CCSS)
    appendices, 9, 29, 36
    categories and standards, 8–13, *9, 10*
    challenge of, 38
    class discussion requirements of, 114–116
    creation of, 2, 3–5
    goals for writing, 136–137
    key organizations involved in, *6*
    organizational support and criticism of, 5–6
    outcomes testing, 186
    rationale for, 2, 6–8, 16
    rigor of, 2, 4, *4,* 28
    state adoptions of, 5
    state literacy standards versus, *4,* 4–5
    support for strong readers in, 16
    See also Anchor Standards; Implementation
        of CCSS
Communication
    real life, versus school, 176–177
    for sharing research, 176–178
    teacher–student, 25–26
    See also Class discussion
Complementary texts, 52
Complex texts
    anchor standards for reading, 13
    in CCSS program, 7–8, 29–30
    difficult texts versus, 33–34
    exemplars, 29, *30,* 36
    inadequacy of current student preparation
        for, 7, *7,* 56
    motivating students with challenge of,
        23–25, *25*
    qualitative analysis of, 9, 33–35, *35, 37, 37*
    quantitative analysis of, 9, 31–33, 37
    vertical articulation in assignment of, 31
    See also Informational texts
Concept maps, 66–67, *67, 68,* 81–84, *84*
Conflicting texts, 52

Constitutionality of CCSS, 5
Construction of meaning, 42, *42,* 45
    in class discussion, 120
Content knowledge, 62, 63
    for discipline-specific writing, 139–140
    teaching of comprehension strategies versus
        teaching for, 88
Context of text, 62
Contextualized vocabulary instruction,
    11–12
Cooperative groups, 87
    for classroom discussion, 118–119
    creation of jigsawed texts in, 106–109
    formed from Lexile data, *108,* 108–109
    objections to, 91
    PALS system for, 99–103
    rationale for instruction with, 91–92
    Reciprocal Teaching in, 103–105, *105, 106,*
        107
    requirements for success in, 91
    research and inquiry in, 178–179
    to support adolescent reading achievement,
        88–91
Council of Chief State School Officers, 2, 5
Critical-analytic stance, 120
Cross-disciplinary implementation of CCSS,
    7–8, 10–11
CSET strategy, 158–159
CSQT strategy, 155–159, *156, 160,* 166

D

Dalton, B., 176
Dash, Joan, 124–125
Data collection and analysis
    for CCSS evaluation, 186–188, *188*
    instruction in, 166–167, 168–173, *171*
Declaration of Independence, 53–54, 201,
    202–204
Degrees of Reading Power, 32
Dellinger, D. G., 166, 173
Devil's Advocate, 132, *134*
Difficulty, text, 33–34
Digital texts, 176–178
Discussion. *See* Class discussion
Discussion Web, 129, *131,* 132, *133*
Dodson, S., 19–20
Doll's House, A (Ibsen), 40, 43–44, 72–74,
    191–195, *192*

Domain knowledge, 62–64, *63*
Drama, 29, *30*
Du Bois, W. E. B., 201, 206
Dunston, P. J., 23
Dweck, C., 26

E

Earthquakes, 213–215
Eco, Umberto, 45
Educational Testing Service, 32
Efferent stance, 120
English Journal, 165
Experiential knowledge, 60, 61
Expressive stance, 119–120

F

Familiarity of text, 62
FDR's Alphabet Soup: New Deal America
    (Bolden), 142–143
Ferretti, R. P., 164
Fieldwork, 168–169
Flexible writing, 147
Forster, E. M., 81
Fox, E., 17–18, 21–22
Fry, E., 34
Fuchs, D., 99
Fuchs, L., 99

G

Gambrell, L. B., 23
Gender, 19–20
Gist level understanding, 43, 44–45, 47
Glogster, 177
Going Bovine (Bray), 172
Gore, Al, 93
Gradual release of responsibility, 92
Graff, G., 10, 154
Graham, S., 138, 140, 147
Grand Conversations, 119–120
Graphic organizers, 78–81, *80, 81,* 82
Greenleaf, C., 139–140
Guskey, T. R., 181
Guthrie, J. T., 84, 109
Guzzetti, B. J., 20

H

Harper, H., 17
Hebert, M., 138, 140
Hein, T., 188
Heller, R., 139–140
Helms, J. W., 93
Helms, K., 93
Henry, Patrick, 75–76
High-challenge language arts activity, 24
Hillocks, G., 156, 170, 171, 172
History, text set case example, 53–54,
    201–207
Hoover, Herbert, 142–143
Hunger Games, The (Collins), 102

I

iBook Author, 178
Ibsen, Henrik, 40, 43–44, 191
Idea circles, 109
Identity development, 18, 26
Implementation of CCSS
    across all content areas, 7–8, 10–11
    challenge of, 181, 188
    collective teacher efficiency for, 182
    cost of, *6*
    creating vision for, *182,* 182–184
    data for evaluation of, 186–188, *188*
    instruction schedule planning in, 185–186
    professional development outcomes in,
        180–181
    resources for, 184–188
    schoolwide participation in, 36, 180
    selection of instructional strategies for, *183,*
        183–184
    successful example of, 188–189
Informational texts
    CCSS exemplars, 30–31
    CCSS goals for student reading, 29
    current exposure to, 30
    curriculum design, 36
    representational model of comprehending,
        45–46
Initiate–respond–evaluate model, 116–117
Instructional strategies
    for building technical vocabulary, 65–74
    for motivating students to read, 86–87
    for previewing texts, 74–81

to support adolescent reading achievement,
    88–91
use of reading guides in, 92–99
Integration of knowledge and ideas, 12–13, *13*
Interest inventories, 22, *22*
"Interlopers, The" (Saki), 96, *97*
International comparison, 5, 16, 19
International Reading Association, 16
Internet
    access, 186
    research, 173–176, *174, 175*
    resources for teachers, 186, *187*
Interviewing, 169–170
iPad apps, 178

J

Jetton, T. L., 117–118
Jigsawed text sets, 106–109, *110*
Johnson, Samuel, 28, 39, 165

K

Kane, G., 78
Karchmer-Klein, R., 176, 178
Keeling, K. K., 19, 20
Kintsch, W., 41, 42–43, 44, 46, 47, 61

L

Langer, J. A., 63–64, 78
Lapp, D., 117
Lee, Y. S., 52
Lesko, N., 17
Lewis, W. E., 164
Lexile standards, 31–32, *32,* 35
    to form groups, *108,* 108–109
Listen–Read–Discuss, 74–76, *77*
Literacy skills
    assessment, 14, *15*
    in context of adolescent development,
        17–18
    current deficiencies in, 1–2, 14–16, *16*
    definition of, 16–17
    gender differences, 19, *19*
    importance of, 1
    instructional time devoted to, 185–186

linkage between reading and writing in, 138, *139*
support for strong readers in CCSS, 16
text representation theory of, 41–47
Literature instruction
  building vocabulary knowledge for, 72–74
  text set case example, 43, 50–52, 191–199
Longitude Prize, The (Dash), 124–126

M

Magnet summary, 142–147, *148,* 166
Mann, Horace, 14
Manufactured Crisis, The (Berliner & Biddle), 2
Manzo, A. V., 121
Manzo, U. C., 132
Marking comments in a discussion, 125
Matthew effect, 59
McKenna, M. C., 22
McMann, A. D., 109
McNamara, D. S., 47
Mehan, H., 116
Meier, D., 154
Menzer, J., 188, 189
Meyers, W. D., 102
Miller, S., 24
Modeling, 126
Motivating students to read
  by altering student beliefs, 20–26
  in cooperative groups, 91
  gender considerations in, 19–20
  obstacles to, 86–87
  by offering choice, 21–22, *23*
  pathways to, 20
  strategies for, 26–27
  students reading ability as consideration in, 23–25, *25*
  by supportive communication, 25–26
Moynihan, K., 169
Mysteries of Mass, The (Kane), 78

N

Nagy, J., 188
National Assessment of Educational Progress, 3–4, 14–16
National Commission on Writing, 138

National Council of Teachers of English, 6
National Education Association, 5–6
National Governors Association, 2, 5
Neman, B. S., 166
No Child Left Behind Act, 3
Note Launchers, 92–93

O

O'Brien, D., 24
One Hundred Books for Girls to Grow On (Dodson), 19–20
Orchid Thief, The, 169
Orwell, George, 191

P

PACT. *See* Promoting Acceleration of Comprehension and Content through Text
Palincsar, A. S., 103, 122
PALS. *See* Peer-Assisted Learning Strategies
Paragraph shrinking, 100–101
Partnership for Assessment of Readiness for Colleges and Careers, 186
Peer-Assisted Learning Strategies, 99–103, *104*
Perin, D., 147, 168
Persuasive writing, 154
"Pit and the Pendulum, The" (Poe), 93–94, *95*
Plagiarism, 177
Poe, Edgar Allen, 93
Poetry reading, 29, *30*
Prediction relay, 100, 101
Prereading Plan, 78, *79*
Previewing texts, 74–81
Prior knowledge, 60
Professional development
  barriers to effective, 181–182
  consultants and specialists for, 184–185
  shortcomings in, 180–181
Proficiency Illusion, The (Cronin et al.), 5
Program for International Student Assessment, 16
Progressive Era, 201, 205–207
Promoting Acceleration of Comprehension and Content through Text, 90–91

Q

Quad text set
  planning, examples of, 50–56
  to promote speaking and listening skills,
    115
  purpose of, 49–50
  text selection for, 49–50, *50*
Qualitative analysis of text difficulty, 33–34,
    37, *37*
Quantitative assessment of texts, 31–33, 37
Questar Learning, 32
Questioning the Author, 120, 124–126, *127*
Quoting text in writing, 155–161

R

RAFT strategy, 147–151, *150, 151*
RAND Reading Study Group, 36
Ranker, J., 176
Ravitch, D., 16
Reading, Anchor Standards for
  attention to key ideas and details, 10–11, *11*
  categories of skills for, 10–13
  comprehending and analyzing complex
    tasks, 13
  integration of knowledge and ideas, 12–13,
    13
  proficiencies for, 10, *10*
  recognition of craft and structure, 11–12, *12*
  for research and inquiry, 163, *164*
Reading guides, 92–99, *98*
Reading Maturity Metric, 32
Reading road map, 93, *94*
Recapping, 126
Reciprocal Questioning, 121–122, *123*
Reciprocal Teaching, 103–105, *105, 106, 107,*
    122
Reformulation of text, 149
Remediation, 2
Renaissance Learning, 32
Research and inquiry
  categories of tools for, 166–168, *167*
  CCSS goals for, 163, *164*
  collaboration in, 178–179
  conceptualization of skills for, 165–166, 179
  data analysis in, 166–167, 170–173, *171*
  data collection in, 166–167, 168–170

fieldwork, 168–169
  goals for teaching, 164–165
  presentation of findings from, 168, 176–178
  project steps, *168*
  rationale for teaching, 163–164
  resource evaluation in, 167, 173–176
  teaching challenges, 164
Revoicing, 126
Road map, reading, 93, *94*
Robinson, R. D., 22
Rosenblatt, L., 120
Rote learning, 12
Rupley, W. H., 60–61

S

Sabol, K., 188
Saki, 96
Samuels, S. J., 35
SAT tests, 2
Save the Last Word for Me, 159–161
Scholastic Reading Inventory, 35
Science text set examples, 54–56, 209–215
Selection of texts
  basic procedure for, 36–38
  CCSS approach to, 9, 36
  CCSS exemplars and, 30–31
  gender considerations, 19–20
  to match student interests, 21, 22
  for quad text set, 49–56, *50*
  qualitative analysis of difficulty in, 33–35,
    35
  quantitative analysis of complexity in, 31–33
  reader considerations in, 23–25, *25,* 35–36
  See also Text sets
Self-perception, 17–18, 23
Semantic feature analysis, 67–70, *69, 71*
Sentence length, 32
Shanahan, C., 128, 132
Situation model, 43–45
Slavin, Robert, 91
Slough, H., 60–61
Smarter Balanced Assessment Consortium,
    186
Smith, M. W., 19
Social studies, text set case example, 53–54,
    201–207
Sociocultural theory, 87–88

Socratic dialogue, 117
Somebody Wanted But So, 151–152, *152*
Son, E. H., 119, 128
SourceRater, 32
Sprague, M. M., 19, 20
Stahl, S. A., 128, 132
State literacy standards, *4,* 4–5
State of State Standards and Common Core, 4
Story reading, 29, *30*
Structural knowledge, 60, 63
Student-generated questions, *83,* 84–85
Summary writing
    challenges of, 141
    importance of, 141
    ineffective strategies for, 141–142
    magnet summary strategy for, 142–147,
      148, 166
    RAFT strategy for, 147–151, *150*
    SWBS strategy for, 151–152, *152, 153*
Surface code, 43–45
SWBS writing strategy, 151–152, *152, 153*

T

Taboada, A., 84
Teachers
    goals for writing instruction, 139–140
    Internet resources for, 186, *187*
    preparation of, to teach writing, 137–138
    supportive communication with students,
      25–26
    texts for, 186
    See also Motivating students to read;
      Professional development
Team-based learning, 90–91
Technical vocabulary instruction, 65–74
Technology
    adolescent fluency with, 18
    assistive, 109
    multimedia texts, 176, 186
    for presentation of research findings,
      176–178
    skills for 21st century, 176
TED talks, 70
Text base, 43–45
Textbooks, 37, 38, 40, 54, 56–57, 106
Textless approach to instruction, 6–7, 10
Text representation theory, 41–47, *43, 44,* 61

Text(s)
    digital, for presentation of research, **176–178**
    forms of, 12–13, 21–22, 40–41, 49–50, 186
    resources for CCSS implementation, **186**
    for teachers, **186**
    See also Text sets
Text sets
    to build background knowledge, **48,** 191
    conceptual framework for designing,
      39–40, 49–50
    history/social studies case examples, **53–54,**
      201–207
    jigsawed, 106–109
    literature case examples, 43, 50–52,
      191–199
    rationale for, 39, 40, 41, 48–49, 56
    related texts in, 40–41
    science case examples, 54–56, 209–215
    selection for, 191
    textbooks in, 56–57
    See also Quad text set
Thomas Fordham Institute, 4, 6
Tie-in sentences, 155–156, 161
Toontastic, 178
Transparency of text, 62
True discussion, 117
Turning back, in discussion, 125

V

van Dijk, T. A., 42–43, 44
Video, to aid literacy instruction, 70–74
View, C., 188
Visual representation of text, 65–66
    in graphic organizers, 78–81, *80, 81*
    guided, 94, *95*
Visual representation of vocabulary words,
    70–72, *73*
Vocabulary knowledge, 60–61, 63
    for literature instruction, 72–74
    strategies for building, 65–74
    word learning, 65, *66*

W

Warrants, 155–156
Web 2.0 tools, 177–178

Wikis, 177
Wilhelm, J. D., 19
Wilkinson, I. A. G., 119, 128
William Penn High School (New Castle, Delaware), 188–189
Willingham, D., 25
Wilson, E. O., 177
Wineburg, S., 170
Wolsey, T. D., 117
Wood, K., 93, 94, 97
Word consciousness, 11–12
Word learning, 65, *66. See also* Vocabulary knowledge
Writing, text-based
  barriers to, 137–138
  CCSS goals for, 136–137, 177
  citing quotes and textual evidence in, 155–161
  discipline-specific, 139–140
  linkage to reading comprehension, 138, *139*
  See also Summary writing; Writing activities

Writing activities
  assessment challenges, 137
  to build background knowledge, 81–85
  empirical literature on, 141
  to enhance argumentation skills, 152–161
  to improve reading comprehension, 138, *139,* 140–141
  teacher readiness for conducting, 137–138
  See also Summary writing; Writing, text-based
Writing to Read (Graham & Hebert), 138

Y

YouTube, 51

Z

Zakaluk, B. L., 35
Zuzak, M., 102

Meet the Artists!

by M. C. Hall

Scott Foresman
is an imprint of

Glenview, Illinois • Boston, Massachusetts • Chandler, Arizona •
Upper Saddle River, New Jersey

Photographs

Every effort has been made to secure permission and provide appropriate credit for photographic material. The publisher deeply regrets any omission and pledges to correct errors called to its attention in subsequent editions.

Unless otherwise acknowledged, all photographs are the property of Pearson Education, Inc.

Photo locators denoted as follows: Top (T), Center (C), Bottom (B), Left (L), Right (R), Background (Bkgd)

Opener: Smithsonian American Art Museum, Washington, DC/Art Resource, NY; **1** The Gallery Collection/Corbis; **3** ©Pascal Deloche/Godong/Corbis; **4** ©Dennis Hallinan/Alamy Images; **5** ©Vinci, Leonardo da (1452-1519)/Institut de France, Paris, France/Bridgeman Art Library; **6** The Gallery Collection/Corbis; **7** ©Geoffrey Clements/Corbis; **8** ©Erich Lessing/Art Resource, NY; **9** The Philadelphia Museum of Art/Art Resource, NY; **10** Smithsonian American Art Museum, Washington, DC/Art Resource, NY; **11** ©Mohamed Mekkawi, 1989/©Howard University Libraries - Media Center; **12** ©Rwin Nielsen/PhotoLibrary Group, Ltd..

ISBN 13: 978-0-328-47253-6
ISBN 10:   0-328-47253-0

7 8 9 10 V010 16 15 14 13

Artists show us how to see things in new ways. Great artists inspire others to try new ideas. Let's meet some of these artists!

People visit art museums to see the work of great artists.

Leonardo da Vinci

Leonardo da Vinci lived more than 500 years ago in what is now Italy. He created drawings, paintings, and statues. He even drew plans for a huge bronze horse statue. But he never finished it.

The *Mona Lisa* is one of Leonardo's most famous paintings.

Leonardo recorded his ideas about art in notebooks. Today, artists still study Leonardo's notes.

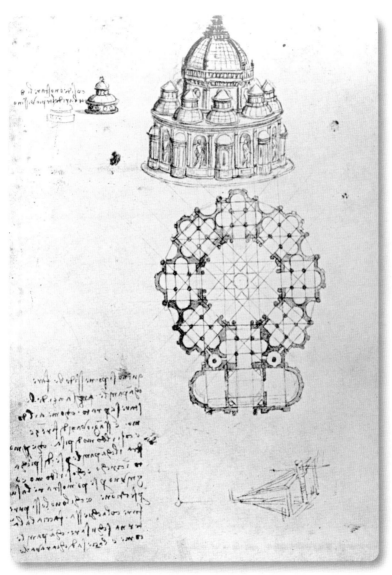

In his notebooks, Leonardo wrote backward!

Claude Monet

Claude Monet was born in France in 1840. His work was different from artists who lived before him. He didn't paint things exactly as they looked.

Monet called this painting *Red Boats at Argenteuil.*

Sometimes Monet painted the same scene over and over again. He liked to show the light at different times of the day. Monet inspired other artists to try new ways of seeing, thinking, and painting.

Painting of the French Countryside by Alfred Sisley

Monet inspired a kind of art called *Impressionism*.

Pablo Picasso

Pablo Picasso was born in Spain in 1881. Even as a child, Picasso had great talent. In his art, people and things looked fresh and new. Sometimes he used shapes and angles to show people and things.

Portrait of artdealer Ambroise Vollard by Picasso

Some artworks by Picasso are full of surprises. He wanted people to think about artists and artwork in new ways. His art still inspires artists today.

Pertaining to Yachts and Yachting by Charles Sheeler

Picasso inspired artists such as Charles Sheeler.

Lois Mailou Jones

Lois Jones was born in the United States in 1905. She was a talented African American artist. Many of Jones's paintings show her African roots.

Does this painting make you think of African masks?

Jones was an art teacher at a college in Washington, D.C. She inspired many of her students to become artists.

Lois Jones taught art for almost 50 years!

Do you remember Leonardo's horse? Five hundred years later, his plans inspired a man named Charles Dent. Dent raised enough money to finish the horse. Today, people can see Leonardo's horse in Milan, Italy.

The horse statue was finished in 1999.